HOMESTEADING IN THE CITY

A survival manual for young people
living in town
or off campus

by NANCY SELIGMANN

**FOLLETT PUBLISHING COMPANY
CHICAGO**

For Michael and the life we have chosen:

That infinitesimal moment
When the waves collided
The bond was indestructible

Copyright © 1975 by Nancy Seligmann. All rights reserved. No part of this publication may be reproduced, stored in a retrieval system or transmitted in any form or by any means, electronic, mechanical, photocopying, recording, or otherwise, without the prior permission of the publisher. Manufactured in the United States of America.

Library of Congress Catalog Card Number: 74-83603
ISBN: 0-695-80513-4

First Printing

CONTENTS

PART 1:
Leaving the Old Nest
and Feathering the New

9

YOUR APARTMENT: Money you must pay before moving in; Finding the right kind of apartment; Your landlord; Moving in; Your telephone **13**

SETTING UP THE APARTMENT: Cleaning; Painting; Plastering; Fixing up; Hanging things; Finding utilities and furniture **23**

YOUR BUDGET—MAKING ENDS MEET: How to set up a budget; A budget chart; Checking account; Savings account; Credit **30**

THE SOMETIMES FUTILE WAR AGAINST COCKROACHES, ANTS, AND MICE: How to prevent them; How to control them **36**

HOUSEHOLD HINTS: How to get rid of garlic and onion smells with vinegar and lemon; Uses of baking soda, canisters, airtight containers, reusable jars, and how to revive yellow window shades; The few cleaning agents required for cleaning the apartment—and more **40**

RECYCLING: Finding a recycling center and being aware of just what the center does and how effective it is; Buying returnables; Saving and using old jars **49**

SHARING THROUGH THE COOPERATIVE SYSTEM: The economics and niceness of sharing; Co-ops, food buying clubs, wholesale buying **51**

PART 2:
Foods for Life, or How to Avoid Scurvy and Slow Starvation
56

SCRUTINY SHOPPING: Learning about prices versus brand, quantity, and quality; How to avoid instant foods and luxury wraps and items **57**

A BALANCED MEAL: The elements which make up a nutritionally substantial meal; A chart containing food balancing and vitamin information.......... **63**

HOW TO COOK: Getting rid of food prejudices; Attitudes; Thinking about what has to be accomplished; Controlling temperature, taste, and quantity **68**

UTENSILS: Basic utensils needed; How one utensil can double as another; A list of utensils and their possible uses **72**

STAPLES AND COMMON INGREDIENTS: Good things to have around the kitchen at all times such as flour, sugar, potatoes, onions, rice; How to store staples so they stay fresh.. **74**

HERBS AND SPICES: A basic list of herbs and spices and their possible uses; A chart of herb and spice uses **88**

CREATIVITY IN COOKING: How to develop originality and create your own touches; How to overcome imaginary barriers in cooking **91**

SUBSTITUTION: What to substitute when you are out of something or how to make Mother's expensive recipe your cheap recipe; A chart of possible substitutions **95**

BIG APPETITE OR UNEXPECTED COMPANY: How to increase recipes without proportionately increasing the price, by doubling up on the cheaper ingredients... **99**

MEASUREMENTS: Abbreviations and what they mean; When measurements may be approximate and when they should be fairly accurate **100**

PRESERVATIVES: Their possible evils; How to avoid them **101**

LEFTOVERS: How to recycle food into something edible; Things that taste good together; Things that may not; Chart of leftovers **104**

HOW TO SAVE TIME: Methods of advance preparation; A list of quick recipes which appears in PART 3 of this book **108**

PART 3:
Bountiful Recipes for the Poor and Hungry
109

THE RECIPES: Beverages, breakfasts, casseroles, desserts, eggs, fish, meats, pastas, potatoes, rice, salads, sandwiches, sauces and gravies, soups, stews, stuffings, vegetables, biscuits, breads, pizzas and pancakes; Sample menus for two weeks; Leftover guide **112**

PART 4:
Country Living in the City
260

INTRODUCTION TO CANNING AND PICKLING: Sterilization and preparation of jars and containers; Canning pickles, tomatoes, and fruits **262**

HOMESTEADING FOODS: Gift-giving suggestions and how to wrap them; Jams, jellies, preserves, and marmalades; Yogurt, yogurt cheese; Granola; Earth snacks and more **267**

A FEW COUNTRY THINGS: Spiced-orange air freshener; Terrarium-potted herb plants; Drying herbs; Candles; Growing house plants............. **279**

INDEX **293**

ACKNOWLEDGMENTS

Thank you people for helping to open my eyes and aiding in the creation of this book. Ellen Epstein, Suzanne Kennedy, Joanne McMillen, Gerard Morin, Char and Jim Stevens, my sister Catherine Winter, my grandmother Hortense Seligmann, Jessie Butler, Grammy Linkevich, Julia King, and my brother Andrew Seligmann, all gave me recipes or tips for this book.

Inés Arias and my mother-in-law Helen Linkevich, my Aunt Sarah Mazzola, my grandmother Angelina D'Amico, aside from giving me recipes or hints, all influenced my cooking style or methods in some subtle way. For instance, without Inés, I would never have discovered nutmeg (one of my favorite spices) as an ingredient with main dishes. I would have thought it was only to be used in desserts. My mother-in-law influenced me toward advanced preparation of meals. I would have forever made scummy chicken soup if it had not been for Sarah. Grandmother showed me how to cut up chuck steaks and increased my knowledge of canning.

My husband Michael Linkevich's contributions are innumerable. He showed me many things about budgeting, turned me off to preservatives, showed me how to make salad dressing and turned me into a salad freak. He suggested additions and corrections for the text and typed quite a bit of it.

At the risk of sounding like a corny greeting card, I'd like to acknowledge the major influencer of various aspects of the way I am, my mother Rosemarie Seligmann. She taught me how to cook, taught me that everyone on earth should have a right to equality, and influenced me against the horribleness of war and destruction. All of these nonacademic lessons—sometimes spoken without a single word—helped to create the person who wrote this book.

My thanks to my brother-in-law, Joel Winter, for naming me Mabel Fitch.

Hello to Rosie King whom I knew at a productive time in my life.

My uncle-agent Jim Seligmann who is both appreciated and loved by me said, "Why don't you write a book?" and brought forward my confidence to do so. To him I am grateful.

Finally, my thanks goes to my editor John Hess and his associate Denise De Clue who turned out to be friendly, helpful human beings, rather than names on a series of correspondences.

PREFACE

"Getting back to the land," rediscovering and living in harmony with nature, and all those other things that are clean, fresh, and good, are many people's dreams and goals and favorite topics of conversation today. Unfortunately, although nature's way seems very enticing, country homesteading and natural food preparation have become rare novelties and environmentally or economically unfeasible for many of us. For some reason or another (like, lack of funds for an initial investment, occupation, or preference), many of us happen not to own a plot of land and a farm house. Our lives are forcibly encompassed by the city or suburbs and a near-total metropolitan existence becomes our "natural" way.

This book is for those of us who enjoy the idea of homesteading and eating wholesome foods but cannot do it in the conventional out-in-the-sticks sense. This book is aimed toward a good, healthful existence in a cramped city or suburban apartment with no peepers singing in the background but rather, a train whose whistle shrieks noisily while its body shakes the breakfast orange juice and flattens one's soufflé.

Young singles, couples, or other economically precarious sorts of people will be interested in the suggestions here toward making ends meet and living on very little money. But, this book also has something to do with overcoming the wasteful garbage-pail trends in our society. Ironically, just as many of us become aware of the need to preserve our environment, the prepackaged, frozen dinner, disposable diaper trends in our society seem to escalate in sickening proportions. Advertising and the accessibility of such commodities have tainted the potential for innovation in the kitchen and elsewhere in the American home. The prepackaged syndrome, in fact, seems to have pervaded our souls. We have lost our creativity; we are not eating sensibly; we waste time and money, and stifle our potential for happiness and fulfillment. This book offers methods for avoiding the use of superfluous household items and foods and gives the reader an opportunity to economize, innovate, and contribute to ecology all at the same time.

Many people spend so much time running around in circles that they delude themselves into believing that they are truly busy. They are convinced that they have no time to do their shopping with scrutiny, or to cook a meal from scratch. (TV dinners can take as long to heat as some scratch meals take to prepare.) Some people, in fact, spend several hours a day over coffee, drinks, dope, or whatnot talking about how busy they are. We have become a twisted and prefabricated society with a limited imagination.

This book will offer suggestions on finding and organizing an apartment, economical recipes and hints on preparation of dishes, as well as foods or ingredients that may be substituted in a recipe. This book includes suggestions on diet balancing, innovation in cooking, and uses of leftovers. It also offers sections on utensils, buying, miscellaneous household hints, how to save time, homemade country foods, how to make candles and terrariums, gift-giving food items, and generally how to enjoy creating without turning it into a distasteful chore.

In this book I wanted to share an enjoyable discovery with people who are either on their own for the first time or who have been out here floundering for awhile. Many mothers kindly offer home-organizing tips to their sons and daughters as they leave home. Unfortunately, few mothers really remember what it was like to be abjectly poor. And chances are, Mom never had her own apartment. The recipes these well-meaning beings have handed down to their children often require costly ingredients that have become too expensive for paupers, though Mom just grumbles and continues to buy the family's favorite items at outrageous prices. Hopefully, novice shoppers and cooks are not yet dependent upon expensive things. The continuing rise in food costs and other prices is frightening. All but the wealthy have no choice but to work around it rather than submit to it.

What I present to the reader is not in my opinion a chore. It is a necessity, and I suppose one could consider some aspects of keeping one's finances, body, and world together a form of task, but it is also a casual art, a pastime, and a way of adaptation toward a not-always-so-beautiful society.

part 1
LEAVING THE OLD NEST AND FEATHERING THE NEW

Shortly after I first left home and moved into an apartment, my roommate called my parents to inform them that I was "starving to death." Though I considered this judgment to be an exaggeration, when I look back on things, it amazes me that I didn't get very sick as a result of the poor diet I maintained. My folks sent me thirty dollars.

Being bailed out by your parents when you are first trying to make it on your own can be an embarrassing and humiliating experience. Those first few months of no free meals at home are especially trying, but you can avoid taking a defeatist's attitude and moving back in with Mom and Dad if you plan things right *before* you leave the nest.

I, like millions of other young Americans, went out to make it on my own and discovered that it's just not that simple. But the experience of life, being more valuable than any degree in economics or nutrition, soon taught me the ropes of survival. We humans are not like the average run-of-the-mill animal. We don't possess the innate ability of knowing how to survive and make things comfortable in our lives. Our superior human intelligence seems to become a lack of intelligence or perception when we are trying to make it alone.

I suppose the primary thing you'll want to do when thinking about leaving home is to define for yourself a few ideas that, as yet, may still be dormant. You should ask yourself why you want to leave your parents' home. Because you're twenty-two years old and all your friends are doing it may not be a good enough reason if your life fits well into the atmosphere which your family offers and all of you are content with your being at home. However, if you have chances at good job opportunities away from home or you feel that the lifestyle you wish to create for yourself does not fit in with that of your parents' or where they live, then you should definitely think about making the big move to your own apartment.

If your parents are not going to be constantly bailing you out, this move will probably be an important episode in your life. It will require some planning as well as an ample adjustment period.

Having made the decision to leave home and move to the "big city" is just the beginning of a long string of judgments that you'll have to make. One of the next problems you'll want to tackle is defining the type of life you'll want to give birth to. For instance, would you like to set up temporary or semipermanent living quarters? Most likely, you'll want to start off by living very cheaply. You'll want to ask yourself if you plan to exist in that manner for an extended period of time or if this extreme frugality is just a stepping stone toward a financially successful and prestigious life.

Your attitudes and the way in which you budget will be influenced by those decisions. For instance, if your first move is to become the transition between leaving home and creating your own comfortable home, chances are you'll want to plan for those future comforts while trying to make your present life as comfortable and productive as possible. However, if you prefer to chance it and live from day to day, you could find a few things in common with my good friend Killer. You may learn some positive things through Killer's resourcefulness, but the tragedy of his life is obvious.

Killer always figured out a way to make money or get something free. He'd walk into my apartment—he never knocked—and as he grabbed an apple out of the refrigerator he'd say:

"Me, Moose and you are going to the dump." Once we found a perfectly good unopened crate of bread at the dump. Sometimes we found bricks and boards and other materials that were helpful in furnishing an apartment. But most of the time we just looked at the rats.

One morning at seven o'clock, I opened my eyes in semishock to find Killer standing inside the door. The city had been pretty well snowed in by a blizzard the night before. Downtown was impassable.

"Come on," said Killer. "Let's make some money." In a little over an hour, three of us had made eighteen dollars shoveling the sidewalks in front of the stores on Main Street.

One time I walked into my apartment to find Killer chest high in bubbles in my bathtub. Killer didn't have an apartment. He just dropped in on his friends. We all thought of him as a loving nuisance.

The incidence of having moved 1000 miles from the city where I knew Killer is one reason why I don't see him anymore. Killer lives at a state mental institution where he doesn't have to make any decisions for himself, and his friends don't have to take care of him anymore.

"I feel comfortable here," he said.

Perhaps you may feel that my account of Killer and its tragic ending is unfair. Most people don't end up in mental institutions because they can't make decisions and keep their lives in order. I've had more than a few acquaintances whose stories are similar to Killer's—save the part about the mental institution. People who, in a seemingly independent fashion, live from one moment to the next and make no attempts to create a home for themselves certainly can't make their lives any happier through this precarious method of survival. Whether they be strong or frail, it is my understanding that most people need some form of roots. Getting yourself organized will probably provide you with these roots —something that Killer never had.

The first section of this book should provide you with some ideas that may be tools toward finding an apartment, setting yourself up, and learning how to budget. Hopefully the inept feelings (that are so easily acquired when you first begin organizing an apartment and doing all those things that are necessary to maintain your new life) will gradually disappear through experience and through the use of this book.

Most of what I offer you through these chapters, I've learned through experience. None of my ideas were developed overnight—it's been a few years since I first made that big move into an unfamiliar world, and still I feel as if I'm constantly going through changes and adjustments. However, these changes and adjustments are not as frightening as they used to be. I look forward to most of them as a challenge.

1
YOUR APARTMENT

You may think that you're ready to start looking for an apartment. Hold off for a moment. Do you have money for your first month's rent and for any utility or security deposits you might be required to pay? In fact, do you know what a security deposit is? Do you have some ideas about the kind of apartment you're looking for and approximately how much you are willing (or can afford) to pay? If you've thought of a few or none of these things, chances are you should slow down and do some heavy thinking—and read the following.

MONEY YOU MUST PAY BEFORE YOU MOVE INTO AN APARTMENT

There are quite a few expenses that you should be prepared for before you begin looking for an apartment. Landlords generally require a month's rent in advance plus a month's rent as security against damage (when you move out, the security should be returned to you if nothing has been damaged in the apartment). So be prepared to pay two months' rent when you move in. If you go to a realtor who has apartment listings, he may either charge you approximately one month's rent (meaning you will have to shell out *three* months' rent instead of two, as you move into an apartment) or the rent of the apartment will have been increased to include his fee for "finding" the apartment for you.

Security deposits are an insurance to the landlord that you will keep his place in good condition. They also insure him that you will give him a month's notice before moving out of your apartment. If you don't, in many cases, the landlord will keep all or some of your security to make up for his inconvenience of possibly not having a renter in the apartment for a month. (Because there is a shortage of economical apartments in most cities, it is highly unlikely that this will happen to the landlord, but he might keep a renter's deposit anyway.) Some landlords attach a rather broad interpretation to the potential use of this security deposit. With some landlords, no matter what you do, there is no way you're going to get your security back. They will say that the money went toward usual wear and tear of the apartment, or that it went toward cleaning the rug—which they will tell you (as you are moving out) is routine procedure. But they won't tell you this as you're moving in. If the garbage disposal happens to break down through no fault of yours, these types of landlords will make you pay for it. You will also never see receipts for rug cleaning or for a new garbage disposal. You will simply be told by these exploiters that the bill was fifty dollars (subtracted from your security). Some cities require that security deposits be held in trust in a bank by the landlord for the renter. This deposit can collect interest which the renter should receive upon leaving the apartment. Find out whether the law applies in your city.

If you pay for your own utilities (such as gas, electricity, water, or oil), then the utility company(s) may require a deposit as insurance that you will not skip town leaving an unpaid bill. This deposit, if there is one, will probably be about twenty-five dollars. Not all utility companies charge a deposit, but you should be financially prepared to cope with this possibility just in case.

I'd like to mention a few things to consider when trying to decide on the cost of an apartment. The rent sometimes covers the expense of water, electricity, heat, and gas, or some combination of these. A $100-a-month apartment in which you must pay all of the water, electric, gas, and heat will cost you more than a $115 apartment in which all of these utilities are paid. These factors must be taken into account before deciding on an apartment.

FINDING THE RIGHT KIND OF APARTMENT

There are innumerable types of apartments in the many cities of this country. Some are large, others are small. Some have reasonable rents and many do not. Some are in good condition and others are not. Unless you are willing to put a fair amount of work into an apartment, keep that in mind as you are looking. Some landlords require that you sign a lease, while others do not.

THE LEASE

A lease is an agreement between you and the landlord. It is usually binding for a year or two and is renewed as both parties see fit. The lease insures you (and obligates you) to a particular apartment for the duration of the lease period. Leases can be broken by either party in some instances. Leases are supposed to reflect the interests of both parties, but it often looks like the lease was composed with only the landlord in mind. Be aware of this before you make the decision about whether or not you want to sign a lease. Chances are, that if you plan on living in one place for any length of time, it would not harm you to sign a lease and it might be of some benefit in the sense that you are guaranteed a place to live.

HOW TO LOOK AT AN APARTMENT

You have not yet begun to look for an apartment—you are still planning out the preliminaries. By not rushing into things, in most cases, you'll do better in the long run. You have to train your eyes and your nose to those things that may not be obvious when you first look at an apartment, but will be ever-present once you move in: shabby walls and floors, excessive filth, bugs, and peculiar odors. I've been told that a smell similar to that of urine indicates that there are roaches in the building—but then again—rotting and decaying wood also can give off that odor (as can urine itself). In any case, reject any apartment with a urine-type of smell. Back to bugs. I once looked at an oppressive apartment that was being "renovated." The developer—who looked like the "Godfather"—flicked on the lights to show me the apartment. A roach scampered across the floor. He slyly crunched it with his foot and then went on to tell me how wonderful the apartment was.

LOOKING FOR AN APARTMENT

You are now just about ready to start looking for an apartment. Finding the suitable place to live is often quite frustrating and seemingly impossible. So tap every resource you can think of while looking for an apartment. Previously, I mentioned the instance of going to a realtor who will "find" an apartment for you. ("Find" is in quotes for the simple reason that landlords list apartments with realtors—the realtors do not go hunting for apartments.) Avoid this method (unless you've tried everything else) as it will be an extra expense to you.

One way to avoid the realtors is to ask friends if they know of vacant apartments or look in the local newspaper(s) for vacancies. Or ask local merchants if they know of any apartments for rent. Don't be afraid to walk into a small grocery store or bar and ask the owner if he knows of any empty apartments. Many merchants have apartments above their stores. Even if he does not know of any, someone in the store might. You can even walk down a residential street and ask the people who are sitting outside if they know of a vacant apartment. You might think this takes a lot of nerve, but it certainly beats paying a month's rent to a realtor. Also, colleges and universities usually have lists of available housing.

If you work, in a few rare cases your company will have leads for getting an apartment. But be sure to ask all of your coworkers if they know of vacant apartments—and don't forget to ask the personnel director who interviewed you. If you are a student and plan on getting an apartment for the following school year, try to find a senior who is vacating his apartment and make arrangements with his landlord to rent the apartment.

FINDING AN APARTMENT: YOU AND THE LANDLORD

When you feel you've found an apartment that you are seriously considering, you should try to have a talk with the landlord. If there is a lease, make sure you ask him questions about the things you don't understand, and make sure he gives you straight answers. Ask him about the security deposit, if there is one. Commit him to telling you (in writing if necessary) just exactly what that deposit is for. Even if he seems like a nice guy, your questions and his answers are necessary. If he's really a nice guy, he'll gladly answer all of your questions, so you needn't feel embarrassed. Find out which utilities he pays for and which ones you pay for. If he is paying for the heat, ask him if it is shut off at night. It's awfully hard to study or just stay up until midnight on a cold night if the heat has been shut off at nine o'clock. Be on the lookout for subtle hints or direct statements about your obligation to paint the apartment or fix it up in any other way. If his requests for repair sound fair to you, accept them. If they do not and the two of you can't come to an amiable agreement, then it would be best for you to look for another place.

Before you move into an apartment, try to compare and find out if your rent is "reasonable." Unless you are getting a rent-controlled apartment, you apparently are stuck with whatever price the landlord puts on the apartment. If you are planning to move into a rent-controlled apartment, call the Housing Authority or an equivalent agency and find out if the landlord is charging you the correct amount.

If you feel it's suitable, you should approach your potential landlord in various tactful and well-thought-out ways as to the possibility of his lowering your rent in exchange for chores such as emptying the garbage throughout his building. This potential deal could also be struck up between you and the landlord after you move in. It all depends upon which time seems right to you.

So long as you are relatively quiet, pay your rent, and don't turn your apartment into a store, crash pad, or house of prostitution, your landlord cannot tell you who is and who is not allowed to visit you. Some landlords will try to restrict you from visitors of the opposite sex or of a different race. The Housing Authority, the Human Rights Commission, and the Legal Aid or the Legal Services are some agencies that might be able to help you with such hassles with your landlord. Some of these problems can be avoided before the fact, if you directly ask the landlord what his policy is about visitors. If you feel it's best to not just pop the question on him (so he won't get any ideas about limiting your visitors), at least try to sense his attitudes on this matter. Sometimes you can simply tell that this will or will not be an issue with a particular landlord.

YOU AND YOUR ROOMMATE

If you decide that you will have a roommate, this person should probably be going through all the apartment research and hunting with you. Hopefully the roommate will either agree to your approach to the problem or both of you will be able to agree to a compromise. If you don't have a particular roommate in mind, you might take the chance of renting an apartment and then finding a roommate. This could be a risky business, but you'll have to make that ultimate decision.

After you've chosen a roommate (or roommates), make sure that the two (three or four) of you get things straight as to your expectations of one another. You should mutually decide whether you are going to share food expenses, eat together, shop together, or if you will do everything separately. If you decide to share in these things, some sort of rotating schedule might be worked out for turns in shopping and preparation of meals. If you have quite different working or other schedules, this may be reason enough to do all these things separately. In that case, you must also decide how you are going to divide shelf and refrigerator space. All these discussions help to prevent future confrontations.

Another hint about you and your roommate: I've found that if you don't spend all of your free time together and become inseparable, you will avoid emotional arguments and an eventual unfriendly breakup. You can become very sick of a roommate living in the confined quarters that most apartments offer, unless you make efforts to spend a lot of time away from one another. Also, if you don't lend money to or borrow money from a roommate, you'll be forever happy that you made that decision. You'll probably, at least once after you've lived on your own for a while, be a third party to some uncomfortable situation where roommates or friends have lent money to one another and have never been repaid. If you can stay clear of the lending and borrowing business, you'll be respected more in the long run.

MOVING IN

I wish I could advise some logical way of moving your things into an apartment. If you just have a few things, you'll most likely have no real problem because someone will probably lend you a car so you can move in. As for large items, it's really difficult to say what the most effective method would be for hauling your stuff. Some people make twenty trips in a VW bug. Others rent a small trailer or a truck.

YOUR TELEPHONE

With all of the aforementioned expenses, you may have to wait a while before you can afford a telephone and its additional expenses. Unless there is already a phone in the apartment and the previous renter is willing to sign it over to you, you must pay an installation fee. This fee ranges from five dollars to twenty-five dollars. If you have never had a telephone before, or, if you did not previously pay your full bill, you will be asked to pay a deposit for your phone service—a cost of about twenty-five to fifty dollars.

One way to alleviate a portion of the fees and deposits is to share the phone with your roommate who must share the costs equally with you. You can eliminate the telephone deposit if a roommate who has had a phone before is the person who orders the phone. Even though this person is responsible for the phone, you too can have your name in the directory. But beware, extra listings cost an additional fee each month.

When you order your telephone, the representative with whom you talk will undoubtedly try to convince you to get either a Princess,

Trimline, or Touchtone (push-button) telephone. The representative will probably not tell you of the extra monthly expense. If you are trying to save money, do not order any of these, because the extra $1.15 to $2.33 (plus taxes) each month can wreck your budget.

You may be wondering if there is a way to get a telephone in your name without ever paying a deposit. The answer is yes. If you have a roommate who has previously had a phone, have him order the phone for your apartment. After a few months, have this roommate sign this telephone (account) over to you. When a phone is signed over from one person to another, the telephone number remains the same and the phone stays in the same apartment. Simply call the telephone company and tell the sales representative that your roommate who has the phone wishes to sign it over to you and have it placed in your name. Do not let the sales representative tell you that the phone cannot be signed over. If you are told this, then ask to speak to another representative or a supervisor. Eventually, someone will be familiar with this procedure. Remember to keep insisting that you paid the bill with your roommate so you can be responsible for the phone. The telephone company will then send your roommate a form to fill out on which he will state that you may assume his present telephone account and number.

By now, you're helplessly looking at your possessions that lie in little heaps all over your new apartment. You're probably wondering if this place will ever look like home. Before you know it, you'll start adding your touches and you'll begin to feel comfortable in your new dwelling.

LANDLADY

My husband, Michael, had just been hired to teach at a private school in the Bronx. It was February, and he was replacing a religious brother who was taking a sick leave. A few days before he was to begin teaching, he was informed that he had the job. So we drove from New Jersey, where we had been staying, to the Bronx to find an apartment.

As we drove around, I decided that I wanted to live in one of the old brick houses in the residential section near the school. I knew I couldn't be fussy, but that was my fantasy, at any rate. Because we didn't have much time to lose, we went to a realtor who said that she knew of a place on a street a few blocks from the school. The realtor, a woman named Sylvia, called about the apartment. She spoke to the landlady who was also a resident of the house and assured her that we were reputable people (which can be translated to mean that we were white), and that Michael was a teacher at St. Stanislaus's Point.

"Boy, what a pineapple," Sylvia said as she hung up. I thought a pineapple was a prejudiced way of referring to someone who was Hawaiian or Polynesian until I discovered that Rosina Flatbush, the landlady, was neither. The owner of the real estate agency walked in.

"Ah, so you're teaching at 'The Point,'" said Ernie Trebba, whose name appeared on billboards and buildings throughout that section of the Bronx.

"My son went to 'The Point.' My four nephews go there now. Is Brother Harold still there?"

Michael said he didn't really know. Ernie smiled and told a few reminiscent 'Point' stories. At the time, we did not know that we would owe good old Ernie a rather large sum of money for "finding" the apartment for us. We had just assumed that a landlord or landlady paid the realtor a fee to rent out his or her apartment. Sylvia gave us directions to Rosina's house. Her job was done. She had made one phone call and her agency was now owed $140 by the still unsuspecting Linkeviches if we agreed to rent the apartment.

We easily found Rosina's house—a converted two-family brick structure which was forty or fifty years old. The green and white metal awning in front was rather ostentatious, but aside from that the house was approximately what I had been imagining. The street was also in a semiquiet residential section a block from Westchester county. We were later to find out that although you could hear the elevated trains through the night, it was one of those things that, from the distance, rattled you to sleep.

Rosina opened the door for us.

"So you're gonna teach at 'The Point,'" said Rosina. "My nephew went there. Also my sister-in-law's brother went there. Are you a Brother?" (By this she meant religious brother.)

"I wouldn't be with him if he was," said I.

"Oh yeah," said Rosina, totally unembarrassed by her blooper.

The apartment was the right size, a reasonable price for that neighborhood, and we liked it—so we consented to rent it. It was then that Rosina informed us that we owed Ernie Trebba $140. When we told her we knew nothing about that policy, she said, "Tell him you can't pay that much. Make a deal with him." We payed Trebba $70. We tried to get away with less.

Little did we know as we naively stepped into Rosina's house what we were getting ourselves into. Sylvia, the realtor, had said that Rosina was nosey. She was nosey alright, but, in addition, she was one of those characters who was definitely worth knowing, just for the experience.

Rosina had a very loud fog-horn voice. You could hear her yacking outside the windows to the neighbors every morning. She was usually, in most defiant terms, giving the victim a piece of her mind.

"What the hell you doin' that for? You ain't supposed to trim roses like that. What, you crazy or somethin'? And keep your dog from you-know-whatting all over my lawn. He did it again this mornin'. I had to take a shovel and stick it in the garbidge. And what with my arthritis. . . ." You never heard what the other person was saying. On a warm morning when our windows were opened, the smoke from Rosina's cigarettes wandered into our windows. Rosina was a heavy smoker and coughed like one.

Rosina told me about three times a week what a skinny little girl I was. (In my opinion I'm just an average-sized person.) One day she smiled and said I looked healthy because I looked as if I had gained weight. To her that was a compliment. To me, it was an insult. Rosina was a squatty person whose shape from shoulders to hips was symmetrical. Two skinny legs were attached to this torso. Her reddish dyed hair, cut as if there was a bowl around her head, and her tremendous eyes, were the two things which made her recognizable in a crowd.

Rosina was an incessant talker and a worry wart. Out loud she worried about the plumber, the garbage man, the water department, her garden, the black people next door, the Spanish people across the street, whether her roof would begin leaking, her bills, and whether she would receive her rent money from us. She always reminded us even though we were never late in giving it to her. Because of Rosina's ability to gab, I felt as if I knew everything about her. She knew nothing about us, even though she tried hard to find out. When we were off somewhere, she'd try to find out where we'd been, but we'd never tell her. It was a matter of principle. It was simply none of her business.

Rosina was paranoid about muggers and thieves. She would lock her door even when she stepped out to empty the garbage. A few days before the Fourth of July, kids in the neighborhood began exploding fire crackers. We all went outside to watch. Rosina, anxious to see all the commotion, left her key inside and locked herself out.

"Oh no, what am I gonna do, oh no, oh no," blubbered Rosina. "You got a credit card or somethin'?" she sniffled to Michael. The credit card, when slipped the right way into the crack between the door and the frame would unlock the door. Michael determined that Rosina just wanted to know if he had a credit card, so he took out his old student identification card and unlocked the door. A few weeks later, Rosina locked herself out again. This time neither of us had any plastic cards to open the door with. Rosina and I boosted Michael up to a window that was unlocked so he could get in and open the door.

"Oh no, oh no, he's gonna break his neck. Be careful. Oh no, what have I done? He's gonna kill himself," she cried.

With all of Rosina's nagging about the rent, she was a generous person. She gave us, at different times, curtains, clothes pins, a bureau, and a storm window, after we broke one of the windows in our apartment. She also gave us many figs from her trees and was forever offering me coffee, cake, lasagna, and whatever she happened to have around. We never took her up on an invitation until the day we moved out when we sat down to tea with her. We were afraid that she'd drive us buggy if we ever got too friendly with her. But looking back, I don't think that was true. Rosina just wanted a little friendship now and then—something that we never gave her.

2
SETTING UP THE APARTMENT

Chances are, that the first day you go to your apartment with dust pan, broom, and various cleaning agents, you'll be a bit shocked. You'll probably be amazed at how dirty the place is. People who are moving out of an apartment don't usually clean it as well as they would for themselves. So unless you are moving into a new or newly renovated apartment, or into a complex where landlords often hire people to clean up for the next renter (often paying these people from the previous renter's security deposit), expect some dirt.

Clean up your apartment before you settle in. You could find that other people's messes and smells get to you, and you'll be happy if you eliminate them soon. You may be one of those people who never notices cobwebs in corners, but a previous renter's grease spatterings on the wall above the stove may really turn you off. The point is, you'll feel more comfortable with your type of mess than with someone else's.

In preparation for cleaning, bring with you to the apartment a broom and dustpan (or vacuum), rags, sponges, buckets, and the cleaning agents you'll need as suggested on page 43 under Household Hints.

If you plan on painting the apartment, check with the landlord and find out if he's paying for the paint. Some landlords do and some don't. Also, if the walls are made of plaster and are badly cracked, chipped, or gouged out, you may want to repair them with plaster of Paris (usually obtainable at hardware stores or in the hardware section of department stores). Again, ask the landlord if he's paying for this repair. The tools and equipment you'll need for painting are a roller and a roller pan (if desired) and a brush. You'll need plaster of Paris and a putty knife or similar tool, to spread the plaster. Use a water base paint and don't get the most expensive kind (if you're paying) unless you plan on living in the apartment for several years or more. Most paint is quite expensive and there is no reason why you should pay for a job that might hold up for years if you're not going to be there to appreciate it.

Before buying the paint, think about what colors you may want in your apartment. If you have roommates, all of you should discuss this.

Light colors give more of an appearance of spaciousness. Dark colors could make a room look very small and closed-in. Medium-toned colors can give a place a feeling of warmth, but like dark colors, will make a small room look even smaller. The novelty of fiery or psychedelic colors will most likely soon turn into an annoyance or an eye sore. If you want some sparkling colors in your apartment, paint a door bright pink, but don't do it to an entire room. If you do, there will be times when you feel as if you're suffocating.

Plastering is done before painting. Make sure the walls are free of grease, dust, and excessive dirt before you plaster or paint. Follow directions for plastering on the back of the plaster package. There should be instructions on the label of the paint can and the number of square feet the paint will cover, should also be indicated.

You can estimate how many feet you have to paint by estimating the height to the ceiling by using your body as a tape measure. For example, I'm about five feet six inches tall. If I stretch my arm above my head toward the ceiling, the inside of my elbow will be approximately level with the top of my head. The length from the inside of my elbow to the tip of my middle finger is more or less one foot four inches. When I reach toward the ceiling against the wall, my middle finger is about one foot two inches from the ceiling. Now I add everything up. $5'6'' + 1'4'' + 1'2'' = 8'$. (It certainly is amazing how the figures came out so well for my own personal case.) You can pace off the width of the wall —estimating the number of inches to the pace. Let's say you get twelve feet. Now multiply twelve feet by the eight foot height and you get ninety-six square feet of wall space. Remember, this is just one wall. Pace off the adjacent wall, add in the other two walls and you have your total square footage of wall space. If you have a tape measure, you can use it to do all the measuring.

Some "holidays" (as my father-in-law calls the sections one misses while painting) can be seen only in good light. If you can bring a lamp with you to the apartment, do so. Remove the shade so that you can use the bulb to its full potential. As you are painting, move the lamp around the wall area in search of "holidays."

After you've painted the walls and have allowed them to dry, you'll then probably decide whether you want two coats of paint. If the walls were in especially poor shape or the walls had been painted previously with a darkish color, you'll most likely need two coats.

Fixing up most apartments requires a little bit of handy work so you'll probably want to make up a little tool box for yourself. This box does not have to be an elaborate affair—in fact a shoe box would be good. You might need two screwdrivers—one regular and one Phillips (Phillips are those screwdrivers with the funny four-sided tip). Some cabinets have Phillips Screws on them. If none of yours do, then you can forget about the Phillips screwdriver. You'll need a fairly well-balanced medium-sized hammer (try it out before settling for it). If it wavers from one side to the other as you're trying to hammer down, it's a poorly balanced hammer. You'll need various sizes of nails—mostly with medium to large heads, some screws, and possibly a pair of pliers. Pliers are useful for various things—one being that you can hold a nut in place as you are turning a screw or bolt into the nut. If the bolt moves around while you are trying to tighten a nut, you'll never be able to tighten it. Using pliers on the bolt will prevent this. You may need a large wrench at some time to loosen fittings around pipes in the event that your sink becomes clogged. But this expensive tool should be borrowed. Screwdrivers and hammers are tools which many families have duplicates of. Before you leave home, you should see if there are any spare tools lying around.

[Also try to find an extra shovel. If you live in the city, a shovel is a special and essential utensil for cleaning up dog dung on the sidewalks near your apartment. (You might also want to get a scraper for your corrugated soled boots.) A small shovel will do if you live, for example, on the mid- to upper-east side of Manhattan where the canine inhabitants are dainty, curly poodles with pink plastic barettes on their heads. However, if you live on say, "two hundred toidy terd" street in the Bronx or in downtown Manhattan, a large shovel is needed to remove what is left by ample sized, drooling, growling mongrels.]

You are now ready to do a bit of handy work around the apartment. If linoleum is coming up in the corners of a room, tack it down with large, one-inch to one and one-half-inch nails. If screws are missing from cabinet doors, replace them.

Some landlords forbid tenants from putting nails or hooks into the walls. You can hardly blame them the way some people massacre plaster when they nail into it. If your landlord does not want you to nail into the wall, buy the type of picture-hanging hook which can be stuck onto the walls. Utility hooks of the same design can also be purchased.

Hanging kitchen utensils from hooks or from long sturdy nails will help you organize things better. And if you have limited cabinet space, you'll need some wall space. Arrange these hooks so that they are out of the line of apartment traffic, so you won't tear your clothing on hooks as you walk by them. Do not put hooks in walls which will have doors slamming up against them because eventually the hook will poke a hole in the door. Don't just go madly hammering away. Think before you arrange your hooks.

If your apartment is without a refrigerator and/or stove, chances are you can pick up these items at a price that you can afford. Look in the classified section of the local newspaper(s) for used refrigerators and stoves. When looking at a refrigerator, if at all possible, plug it in and see if it runs. If the gasket—the rubber around the door—is old and leaky, it can be replaced with foam weather stripping. Leaky gaskets place excessive wear on the motor causing it to use at least twice as much electricity. If you have a choice in your kitchen, put the refrigerator in a place where it is not surrounded by walls. If air circulates freely around it, the motor will not have to work as hard.

As for stoves, you can purchase either an electric or a gas range. In most cases a gas stove is easier to install. You need a special 240 volt hookup for an electric stove. An electrician will probably have to come in to install it. Most apartments have a gas outlet. Check with your landlord about this. If there is one, you should be in the market for a gas stove. At any rate, these outlets are less complicated than the voltage outlets for the electric stove. When you find a stove, if it is connected, check the burners and oven to see if they work. Ask the seller as many questions as you can think of. For instance, you might get instructions on how to use the stove and find out if you must light the burners and the oven (if the stove is gas) or if the pilot is automatic. Ask whether all burners are working and if they are not, find out if they can be repaired easily. Also, many oven gauges are inaccurate. If you set the temperature for 375° F. the oven may actually be at 350° F. or 400° F. depending upon whether its tendency is to run cooler or hotter than normal. If you ask questions before you buy the stove, the chances of getting a poor deal will be slightly diminished. You will also be getting an account of how the stove works which will make your adjustment to it a bit easier.

Your apartment by now is probably starting to look pretty nice, but it is most likely very sparsely furnished. Quite often parents have furniture, throw pillows, and kitchen utensils that are gathering dust in the attic. You will probably be doing your folks a favor if you take these articles off their hands.

Some cities offer many opportunities for you to pick up old or new household and personal items at reduced prices. Rummage, garage, and basement sales seem to be the mania in some small and average-sized cities. Chances are that your city may even have a newspaper that comes to you as a boxholder and acts as an advertiser for the inhabitants of the city. Papers such as these advertise articles for sale—both used and new—and also request items wanted by individuals. If your city does not have such a paper, look in the regular city paper under "classified" for such offerings.

People are discovering that it's easier to have a garage or basement sale than to pay someone to haul their unwanted articles away. Rummage sales are no longer solely for charity—people have them in their homes for their own benefit. Some of these sales are really great—while others are lousy. If you're lucky, you'll come away with a mattress, pots and pans, eating utensils, shirts in good condition, and other similar items at really cheap prices. If you go to a real bummer of a sale, the most valuable items you'll see will be photographs of Mary Lou's graduation, some plastic roses, and three *Bugs Bunny Goes to College* books. If you hit a few crummy sales, don't give up right away on the whole idea. You will most likely hit several good sales in due time.

In some cities, people leave large items out on the curb on certain days for the sanitation department to pick up. It is understood that if you see such items on the street, they are yours if you want them. You may find mattresses, chairs, couches, laundry baskets, and tables. If you look through these things carefully and they seem to be clean and vermin free, grab them before someone else does. If there is a roach problem in your city, it's best to stay away from mattresses, stuffed chairs, and couches.

If you are looking for plumbing supplies such as sinks, toilets, bathtubs, or other miscellaneous items, see if you can find a plumbing supply company or a wrecking company. These outfits take old fixtures out of houses and then sell them, give them away, or dump them. If a company is about to dump an item you desire, convince them that it would be cheaper for them if you just took it off their hands. If they are not willing to give away an item, bargain with them. "How about five dollars?" you say.

"Give me ten," he says.

"Seven dollars and fifty cents," you say.

If they don't go below $10, and $10 is still a good deal, then pay it. If it's not what you consider to be a good deal, then go elsewhere.

If you are looking for a particular item, and you've been striking out at sales and on the street, put an advertisement in the paper under "wanted"—if the cost of such an ad is reasonable. Some stores, such as supermarkets, often have free bulletin boards where the customers can advertise articles they wish to sell or buy.

Also, be on the lookout for sales at supermarkets and department stores which are advertised in the paper. Calculate transportation costs versus how much money you can save on the sale item and decide whether or not the trip is worth it. If you're getting sixty cents off a bottle of oil and it costs you fifty cents to get to the store, the ten cents you save is not really worth it. A slightly larger savings just might be worth it—especially if you can find more than one item you want on sale.

Next time you pass a street vendor, look to see what he has to offer. Occasionally, these people sell things besides costume jewelry and belts. They also sell panty hose and kitchen items—often at better prices than in the stores. If you're looking for furniture and you've struck out at rummage sales, the ads in the paper, and no one has left a gem on the curb, look for thrift shops such as Goodwill and the Salvation Army. Cleaned, used mattresses can sometimes be purchased at these stores. Unfortunately, some thrift shops don't live up to their name, and offer no bargains at all.

Whatever you do, don't buy new furniture while you're still budgeting and trying to make ends meet. This would be especially foolish if you don't plan on living in the apartment you're in now for at least the next five years. Moving furniture any distance costs a fortune, and besides, your tastes may change or your furniture may not fit into your future home. There's something very comfortable about furniture you've acquired cheap or free or have made yourself. No matter how ugly it is, it fits in.

Making your own furniture is, of course, the most satisfying method of furnishing your apartment. Rummage for used brick and old pieces of wood at sites where buildings have been torn down. Portable, adjustable bookcases can be built by stacking bricks at both ends of boards that are laid across as shelves. Books will stand best if this structure is placed against a wall, as it has no back. Tables can be built from old weathered wood in various designs. A basic design would be as diagrammed in Figure 1. Select wood which is at least one inch thick. Use nails which are about two inches long and have medium heads. You'll need seven boards: one for the table top; two identical boards for legs; two identical reinforcing boards; one shelf board which is as long as the width between the two legs and as wide as the leg boards; and one "lean" board which is the width you desire and as long as the distance between the two legs. To assemble, follow the diagram, nailing boards together in appropriate places.

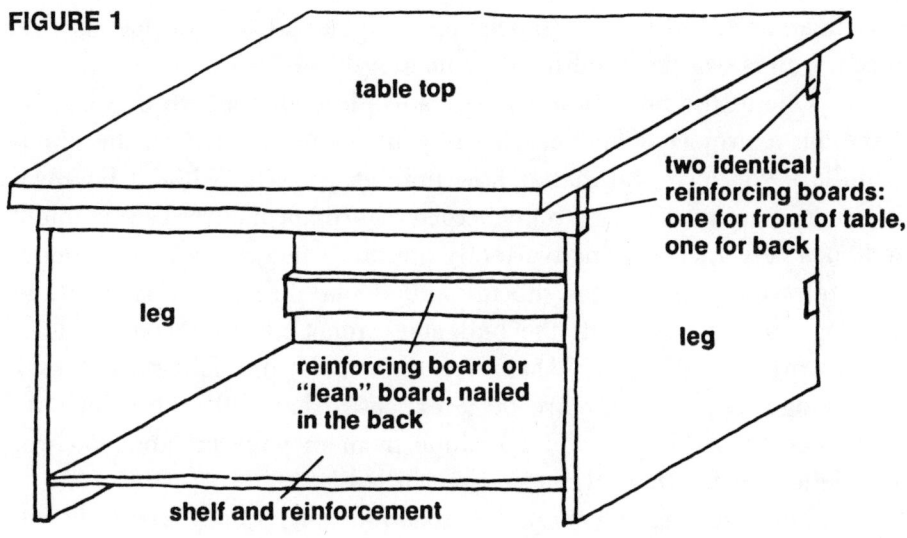

FIGURE 1

Old telephone cable spools can be used as tables. They come in various sizes and can be painted, shellacked, or left natural. Orange crates[1] can be used as tables, cabinets, or bureaus. Crates can be lined up, stacked, or attached together in various patterns.

Do not expect that you will run into so many good deals at once that your apartment will be instantly furnished. Chances are the furnishing will happen gradually, over a period of weeks or months.

---

[1] Orange crates, though hard to find these days because fruits are now shipped in cardboard boxes, can sometimes turn up at rummage sales, on the street, or in people's garages.

3

YOUR BUDGET—
MAKING ENDS MEET

On paper, survival may seem not all that difficult to achieve, but the reality can be somewhat eye-opening. Making ends meet is one of the daily hassles a low- to no-income person will encounter. But a good healthful life can be obtained through conscientious budgeting and economizing. Current trends and fluctuating prices will play an important role in how well one's money will stretch. There will most likely be times of near financial disaster in every novice budgeter's life; but one can learn to compromise, adjust, and juggle, and simply survive.

One of the most practical ways to plan your month or week is to make out a projected budget. See if you can plan it within the number of dollars you have, no matter how limited they are, without borrowing or going into your savings. Some expenses are not incurred every month, and, as a result, can be inadvertently omitted when making out a budget. Hospitalization, insurances, doctor and dental bills, prescriptions, and clothing are expenses that the budgeter cannot afford to pay suddenly without previous planning. Don't forget to make provisions for these in your budget because they are large expenses that will take a lot out of your pocketbook. If you don't include them in your budget, you won't be able to pay for them when you are billed.

For instance, if your hospitalization is $168 a year, divide that into twelve equal parts and you get $14 dollars, which is the amount you must put aside each month for hospitalization. Or, if you work, then you probably get paid each week. Therefore, consider each month to have four weeks. Divide the fourteen dollars by the four weeks to get $3.50, which is the amount you put aside each week for hospitalization.[1]

There is one very nice benefit in budgeting your money as outlined above. We generally consider each month to have four weeks. Therefore,

---

[1] It should be noted here that this method does not usually work for car insurance, because the insurance company or agent asks for advanced payment. You might have to pay your 12 months of insurance coverage in seven months. Take extra care in planning your budget for your car insurance.

we would expect three months to have twelve weeks. But if you look at any three consecutive months, you will see that they have thirteen weeks, not twelve. This means that if your bills are due monthly, every three months you get a "free" or bonus check.

Items such as hospitalization or auto insurance, may require a downpayment. When you initially take out any type of insurance policy, you should have saved enough money to meet this first bill, and then incorporate the subsequent payments into your budget. For a sample budget schedule, see Chart 1.

There are times when you will have to use common sense and "juggle" your budget. For instance, if you become ill and have to spend thirty dollars in one month for medical expenses and prescriptions, since you've budgeted ten dollars for medical fees for that month, you're going to have to dig up the extra twenty dollars from somewhere within your budget. Let's suppose you had planned on buying some new underwear. Patch up your old stuff and wait until the following month to buy some. If you're a woman and you wear panty hose to work, you'll probably want to leave something in your clothing budget for them. So let's say you take out five dollars from the clothing budget and you put it into medical. You are now still short fifteen dollars. Suppose you take the subway or bus to work or school. You figure if you walk six extra blocks a day for a month you can avoid changing trains or buses, and you can save thirty-five cents a day or $7.70 for twenty-two days (or the number of days you take the public transportation in a month). You now need $7.30 more for your medical bills. Chances are you'll be able to take it out of the Miscellany part of your budget. Being sick however, while it robs you on one hand, may save you a bit of money on the other. If you are paid for sick days, you won't lose any salary—and to top things off—you won't have to pay for transportation (or panty hose if you wear them). Being sick will naturally not be the only thing which will force you to juggle your budget. Many things will come up, but eventually you'll get the hang of things and you'll be able to feel fairly comfortable with your budget.

CHECKING ACCOUNT

If you don't already have a checking account, you're probably beginning to run into a few problems. It's not a good idea to send cash through the mail, yet it's much easier to pay some of your bills by mail.

CHART 1

SAMPLE BUDGET FOR ONE MONTH BASED ON A TAKE-HOME INCOME OF $230 PER MONTH

EXPENSES	PROJECTIONS FOR ONE MONTH	ACTUAL AMOUNTS PUT ASIDE OR SPENT[1]				ACTUAL AMOUNT SPENT IN ONE MONTH
		Week 1	Week 2	Week 3	Week 4	
Rent	75	18.75	18.75	18.75	18.75	75
Phone	8	2.00	2.00	2.00	2.00	8
Utilities	27	6.75	6.75	6.75	6.75	27
Transportation	22	5.50	5.50	5.50	5.50	22
Medical, Dental, and Prescriptions	12	3.00	3.00	3.00	3.00	12
Food	40	10.00	10.00	10.00	10.00	40
Clothing	10	2.50	2.50	2.50	2.50	10
Insurance and Hospitalization	14	3.50	3.50	3.50	3.50	14
Miscellany (Savings, Entertainment, Gifts, Emergency, School, Reading Material)	22	5.50	5.50	5.50	5.50	22
TOTAL	$230					$230

[1] Money for bills due monthly such as insurance and rent, should be put aside weekly and recorded on your chart as "spent."

And money orders, which can substitute for checks, cost at least a quarter apiece.

A checking account can be opened at a commercial bank. If a bank has the word "savings" in any part of its name, it is a savings bank and it does not handle checking accounts in most cases. Checking accounts are easy to learn about and maintain; so it's worth your while to begin looking for a commercial bank that will satisfactorily meet your checking account needs.

Different banks charge different amounts for the maintenance of checking accounts. Shop around for the best deal if there is more than one commercial bank in your area. Although there are other types and variations of the checking account, the two most common types are the Special Checking Account and the Regular Checking Account.[1] If you decide upon a Special Account you will be charged for each check you write out. (You may also be charged a monthly fee in addition to the check charge.) With a Regular Account you are not charged anything for the checks or the account, but you must maintain a minimum balance (usually $100 or more) in your account.

When weighing the odds regarding the type of account to open, note the following: Assume that for a Special Account the bank charges ten cents a check and requires no additional maintenance fee. If you estimate that you'll write forty checks annually, the account will cost you four dollars a year. If you choose the Regular Account and leave $100 in it, you will lose five dollars by not putting this $100 in a savings account at five percent interest. If you write forty checks in your Regular Account, because you have not been charged anything for the checks, you gain four dollars. Subtract the four dollars from the five you lost by not putting the $100 into an interest-yielding savings account, and you've lost one dollar by using the Regular Account instead of the Special. If you write more checks a year (say over 50), chances are that the Regular Account might benefit you more. But on the other hand, if you can get a high enough interest rate on your $100, the Regular Account may *not* be worth it. And finally, you may feel as if you can't maintain a minimum balance of $100 —or whatever amount the requirement happens to be. Think about the

---

[1] Some banks offer free checking accounts to students. If you are a student, find out if any banks in your neighborhood offer this service.

whole situation and its various possibilities and consult your local banks. *Then* open your account.

Once you've opened your account, it's important to keep careful track of your money. Checking account balances are easy to figure out. Usually it's little more than a simple case of subtraction or addition. If you overdraw (meaning that you write a check for an amount which is greater than what you have in your account), you could create a few hassles for yourself. You will be charged a fee for this error, and it might take a while before the bank clears things up in your account. The whole thing is an embarrassment and a nuisance. So make sure that you don't make any mathematical errors when recording checks and deposits in your book, and don't "cheat," thinking you'll put more money in before the bank gets your bad check. Checks are returned to your bank very quickly.

SAVINGS ACCOUNT

You can also open a savings account at a commercial bank, but savings banks offer you a little more money in interest. The larger interest may or may not be worth it to you. It will depend upon the location of the banks, the amount of money you plan on putting into a bank, and just how much more interest the savings bank offers. As with checking accounts, there are also different types of savings accounts. Depending on the account you decide upon, you can receive the minimum, or average, or maximum interest that a bank offers.

There are accounts called Time Savings Accounts from which you can receive a higher interest rate on your money if you deposit a minimum balance (usually $500 to $1000) for a minimum amount of time. Some Time Accounts require a minimum balance for two or three or more years. If you deposit your money in these accounts, your interest rate will be even higher than with a Time Account which runs for a year or less. If you close a Time Savings Account before the time period is over, you will lose some or all of the interest. The Regular Day to Day Account which requires a minimum balance of one to five dollars and no time period, offers the lowest interest because it does not commit your money for any length of time. It might be the right account for you. Shop around for the account that seems most suitable for your needs. If your needs change, you can open other accounts and still maintain your original account.

CREDIT

Don't be deceived by the ads you see on TV about borrowing money. It is simply not that easy to decide to go camping in Maine for the weekend and then to walk into a camping supply store, charge $200 worth of tent, sleeping bags, and canteens and then take off for the woods without a care in the world. Even if it is that easy to get credit, you will not necessarily want it. To pay the loan plus twelve to eighteen percent interest charge, is no picnic. And as far as I'm concerned, you're simply living beyond your means if you get into the credit scene. You could end up declaring bankruptcy at a tender age if you get caught up in that mess.

The old story (which happens to be true in many cases) is that you need credit to get credit. If you want to get a loan at a bank (which I would recommend above a loan anywhere else—even though I'm not recommending it), chances are you will have to prove that you have received credit previously and that you have successfully paid on previous loans.

If you don't pay the money you owe on a loan, you'll get a bad credit rating which goes down as a "judgment" against you in the books at the Credit Bureau and at city hall. Chances are if you have a judgment against you, it will be very difficult to get any future loans until it is cleared up. These books of Judgments are opened to anyone who cares to see them, so you're a marked person if negligence ever carries you as far as these books.

If you live frugally and take out health and car insurance, chances are, there is not too much that could happen to you that would force you to take out a loan or buy on credit. A new carpet bought on credit is not an emergency or a necessity. (If your floor is cold, find a used rug and wear shoes.) If your car breaks down, you don't need a $4000 new car. Shop around for a good used car. If you borrow $1000 at eighteen percent interest, you are throwing away $180 each year you have the loan. One hundred eighty dollars can buy ten to twenty used rugs and a quarter to half of a used car. So think about it. There are many pleasant ways of surviving in this world without selling your soul to the Credit Bureau.

4

THE SOMETIMES FUTILE WAR AGAINST COCKROACHES, ANTS, AND MICE

A cockroach's only claim to fame is the incident of a song having been written about him. Cockroaches are disgusting. If they live in your apartment, they force you to become the secondary inhabitant of your own dwelling—and they don't even pay rent. As you lie in bed you begin to imagine them crawling over your body. Nights are spent twitching and scratching. Everything you crunch into as you eat is imagined to be a roach. Now, as I sit in a car writing (because it's too cold outside, but too drab inside on this beautiful, sunny, almost spring day) ten miles from any city, I look through the corner of my glasses. And as the sun plays with the glass, I see cockroaches crawling up the armrest of the car.

Cockroaches (called cocker-roaches by some New Yorkers) can inhabit your apartment even if you are impeccable. Thinking about the ways they can force themselves in and become members of your family can make you crazy. Sometimes they just come with the fixtures. Many apartment complexes have been built over former garbage dumps, so there is little chance that the apartments in these complexes won't have roaches. If your neighbor is renovating his home (which has roaches), tearing out plaster, or just moving out old furniture, he may disturb the nest of the roaches who may take a walk over to your place to find new settling grounds. Roaches can also come in grocery bags as eggs, babies, or full-grown bugs.

If you live in a place where roaches have been seen—or they are common inhabitants of your city—you must take many precautions against turning your apartment over to these creatures. Keep *all* your food tightly covered and your counters, stove, and table free from crumbs and grease. Dry bathroom tiles after you use the shower. Some people say that roaches don't like dampness, but I think it's the opposite. I've seen them in more than one bathroom. Do not keep stacks of old newspapers lying around. Roaches lay their eggs in these ready-made nests. Above all, empty your garbage often—at least once a day—and always before you go to bed.

Commercial insecticide sprays kill roaches when a large enough quantity is applied to a roach who has no escape, but more often, the fumes of these sprays do little more than annoy or irritate the roaches so that they leave wherever they are when they detect the spray. So the sprays are frequently acting merely to repel the roaches. Let's say you spray your apartment. The roaches will hike over to your neighbors' or just hang out between the walls until the spray residue is gone. Then they'll come home again when they feel the coast is clear.

Even though a direct hit of an insecticide might kill a roach, it's unlikely that you'll often make a direct hit because these sneaky little characters are not only fast, but they come out in the dark nine out of ten times. They also have the ability to develop an immunity to insecticides. Insecticides are also very unhealthy to have near people and their food. Some folks have developed uncomfortable diseases from the fumes of such toxins.

So if you are doing the best job you can to prevent the beasties from living where you live, and they seem to be defying your efforts, you should begin an all-out crusade to eliminate them—but without the use of the above mentioned insecticides. Go to a pharmacy and purchase a jar of boric acid powder. It is not toxic to human beings. In fact it has been used over the years as an eye bath when mixed with water. At night before going to bed, either spray or spoon out boric acid powder along corners and edges between floors and walls. Also put some boric acid near your garbage area (even if it's empty), behind the stove and refrigerator, along the edges of your bathtub, under your sink, and any place roaches have been seen. Do this at night, because roaches are predominantly night creatures. When they come out of their corners and crevices, they will step through the boric acid and burn themselves. As they try to rub the powder from their bodies, they make the situation worse for themselves by rubbing it into their skin, and eventually they die. In the morning, chances are, you will find dead or dying roaches scattered about your apartment. Flush them down the toilet or incinerate them as roaches sometimes lay eggs as they die. Frequent boric acid sprayings should work miracles in your apartment. Boric acid does not repel roaches. As far as the roaches can detect, it is merely a benign substance. And this is why boric acid is so effective—the roaches will walk right through it before the burning action occurs.

You can make a fairly good boric acid sprayer with a plastic bottle with a nozzle like the catsup containers you find at restaurants. Some hair conditioning containers also are good. If the nozzle opening is too small, cut it larger. Spray the powder and then allow the air to get back into the bottle before spraying again. The method is not perfect but it is sufficient. You may be able to develop a more convenient method.

One word of caution, though, about using boric acid. When spraying boric acid from a homemade container, don't spray so vigorously that you create a dust cloud—you shouldn't want to breathe in boric acid dust. Spray the boric acid gently, or spoon it out easily. Also, wash your hands after using it since it can be mildly irritating to the skin. This makes boric acid significantly better to use than the commercial insecticide sprays whose fumes you cannot control because you must use the aerosol spraying device on the can. You can control the boric acid dust. It is about as irritating to your skin as some cleaning agents.

Ants are not nearly as annoying as roaches, and they don't usually plague people at all times of the year. However, they can be a source of irritation. Sugar and other sweets are ant favorites, so they should be kept in tightly covered containers. Usually, if you keep a kitchen area free of crumbs and other food particles and you empty your garbage often, your ant population should not be too bad. Some country folks plant a bitter herb called tansy outside their kitchen walls to keep ants, which are repelled by this herb, from entering the house. You might want to plant tansy in a pot and put it in your kitchen. To grow tansy just follow herb planting directions in Chapter 24. Tansy can be purchased in the typical seed packets but will most likely be difficult to acquire in your city. If so, find someone who can get it for you in a more suburban or rural area. Or, write to seed companies and ask for their catalogue. Not every seed company handles tansy, however. If you don't know of any seed companies, ask a nearby florist—they might be able to steer you in the proper direction. Or, look at the seed catalog guide at the end of the section on potted herbs on page 286.

Also, if you see ants congregating near cracks and crevices, pour a generous amount of common salt around the area. The salt quite often repels the ants. Some people claim that baking soda also repels ants, but the times I tried this method, I caught the ants having a good old time lapping it up. Another time, I think I smothered them with baking soda.

Don't feel embarrassed about the buggy pests that keep you company in the city—after all, you can go for a nice invigorating walk in the country and come home with chigger, black fly, or mosquito bites, or even with cute little ticks clinging to your body. (Just the same, I hate cockroaches more than almost anything.)

The problem with mice in your apartment is perhaps a bit more challenging than that of cockroaches and ants—that is, if you're soft like me and you think that mice are cute. If mice give you the creeps, then you have less of a problem. Half a dozen mice, as far as I'm concerned, create few problems in an apartment. I grew up with the noise of mice in between the walls of my parents' home in the country. Their incessant scampering against the insides of the walls, lulls you to sleep after you've heard it for years on end. We rarely knew that the mice were around except for a few obvious traces they left. They had a particular fondness for the drawer that my mother liked to put the dish towels in. They liked to leave their droppings there. And underneath the drawer where the silverware was kept they would make meticulous nests out of cigarette butt filters. The strange thing was that they never seemed to get into any food.

Regardless of what anyone says, I'm convinced that city and country mice are of the same species and do about the same things. Some people like to theorize that city mice are filthier than country mice. I think that's a lot of ridiculousness. So if the idea of a little field mouse doesn't offend you, your city mice really shouldn't either—unless they begin to infringe upon your rights. If the mice in your apartment begin eating your plants and getting into food which has been covered, if they start eating your shoes and dropping their delicate loads in your underwear drawer, you'd even begin to convince me that they are not cute. Mouse traps will probably get your problem under control. They are still fairly inexpensive and beat the hassle of cleaning up after the mice. A cat will also curtail your problem, but caring for a cat in the city poses other problems that I'm not sure you'd want to get into.

As I'm discussing mice, your mind might be wandering to their relative, the rat—that horrible rodent which reputedly bites babies and kills them. I've never rented an apartment where there were rats. But I suppose if I discovered more than one rat in my apartment, I'd move out. Finding rats would probably be reason enough to break a lease.

5
HOUSEHOLD HINTS

Most of the neat little hints one picks up that help to make things a little easier around the apartment are usually discovered gradually. For instance, my Aunt Sarah is always giving me hints. It seems that every time I visit her—which is not too often because we live so far away from one another—she gives me another little tip that is very helpful in making my apartment a bit more organized. Other hints I picked up the hard way. For example, when my cutting board no longer smelled like the wood it was made of, I decided it was about time I experimented and attempted to get out the garlic and onion smells.

I've seen household hints off to the side of calendars. You get twelve recipes and twelve hints—one of each for every month. I don't think I've ever taken advantage of any of these hints. It's not that they're unreasonable, it's simply that they just seemed unnecessary for me. One such hint I recall was to put dust rags in an old shoe bag and hang it inside a closet. There's nothing the matter with that at all—in fact you may like the idea. But I was happy enough to keep my dust rags in a plastic Macy's shopping bag in the cabinet underneath the kitchen sink. Besides, I didn't have a shoe bag.

Those calendars always frustrated me. I was forever wanting to see all the hints and all the recipes at once but somehow felt like a cheater if in January I started peaking at the recipe and hint for February. All this rambling is to tell you that with my household hints, you can read them all together. It's not like those calendars where you have to wait.

Some of these hints, you'll never find a need to apply. Others you've probably incorporated into your life already. But there are most likely a few, that you'll find invaluable, as I have.

REMOVING THE SMELL FROM A CUTTING BOARD

Wood soaks up smells like garlic and onion. The potency is overwhelming—especially after it's been sitting around for a while. Rub vinegar, lemon, or baking soda on the board. Remove the smell from your fingers in the same way.

HOW TO TREAT
SKIN BURNS

Put the affected area under cold running water or in ice water. In the case of a moderate burn, this should prevent a blister. If the burn seems serious, submerge the affected area in ice water and call a doctor. Under no condition should you rub grease, butter, or vaseline on the burn—they only add fuel to the fire.

REVIVING
OLD WINDOW SHADES

If your window shades are dingy, yellow, or cracked, draw a picture or design on them. Use felt tipped pens, fountain pens, crayons, paint, colored pencils, or dye. If you want, create a picture that will be enhanced by the cracked or yellowing background. Simulate an ancient, cracked, and yellowing scroll or modern batiking, or use lines and cracks for mountains and ravines. Use your imagination.

Patch rips and tears with tape on the outside of the shade. The tape will show through in the sunlight but will not really detract that much from your artistic endeavor.

THE USES
OF BAKING SODA

Baking soda (bicarbonate of soda) has more uses around the house than anything else I can think of. Here are some of its uses.

Fire Extinguisher: Pour baking soda on the flame. It will smother the fire.

Bad Odor Eliminator: Put a completely opened box of baking soda in the refrigerator. It will absorb odors such as onion, garlic, and fish. The box should be effective for two months (according to the Arm and Hammer people). They also suggest that you pour the two-month-old baking soda down a drain—to improve the smell of the drain—rather than discarding it. Wipe baking soda on ashtrays to remove tobacco smells. Remove smells such as coffee by putting a few tablespoons of baking soda in the coffee pot with warm water. Soak it for a while and then wash the pot. To remove the garlic or onion smell from a cutting board, wipe it with baking soda.

As a Cleanser: Dishes may be washed with baking soda but do not expect any suds. Pots and pans may be scrubbed with baking soda as it is a mild abrasive. Bathtubs, sinks, and counter tops are cleaned well with baking soda.

For Your Body: Use baking soda as a soak in the bathtub or in soothing sore limbs; use a few teaspoons in water as a mouthwash or as toothpaste. Use it in a paste form to soothe insect bites. For indigestion, put half a teaspoon in a glass of water and drink.

In Cooking: Various recipes call for baking soda, but make sure you do not confuse it with baking powder. Baking powder is bicarbonate of soda plus cornstarch and other ingredients (depending upon brands) while baking soda is straight bicarbonate of soda.

WASHING WOODEN UTENSILS

When you wash wooden utensils such as bowls and cutting boards, quickly wash them and try to avoid submerging them in water. Then quickly dry them. Good care of these utensils will prevent warping and splitting of the wood. Wooden spoons should be washed as quickly as possible, though they will probably have to be subjected to more water and a bit more scrubbing than most of your other wooden objects. Dry the wooden spoons with a towel and then allow them to air dry.

STAINED PORCELAIN POTS

Tea- or coffee-stained porcelain kettles can be bleached by putting a small amount (say a capful) of liquid bleach with hot water in the pot. Soak for at least an hour and then wash the pot with detergent. Rinse well.

CANISTERS

Canisters for storing sugar, flour, rice, tea, and other staples do not have to be purchased at a store. Try to acquire large institutional jars. The cafeteria at your school or place of work might have some. I purchased several gallon mayonnaise jars for ten cents apiece. You might be luckier and get them free. For items that you do not buy in a large enough quantity to require a gallon jar, save smaller jars such as quart jars and off-size jars. Fat pickle jars are good storage containers. Soak them in water and baking soda to remove the pickle smell. Make sure all jars are thoroughly cleaned and dried before you use them. Let them dry on a draining board so that air will circulate freely through them and they will dry completely. Jars with screw-on lids protect your foods against bacteria, bugs, moisture, dirt, and other disagreeable entities that easily find their ways into your things. Protecting your food effectively saves you money because it discourages pests.

MAKING YOUR LIDS AIRTIGHT

When you intend to reuse a jar lid, the cardboard liner that is wedged into the lid should be removed and thrown out unless some dry ingredient has previously been stored under that lid. If your lid does not seem airtight enough without the cardboard liner, just make another one. Trace the narrow side of the rim on cardboard, cut out, and wedge in.

CLEANING AGENTS

Most of the cleaning agents that are available to the public are really unnecessary. You're a sucker if you pay money for one thing to clean your sink and tub, one for your tiles, another for floors, another for counter tops, and so on. You can buy just a few cleaning agents and they will provide for all your needs. Baking soda as a cleaning agent is described on page 42.

Cleansers such as Ajax, Bon Ami, Comet, or a store brand (they all seem to be good) are very helpful for cleaning tubs, sinks, the inside and outside of toilets, counter tops, stove tops, and small stains on linoleum floors. Ammonia is a good all-purpose cleaner and so is bleach. You can use both of them for cleaning counter tops, floors, and painted wood. DO NOT MIX AMMONIA WITH CHLORINE BLEACH OR WITH ANY OTHER HOUSEHOLD CHEMICAL (CLEANSER CONTAINS BLEACH). DO NOT MIX BLEACH OR AMMONIA WITH BOWL CLEANERS. Fumes from these combinations can be deadly. Cleanser, ammonia and bleach are just about the least expensive cleaning agents on the market. If you really prefer to buy something that is sudsy, Top Job, Mr. Clean, Ajax, and Pine Sol are good and are not as expensive as some of the other cleaning agents.

Dishwashing detergent and water can be used in place of rug cleaners. If your rug is wool, use cool water. Otherwise use warm water.

If you want to wax your wood furniture and wood baseboards and paneling, do not be fooled into believing that you need a different wax for each job. One all-purpose wax will do.

KEEPING BREAD FRESH

Many city apartments have a tendency to be damp or humid, especially in the summer. Your bread can sometimes become covered with fuzz overnight if moisture gets into it. Moldy bread is very interesting to look at but that's as far as it goes. Wrap all bread in dry plastic bags (many breads come in their own plastic bags), and store your bread in the refrigerator.

CRUSTY POTS

Pots and pans that are coated with hard-to-remove food should be filled with water and put on the stove at a medium heat until the water just begins to boil. Turn off the flame and allow the pot to soak for a few additional minutes. This process should loosen the food. Do not try this method for baking dishes unless you specifically know that your dish can be placed on a flame. Baking dishes can be soaked with hot water in them—just don't put them on a burner.

SILVER SPOONS

You may have some old silver spoons in your possession. Do not leave these in bowls in your refrigerator; they will taint the flavor of your food.

OLD NEWSPAPERS

Do not keep large stacks of newspapers lying around your apartment. As soon as you accumulate a pile that is about twice the size of the Sunday paper, it should be recycled or at least thrown out. Piles of newspapers attract bugs (particularly roaches) and moisture. Also, if you have a paper-trained dog, he may surprise you some day and wet on your pile of papers.

STOCK UP
ON SPECIAL FOODS

Build up a stock of natural grains, honey, herbal teas, and things you might not be able to afford but would like to have, by asking for such items as birthday, Christmas, Chanukah, or house-warming presents. The last three jars of honey I acquired were free because people gave them as gifts.

RECYCLE
PLASTIC FOOD BAGS

Acquire plastic bags at the supermarket. Many times such bags hang above the produce. Don't just steal them—use them for the fruits and vegetables you buy. These bags can be washed, hung up to dry and reused many times before they are thrown away.

ALUMINUM FOIL

Aluminum foil can sometimes be reused. If you put aluminum foil over a baked casserole, the foil may get greasy in several places, but it soon dries out. It can then be reversed and reused.

Don't use aluminum foil over a dish which is warm or contains a lot of moisture. Aluminum foil exposed to steam or other types of dampness, often oxidizes and little holes form in the aluminum foil. Specks of aluminum drop in the food making it inedible. If you make this mistake, often you'll find you can scrape off the top layer of food and salvage the rest.

MAKE YOUR OWN
BREAD CRUMBS

Bread crumbs can be made from stale bread or from bread crusts. To make sure the bread is thoroughly dried out, place one layer on a cookie sheet or on your *clean* oven rack. If you have a gas stove with a pilot light, the bread should dry out easily. Otherwise, set the oven to its lowest temperature and keep the bread in the oven until it is hard and dry. Grate or crumble the bread into crumbs. If the bread has been dried out properly, you will not have to refrigerate the crumbs. Just store them in a jar that has a top. Damp crumbs will become moldy if they are not refrigerated.

CLEAN STOVE

If you wipe out your stove after you use it each time, you will never have to go through that gruesome housewifely chore—that is so often dramatized on TV—of cleaning your oven. Commercial oven cleaners are dangerous to lungs, noses, and skin and cost too much anyway. An abrasive cloth and suds or cleanser can be used, but that's a hassle. Wait until your oven has cooled down enough so it can be wiped but is still warm enough so you can easily remove the spilled food. A rag and warm water should take care of most recently spilled food. Use an abrasive cloth for large crusty spills.

DON'T DRAG OUT BAKING TIME

The best way to prevent something from cooking, is to constantly open the oven to "check it out." Much heat escapes when you do this and the oven, as a result, cools down tremendously and takes a while to get up to the original temperature again. Try to become a good judge of cooking time. Once you get to know your oven and your recipes, even a few peeks can be avoided.

CAKE AND BREAD TESTING

Check out a cake or bread to see if it's done by putting a broom straw or toothpick through the center of it. If the straw comes out gooey or sticky, more cooking time is needed.

PREVENT DISCOLORED POTATOES

If you are preparing potatoes for cooking, put them in cold water as you slice them to prevent the white of the potato from turning brown.

NO MORE TEARS FROM ONIONS

Slice onions under cold water. This will prevent you from crying all over your food.

FINDING A SURFACE FOR KNEADING BREAD OR ROLLING OUT DOUGH

If you only have a small cutting board, clean off counters, your kitchen table, or your stove, and knead or roll your dough on one of those surfaces. Or, scrap, off-sized formica can sometimes be purchased cheaply. It makes a great utility board.

KNIFE SHARPENING

Electric knife sharpeners and manual honers are nice to have, but it's not that easy to get them inexpensively. If you don't have a knife sharpener, sharpen your knives (all but serrated ones) by scraping the blade of one knife against the blade of another. Scrape the blade of the knife in your left hand against the blade of the knife in your right hand, and then alternate. Scrape the blade of the knife in your right hand against the blade of the knife in your left hand.

EGG YOLK REMOVAL

Egg yolk is more easily removed from a pan or plate with cold water rather than hot.

COMPROMISING OVEN TEMPERATURES

If you are cooking two things in the oven and they both call for a different temperature, chances are you can compromise on a temperature if they are within reasonable degrees of one another. For instance, if one thing is to be set at 300° F. and the other at 375° F., set the oven for 350° F. and give the food that was supposed to be set at 300° F. less time. If you see it is cooking faster than usual, give more time to the dish that was to be set at 375° F. Chances are, you'll be able to do this sort of compromising often because many oven meals require that they be cooked at a temperature of 300° F. to 400° F.

REMOVING NASTY SMELLS FROM THE AIR

If your kitten wets on the floor, quite often there will be a rather nasty odor in the air. But once you've cleaned up the spot, the odor may no longer be in the atmosphere. Occasionally, however, there are odors that are so bad that even cleaning the spot with a disinfectant doesn't completely eliminate the odor. For instance, if your dog vomits after having gotten into the garbage on a rainy day (when any odor will linger inside your apartment anyway), you've really got a problem.

If you eat citrus fruits daily, you're in luck. For not-so-bad, nasty odors, take citrus fruit peels and slice them with a knife at an angle so that the oil of the skin is dispersed into the air. Then place the peels around the room. This oil will improve the atmosphere. Also, open some windows if it's practical to do so. For *really* nasty odors such as the aforementioned example of dog vomit, slice citrus fruit peels and put them around the room as above, and also open the windows if it's clear outside. If it's a rainy day, it may do no good at all and may even be detrimental. Finally, open a bottle of ammonia and just place the opened bottle in the most stinky area of the room. If no animals are left in the apartment, take a walk and maybe things will be more tolerable when you get back.

CLOTHES
WASHING AND DRYING

If you'd like to cut down slightly on the number of trips you take to the laundromat, do washing of small items such as underwear, handkerchiefs, and dish towels at home in your kitchen sink. Use only small amounts of soap powder and rinse your clothing well. Hang these things over your shower by stretching a string above your bathtub. Attach it to the most available fixtures. Clothespins can be purchased relatively inexpensively and will aid in drying clothes more rapidly, because things will hang better. Buy the pins with a metal spring. The other pins might be too wide for the string you use as a clothes line. Plastic bags which you have washed for reuse can also be dried on your clothes line.

6
RECYCLING

Western man has a tendency to take much more that is useful out of the earth than he puts back into it. When we do "put something back into the earth," we usually do so in a most repulsive and ridiculous fashion. For instance, rather than putting what could have been human resources to a profitable use, such as fertilizing the soil, we flush everything down the toilet. This often sends raw sewage into what was once a nice, clean river. We do the same thing with our uneaten food. Rather than composting it and putting the nutrients back into the land, we have it picked up by the sanitation department, and it is either dumped in a place where it can't reach the earth, or it is incinerated and converted into polluting fumes.

If you feel badly about this, there's not much you can do about it as a city person. You can't control the place your toilet flushings go to, and you most likely have no place to set up a compost pile. But you can do your share of recycling of other potential wastes.

Old newspapers, magazines, corrugated cardboard, glass, and metal cans—all would-be polluters—are reusable by industry. Paper is pulped and converted back into paper products. Glass is either remelted to become a glass product again or is mixed in crushed form with things such as concrete and used as a filler. Metal is also melted and reused.

Many cities now have recycling centers for paper, glass, and metal. Find out through your city hall or the yellow pages where you can find such a center. Once you find a center, make sure it's not one of those places that makes a mockery of dedicated recyclists. Some centers become swamped with things to be recycled and the workers secretly end up throwing the stuff into the city dump. Other centers are sloppy or disorganized and as a result, items are not properly sorted and industry refuses to take the stuff.

If recycling is not practical for you through some sort of center, at least do your own mini-recycling at home. Do not buy wasteful paper products. Paper towels are really unnecessary though they are convenient. Rags or old dish towels can be used in place of paper towels.

When absorbing the grease from fried potatoes, eggplant, or meat, clean store paper bags can be used.

Try to avoid the purchase of no-deposit-no-return soda and beer containers. For unknown reasons, returnable bottles are hard to come by in the eastern part of the country. Bottling companies complain to those who push for the return of the returnable, that the cost to convert back to this logical system would be prohibitive. This has been proved in some midwest and western states to be untrue. Luckily, it seems as if the environmentally-minded people might win this battle. But while the conversion is taking place, you can convert your bottles into drinking glasses through bottle cutting. Glass cutting tools for this can be purchased at a hardware or department store.

Glass jars (and bottles) can be used in many ways around your apartment. Mayonnaise jars are especially good for canning as their rims will fit standard canning lids. Instead of throwing out a mustard jar, use it to keep odd buttons in. Glass jars can be used to store leftovers. Rather than spending the money and consuming additional natural resources by purchasing plastic containers, store food in jars, such as those that peanut butter or jelly come in. (Of course, plastic containers that come with food are very good for storing leftovers.) Even oddly-shaped bottles such as those that catsup comes in, can be used as clothing or plant sprinklers. Just poke holes in the top. Smaller jars can be used for herbs and spices since the boxes and metal containers in which herbs and spices are sold are not always airtight. Larger jars, such as mayonnaise, pickles, and tomato juice jars, are good for preventing moisture, ants, and roaches from getting into your flour, sugar, tea, and other dry staples.

Large cans may be utilized as herb or flower pots. As every second grader knows, cans may be painted and transformed into pen/pencil holders. Those cans (like the ones coffee comes in) with resealable plastic lids are especially useful for storing your flours, sugar, tea, and beans. If you do reuse a coffee can for food storage, be sure it has been thoroughly cleaned and aired so that there will not be a residue smell from the coffee.

Grocery bags, aside from being used to absorb excess oil from fried foods, can also be used as garbage bags. Instead of buying wrapping paper, grocery bags can be cut and used to wrap presents or packages —a hand drawn design will make the paper look quite acceptable.

7
SHARING THROUGH THE COOPERATIVE SYSTEM

If you don't make an effort, living in the city can be lonely and depressing because of the lack of community spirit. Back in the pioneer days in this country, "neighbors" were people who lived miles apart—but the miles seemed short to people who wanted to get together. Folks would share and exchange things such as food, wood, and even lit coals for the fire. People had roof-raising parties, quilting bees, and corn shucking parties. Through the cooperation of people, things that would take one man days to do—such as raising his roof—were done in comparatively no time at all.

Of course, neighbors in the city are stacked one layer on top of another and next to one another in endless rows, and yet you may live next to the same people most of your life but never speak to a single member of the family. Borrowing a cup of sugar from a neighbor in some city setups would require a lot of nerve. The irony of this situation is incredible. When people live far apart, they seem to make an effort to get together, socialize, and share. When they live close together, everything, save the physical setup, seems to be separate. But this doesn't have to be the situation; city people are not really as cold and unfriendly as they seem. I theorize that they are somewhat afraid and reserved. It seems that during times of crisis, such as the electrical failure in New York City a decade ago, city people too, can join together in the spirit of community and sharing.

If you are a friendly sort of person—and an opportunist—then maybe you can bring your neighbors around so that all of you can begin sharing in either large or small ways at a savings to all of you. If you can develop with them one of many types of cooperative food buying systems, your grocery bill can be greatly reduced. Sometimes the best way to get to know neighbors is through their children. Most children have not yet learned to be cold city dwellers. Don't approach a child and ask him if his mother wants to join a food co-op. Just say hello and develop a friendly rapport. When you do approach his family, the child will probably let the family know in some way, that you're O.K. At times, neighbors have introduced themselves to me because of the elevator relationships I have developed with their kids. Another good method of getting to know people is through their animals. As you meet your neighbors on the stairs or in the elevator or on the streets with their animals, strike up a friendly conversation with their French poodle. After a few such meetings, the owner of the dog will probably become friendly with you. I also find that many city folks will attempt to strike up conversations with their neighbors, but some neighbors will just grunt in response. After a while friendly people will begin to think that being congenial isn't cool. So, instead of being the grunted at, they become the grunters. Next time when it's thirty degrees out and a neighbor says, "Cold day!" strike up a conversation with him about how you're very warm blooded —if you are—or at least agree with him. But don't grunt!

If none of these methods seem to work with your neighbors or they are willing to be friendly enough but do not want to share, perhaps you can develop a cooperative system with schoolmates or the people with whom you work. The neighbor system works best because you all live in the same locale, making food distribution easier.

There are varied types of cooperative food buying systems but they are all aimed toward similar goals. The major goals are to purchase good food at reduced rates at a more or less convenient location and to join with neighbors in the spirit of sharing.

Usually the farmer sells his produce in bulk to a wholesaler or middleman. The middleman in turn sells the produce in smaller quantities to the retailer—the second middleman—who is the person who runs the store where you buy your fruits and vegetables. Between the wholesaler and retailer (especially the retailer in recent years), the price that you, the consumer, must pay, is many times that which the farmer sold his crops for. Under the cooperative system, prices are lower because the middleman is eliminated and the purchasing members do the work. Co-op members get their food from what is known as a farmers' market or a wholesale warehouse. These stations are found in almost every major city. So, even if you live in a small city, if there is a large one near by, you can take advantage of its market.

There are three types of cooperative food buying systems which you might consider. The food co-op, the food buying club, or wholesale buying for a few specific items. If you can join an existing co-op or club that is functioning well and is within a reasonable proximity of home, work, or school, it is probably to your advantage. To start things from scratch is always a lot more difficult.

Members of a food co-op usually have a store where wholesale food is brought by the workers. The food is then purchased by the members at the store. Some food such as fruits, vegetables, dairy products, and other perishables, must be preordered. Other products are often available whenever the store is open. All members must share in the work to make the co-op work. Each member is expected to donate a certain number of hours per week or month to the co-op. Sometimes a membership fee is also required, but if the co-op is a good one, it's usually worth it. Co-ops are subject to visits from health inspectors, so premises must be kept clean and specific packaging regulations must be followed. Chances are you don't want to belong to a dirty co-op anyway, so you should be happy to follow these regulations.

Buying clubs work on a smaller scale. Neighbors or friends get together and decide to take turns picking up certain wholesale items at a farmers' market. Because vegetables come in units such as fifty pound bags and bushel baskets at wholesale outlets, you must buy the whole thing if you want to pay wholesale prices. If you want to buy potatoes and there are ten members in your club, each member must agree to take five pounds, unless one member wants eight pounds and another wants two. Everyone has to cooperate so that nothing will be wasted. Usually, by looking in the newspaper or from experience, members have an idea of what food items will be available at the market during a given week and at approximately what price they will be going for. Prepaid orders are given to the person or persons who will pick up the order for everyone. Reimbursements for overcharges are returned after the food is received. At least one member of your club must have a car in order for the club to work unless you can devise another successful means of transportation for picking up the food.

Wholesale buying as the spirit moves you or as the opportunity arises for a few specific items with people you know, can also be convenient. Suppose you hear of an outlet which sells a fifty-pound cake of cheese at less per pound than you could ever get at the store. If you can get four friends to buy it with you, you can all have ten pounds of cheese. This method of buying can be more successful than co-ops and clubs because it does not require a long-range commitment from people.

While you are shopping around for a co-op or attempting to organize your own, you'll discover that different groups function in different ways or are dedicated toward different goals. Some organizations do not carry good fresh vegetables the year round, while others do. Other groups buy only products that they consider to be geared toward good nutrition, and they refuse to carry something that they feel is garbage. For instance, you may only be able to get whole grain flour through your group because the members feel that white flour lacks nutrients, and they feel they would be doing their members a disservice by carrying it. Members of successful cooperatives seem to share common philosophies and moralities.

SOMETHING NICE COMES TO BRICKOMANIA

Sections of some cities, no matter how hard you look at them, are ugly—there's not an ounce of appeal in them. These scowling pockets are usually not the slums. One can find an off-beat beauty in the slums—old cobblestone, shadows bouncing off fire escapes on the streets, children play-acting on the sidewalks, an old woman fanning herself. Often the ugliest places, stripped of all aesthetic appeal, are some middle-class, high-rise housing projects. Row upon endless row of forever salmon red bricks engulf scores of city blocks. All buildings are the same height. Just to get a glimpse of the sun, you must walk two blocks to the parking lot—that overlooks the expressway—to peek at a sick white sun which glares off car windshields.

The designers of some of these projects pretend to add variety and creativity to each building. If you ever live in such a project, you will surely get to see the different lobbies of neighboring buildings because one day you will not be paying attention as you walk along Brickomania, and you will wander into the wrong building and you will never notice you are in the wrong place until, as you wait for the elevator and glance back at the lobby, two metal chairs and a "marble" fountain, which are carefully placed around plastic turf, hit you squarely in the face.

"I must be in 'The Garden!'" you say to yourself. You live in "The Mansion" which has a lobby ridden with hideous plaster columns. Someone you know lives in "The Californian" which has a red granite front. To the right of your building is "The Moderne" which has a modernistic reproduction of a painting in the lobby. To your left is "The Athenian," whose lobby displays a white plaster statue of a woman draped in flowing robes on which "Mitch loves Suzi" is scrawled in Magic Marker.

Every day you tell yourself that you have to get out of that section of the city and move into a nice slum downtown. After all, both have cockroaches, both have poor heating systems and both are in a section with a high crime rate. The slum is beginning to sound like a very quaint and charming little place to you.

One morning in winter you wake up in your freezing apartment. At 10 o'clock the heat will go on and the hot air will practically knock you out. You quickly dress and head for the corner stationery store to get a newspaper. There had been freezing rain the night before and it's about fifteen degrees outside. As you go out into the morning wintry air and skid out onto the sidewalk, you are amazed at what surrounds you. Ice is clinging to all the trees and bushes and ivy. You never even noticed there were trees and other foliage in your neighborhood. Now you are pleasantly astounded. The sun shines brightly through the ice-captured trees creating sparkling and rainbow patterns. A lone leaf clings to a tree. Ice, shaped exactly after the leaf, molds itself around the brown form, causing it to bend precariously below its branch. There's something else that is aiding this enchantment which has taken over Brickomania. At first you can't figure it out because you are so taken aback by the glitter—but there is hardly any traffic on the nearby expressway. Occasionally a car crawls along on the icy road, but the usual hum and roar is just not there. Even Brickomania has been forced into beauty which you sadly watch melt away by midafternoon.

part 2
FOODS FOR LIFE, OR HOW TO AVOID SCURVY AND SLOW STARVATION

Even if you're not a food freak, you'll find that shopping, cooking, and eating are important parts of your life. You eat to survive, but you also eat for pleasure, so it's only fair that you should have a variety of foods and recipes to choose from. And with the rising cost of everything, it seems that spending an evening with friends making bread, yogurt, or jam, is a lot cheaper and of more lasting benefit than seeing a movie or going to a club just for the sake of getting out of the apartment. (If you need fresh air—such as it is in some cities—walks are nice.) Even if there's a good movie in town, you might not be able to afford it, and you'll find that you can entertain yourself by learning a few things about food.

You really should know as much as you possibly can about shopping and preparing food. You don't want to get ripped off when you buy or when you cook. Everything is related: if you don't get the most for your money at the supermarket, your body suffers. And if you don't take full advantage of what you've purchased, again your body suffers.

If you want to use the following shopping and food-related chapters to their best advantage, take something from all of them, because they all have a lot to do with our adjusted and adapted modern day food and survival chains.

8
SCRUTINY SHOPPING

Grocery shopping, if not done with a degree of ingenuity can be disastrous. The most scrutinizing of scrutiny shoppers can, at times, be hoodwinked into purchasing various types of atrocities at the supermarket. This is basically because quality products at the reduced prices that chain stores offer have to be sifted out from amongst the garbage. One must develop nothing short of a radar system to detect the quality, but since most of us are interested in the lower prices we have to resign ourselves to lack of superiority in some of their items.

Shopping for good buys is definitely an art which must be developed and then redeveloped in our erratic economy in which prices fluctuate from week to week. You can learn the general concepts of food shopping, but you must at all times be aware of current trends in prices and of the economy in general.

If you are basically a person with no will power, one of the worst things you can do is to go to the market on an empty stomach. You'll end up splurging on *pâté de foié gras* or asparagus tips, when you really just ran out for margarine, milk, and potatoes. If you want to save money, go grocery shopping after supper and take only the amount of money you intend to spend. Full stomachs protect one against silly splurges. Also, grocery lists can be very helpful. If you generally know what items you want and specifically know what items you need, you'll save both time and money in the market. You will either want to loosely plan a menu for the week and do your shopping around the foods needed for that menu, or you may want to buy first, according to the best bargains or qualities for that week, and then plan your menu around what you have bought.

It is extremely difficult to get all the groceries you want at the best possible prices and of reasonable quality at one supermarket. After you familiarize yourself with the stores in your neighborhood, you will notice several trends. One store may have reasonable sugar, flour, and vegetable oil prices and have outrageous meat prices. The reverse may be true at a market a few blocks away. One week prices may be reasonable for produce (fresh vegetables and fruits) at one store and ridiculous at the same store the next week. Prices fluctuate for many reasons: they are dependent upon growing seasons, the weather, labor disputes, political trends and the general chaotic state of the world. So you must watch the prices carefully and make mental notes so you'll know when you're getting a good deal. Hamburger might be truly economical one week and a delicacy the next.

Obviously what you want to do when purchasing food is to choose those items which are both of decent quality (or at least palatable) and are not of an outrageous cost. (To use the word "reasonable" with cost, though I may unintentionally do so somewhere in this book, would be outrageous, because the only things which are still reasonable are salt and Kool-Aid.) You will also most likely be searching for some variety in foods. Weighing all these factors you will probably, even if you must go shopping on two separate days, want to scan the neighborhood for the best possible purchases.

You might want to note the following information on prices, unit prices, price lists, and price vs. brand and quality, instant foods, and luxury wraps and items:

PRICES

After you have become a little experienced as a grocery shopper, you should be able to tell if, in the general scope of things, a price is acceptable or unacceptable. If you have a question as to whether or not an item should cost as much as the store is charging, pass it by if at all possible and hope to find a more acceptable price elsewhere. Or, substitute a less expensive item for your first choice, or pass up the whole thing. Foods which can be substituted are innumerable: beans for asparagus, lettuce for chicory, onions for scallions, chicken for turkey—the list is endless. (For more ideas on substitutions, see Chapter 15.)

UNIT PRICES

According to the Manhattan office of the Consumer Affairs Department, supermarkets in New York and some other states are required by law to post the unit price of all food items in the store. Unit price is simply a statement of how much a particular item costs per pound, per ounce, per quart, or any other specific weight or volume unit by which a product may be represented. This relatively recent development avoids the mathematics involved in determining the size or brand that gives you the most for your money.

PRICE LISTS

Current price lists for all foods in the supermarket are also required by law in New York and elsewhere to be readily available to the consumer. These lists are usually in the manager's office. If you want to know what you are getting yourself into before you fill your cart, check the price list. If you encounter a supermarket which does not post unit prices or make current price lists available and you know it's a law in your state, report them to Consumer Affairs or an equivalent organization. The Manhattan office says they want to know about delinquent supermarkets. Some individual managers or personnel at supermarkets will try to convince you that these price requirements do not exist by law in states where they do. Do not be fooled by these people.

PRICE VERSUS
BRAND AND/OR QUALITY

Selecting the overall most satisfactory brand of a particular item, in some cases, may take a bit of experimenting. Some store brands or relatively unknown brands for particular items are quite decent. Others are atrocious. Generally, I've found most store or unknown brand vinegars, flours, nonfat dry milk, saltines, macaroni, spaghetti, canned fruits, and tomatoes, catsups, spices, rices, corn meals, and baking powders to be almost always of decent quality. Of course, there could be some deviation. The store's brand of teas, mayonnaise, oils, and margarines can fall either way—you may have to experiment. Tuna at a low price in an obscure brand or store brand is usually flaked instead of chunk and practically always (in my experience) tastes more fishy than other brands. However, tuna of lower quality, if economical to buy, can be made quite tasty with a squeeze of lemon. Until you have accustomed yourself to particular brands and have discovered the bargains, you might want to lessen the risk before you purchase an item by comparing ingredients on the labels. For instance, if a less expensive product seems to be loaded with fillers, fats, or more weird chemicals than other products, chances are that you wouldn't be getting a great deal for your money.

When pricing things of no specific brand, such as produce and meats, several things must be taken into account. You will soon realize, for instance, that a cheap, beat-up head of lettuce which will have to be discarded in part is less economical than a healthy head which costs more per pound, or beets at a lower price without the tops might be less of a bargain than beets at a slightly higher price with tops. Beet tops are delicious and provide an extra vegetable and good nutrition. Fortunately, vegetables can be looked at and gently felt before being purchased. Try to avoid plastic wrapped fruits and vegetables which are placed in cardboard trays (although this is not always possible), because you simply cannot get a fair view of the fruit or vegetable. Fruits and vegetables generally should be firm; very few items are in good condition when they are soft or mushy. If you discover that the fruits and vegetables at the supermarkets are of poor quality, you might want to try a produce market where you could get more for your money. Or, look into the possibility of going to a public farm market to get such items. See Chapter 7 on Sharing for information on wholesale buying.

Meats practically always have to be examined under plastic wrap. In examining price per pound, realize how many edible parts of meat you are getting. For instance, fat and bone weigh a lot and you end up paying for it. Obviously, you cannot avoid fat and bone, and in fact they are sometimes usable. But you must realize that the price of meat includes the bones and fat. Another thing you might note about nice red, healthy-looking beef is that it is usually dyed. One test you can make to see if meat is dyed is to leave it out of the refrigerator for a few hours. If it does not turn brown, it is most likely dyed. Of course, there is not much you personally can do about dyed meat unless you intend to hound the Food and Drug Administration—and somebody should.

INSTANT FOODS

The entire TV dinner, instant food syndrome is representative, in a sickening sort of way, of a large aspect of our society. Centuries from now, archeologists will unearth aluminum foil trays and perhaps a petrified toaster waffle—the things that symbolize our great society. Promotion of prepackaged dinner items on the television is nothing short of a crime when you consider the fact that innocent children are actually watching these ads. The height of frozen dinner ridiculousness is a hamburger, soup, fruit, and a package of instant chocolate milk mix. (This exact frozen dinner actually exists.) Television ads lead children into believing there is something special about that particular hamburger, soup, fruit, and package of instant chocolate that is somehow lacking in the same product that is prepared by mother. I frankly do not know how the kids' parents are enticed into buying such wasteful items. Perhaps, they are incredibly inane and think they are saving a significant amount of time, or perhaps they are simply submitting to their children. I must admit that I have never heated up a frozen hamburger dinner, but I would think that a hamburger fried or broiled from scratch would take less time.

Whether you buy a prepackaged meal or not is, of course, your own business. The example of the frozen hamburger is naturally one of extreme—frozen dinners come in a variety of selections ranging from macaroni and cheese to a German-style meal. But frozen foods generally cost more. During my last survey of the unit prices of frozen dinners, I found a range of 65¢ to $1.84 per pound. This is not solid meat, remember. It includes starch and vegetables. Cooking time for the dinners ranged from thirty minutes to an hour (innumerable scratch meals can be prepared in that time range). Finally, frozen dinners are expensive, of questionable food value, have been known to contain such delicacies as legs and hairs of cockroaches, and really do not save that much time.

LUXURY
WRAPS AND ITEMS

No doubt you are aware of the innumerable bags and wraps (mostly plastic) which came into vogue a few years back. These bags and wraps are very convenient—plastic garbage bags are available in different sizes for individual garbage pails and trash cans, and plastic food storage bags come in many dimensions. Bags for cooking are designed to speed up time involved and eliminate a greasy pan. Some of these bags and wraps are quite tempting. But let's look at the other side of the picture. Who wants to spend all that money on something so disposable? These bags cannot be properly decomposed and they contribute greatly to an already disastrous pollution problem. The next time you are walking down a street on garbage collection day, observe how many plastic bags have replaced garbage cans.

Because just about everything used to wrap, bag, or dispose of an item is a probable polluter, we face a problem of having to compromise. Many stores carry free plastic and paper bags which are available above or below the fresh fruits and vegetables. When purchasing fruits and vegetables, make sure you put your purchases in these bags. You can use them many times before they wear out. The plastic bags may be washed out and hung up or turned inside out, and the paper bags can be used for things like lunches for quite a few days before they wear out. Large grocery bags can be used as garbage bags; just be sure you empty your garbage often.

Chances are that you will still want to buy such things as wax paper or sandwich bags, aluminum foil and possibly some plastic wrap. Naturally, you are still polluting, but if you are frugal with these items you will at least cut down on the amount of pollution you are contributing to the world.

The fact is that anything disposable costs more than something that is supposed to last longer. Disposable broiler and pie pans should be avoided. Reusable pads for scrubbing pots and pans are a lot more economical than the soap and steel wool soap pads. The reusable cleaning pads can last for months whereas a steel wool soap pad may lose its soap and rust after one use.

Innumerable cleaning agents intended for each household chore and every corner of the house are now on the market. To buy more than a few basic cleaners is unnecessary. One can get by with purchasing only a few of these items, such as ammonia or disinfectant (such as Lysol), cleanser, and dishwashing detergent. (For more hints on how to conserve on luxury wraps and items, see Chapter 5 on Household Hints.)

9
A BALANCED MEAL

When you were a little kid and you got sick, it was a comfort to know that your parents were there to help you out. Chances are, they put you in their big bed and brought in the TV and let you watch all the soap operas and they forced liquids on you and took your temperature every few hours. It was encouraging to know that they really cared about your health—they made you feel as if everything was going to be O.K. But most importantly, if you were sick enough so they couldn't take care of the problem themselves, they called a doctor and then he made sure that you became healthy again.

You may think that you're all grown up and that my reminiscing about being taken care of by Mommy and Daddy represents some inner need to return to the womb. But unfortunately you'll probably see my point if you ever do get sick when you're on your own. It can be a frightening experience. I've found that roommates are really not all that sympathetic when you're sick. In most cases they will flit into the apartment, ask you how things are going, and then flit out again.

Some diseases or illnesses are very hard to avoid, so chances are that you'll be stricken at some time and you'll have to cope with it as best you can. By all means, if you feel you're quite ill, see a doctor.

But as best you can, you'll want to try to avoid getting sick, and one big way is to make sure that your diet is properly balanced. If you don't take care of your body, scurvy, beriberi, and other diseases which people make jokes about, could become realities.

Balancing your daily intake of the foods that contain different vitamins and minerals is very essential to your health and well-being. If you've been feeling crummy lately, it could be due to a poor diet. Just for example, you could be lacking calcium, because you haven't been drinking milk or taking in enough of the other calcium-yielding foods. Women who lack calcium can become tired, irritable, or have severe menstrual cramps. Or, you could have a deficiency of vitamin C which can cause severe damage to your system—even intercellular damage.

The human body is an amazingly delicate mechanism. All vitamins and minerals are essential for good health and we get most of them through the foods we eat. True, you can take high-potency vitamins to bring these necessary components into your system, but it's cheaper to eat right. You'd have to take an awful lot of vitamins if you weren't eating properly to make up deficiencies. Taking vitamins and balancing your diet properly *might* make you even more healthy, but you should know what is in the vitamins you're taking.

It is not necessary to become a vitamin pill freak either. Too much of a good thing can also cause damage to the body. For instance, several years ago it was reported that a teen-age girl was taking vitamin A tablets in large dosages for an acne condition. The overabundance of vitamin A in her system began to create symptoms of mental disorder. Adelle Davis, a renowned nutritionist, was one of several people who claimed that ferrous sulfate, which is commonly sold as iron tablets, can destroy the body's supply of some vitamins and can create a greater need for oxygen in the body as well as cause other difficulties to the human organism.

Basically, vitamins and minerals are chemical compounds which are essential in the diet so that the body may function and grow. Good health or ill health is usually not something that just happens to a person. Quite often, you are in control of the condition of your body and how it looks. I noticed while in college two types of students who stuck out from the rest: the overweight, overstuffed "dormie" who was fed on starchy cafeteria food, and the thinner students who lived on their own and usually had poor complexions and a sallow skin color. Both had lousy diets.

Many diseases are caused by insufficient vitamin and mineral intake. You might have heard of beriberi, a sensory nerve disease previously common in the Orient. Polished rice (the refined rice we call white rice) was seen to be the cause of this disease. Because rice is the main staple of many Oriental diets, and the B_1 (thiamine) found in rice husks was removed, beriberi resulted. A vitamin C deficiency can cause scurvy, a disease which creates aching muscles and joints and makes the victim short of breath and weak. This disease used to be common among sailors, who, because they were on long sea voyages, could not get fresh vegetables and citrus fruits. It's possible that people who claim the change of weather is making them stiff and achy, are in reality low in vitamin C because they are not getting enough fresh fruits and vegetables during the winter months.

An acquaintance of mine claims that a friend of his ate only McDonald hamburger products for several months to see what would happen to his body. The result was a case of scurvy. This is not to say that McDonald hamburgers cause scurvy, but rather, the products offered at McDonald's or any other hamburger stand cannot supply a totally sufficient diet.

Diet balancing is pretty basic. After putting a car engine together, if you have some parts left over, chances are the engine will not run, or will at least run improperly. The same goes for your body.

Your meals should contain different vitamins, minerals, proteins, fats, and carbohydrates. For instance, a meal of potatoes, bread, and ham is a meal of carbohydrates and fats, a few proteins, and some incidental essential vitamins. But a meal of ham, potatoes, a *vegetable* and/or *salad* will give you more of the good nutrition your body is looking for. A sample diet for the day, might be as follows. The vitamins or other nutrients listed in the meals are just some of the things provided by these foods:

BREAKFAST: orange (vitamin C)
whole wheat toast (vitamins B_1, B_6, E, carbohydrates)
margarine (fat)
milk (calcium, vitamin D, proteins, fat, vitamin A)
coffee or tea

LUNCH: tuna (vitamins B_{12}, B_6, proteins, niacin)
whole wheat bread (vitamins B_1, B_6, E, carbohydrates)
raw peppers (vitamin C)
milk (calcium, vitamin D)

DINNER: lamb (iron, fats, niacin, vitamins B_1, B_2, B_{12}, A)
carrots (vitamin A)
potatoes (carbohydrates, vitamin B_6, and traces of varied other vitamins)
milk (calcium, vitamin D)

Vitamins A, B_1, B_2, B_6, B_{12}, C, D, E, protein, calcium, iron, and niacin were received by your body if you had a diet which was similar to the one above. Other essentials were also received as this list is a general guide and is not a complete nutrient chart. For detailed nutritional information you should go to the library and take out a book on nutrition.

Many nutrients can be lost from foods as they are processed, refined, or cooked. Vegetables can lose a lot just by lying around. The beans you pick from the garden are more nutritional than the beans you picked up at the supermarket even though they are both "fresh." You can imagine what is lost from canned beans. Sometimes foods are enriched with chemical vitamins because so much is lost from vine or pasture to the table. White flour, for instance, was once whole wheat grain. Graham flour, whole wheat flour, and white flour come from the same plant. They just represent different stages of industrial refinement. Graham flour and whole wheat flour have more of their original nutrients than does white flour. White flour is bleached in most cases and then enriched. In other words, a few of the nutrients that were lost in the refining process are put back in. This white flour refining process all seems to be a terrible waste of time except for the fact that Americans seem to prefer white flour.

Vegetables that are gently steamed lose fewer vitamins than do those that are cooked to a mush. Meats which are not cooked too long will retain more iron and other nutrients.

Chart 2 will give you a general idea as to what foods provide what nutrients. Make sure your daily intake provides for these essentials.

CHART 2

VITAMIN OR MINERAL	FOODS WHICH PROVIDE A SIGNIFICANT AMOUNT OF VITAMINS OR MINERALS
Vitamin A	carrots, sweet potatoes, leafy vegetables (such as spinach), butter, milk, cheese, eggs, whole grain cereals, beef, lamb, liver
Vitamin B_1 (Thiamine)	soybeans, nuts, seeds, peas, milk, brown rice, whole wheat flour, wheat germ, soy flour, lamb, pork, liver
Vitamin B_2	nuts, seeds, milk, cottage cheese, lamb, pork, liver

Vitamin B$_6$	bananas, whole grain cereals, chicken, dry legumes (peas and beans), egg yolk, most dark green leafy vegetables, most meat and shellfish, muscle meats (liver and kidney), nuts, potatoes, sweet potatoes, prunes, raisins, yeast
Vitamin B$_{12}$	kidney, liver, meat, milk, most cheeses, most fish, shellfish, whole eggs and egg yolks
Vitamin C	spinach, cauliflower, cabbage, raw peppers, tomatoes, broccoli, sweet potatoes, milk, oranges, limes, lemons, grapefruits, tangerines, strawberries
Vitamin D	vitamin D fortified milk, egg yolk, saltwater fish, liver
Vitamin E	vegetable oils, margarine, salad dressing, whole grain cereals, peanuts
Niacin	sunflower seeds, wheat germ, lamb, pork, liver, tuna
Protein (not a vitamin or mineral but grouped here for convenience)	beans, seeds, some nuts, milk, eggs, cheese, wheat germ, liver, fish, fowl
Calcium	sesame seeds, milk, cucumbers
Iron	sesame seeds, soybeans, evaporated milk, wheat germ, lamb, pork, liver, prunes, brown sugar

Some of the preceding information was acquired from the following sources:

Consumer and Food Economics Institute. *Nutritive Value of Foods. Home and Garden Bulletin No. 72.* Washington, D.C.: U.S. Department of Agriculture, 1971.

Davis, Adelle. *Let's Get Well.* New York: Signet Press, 1965.

Stedman, Thomas. *Stedman's Medical Dictionary.* Baltimore: Williams & Wilkins, 1966.

10
HOW TO COOK

If you intend to live economically, one of the first things you're going to have to do is to get rid of a few food prejudices and misconceptions. The only prejudices you should maintain (or develop) are against those foods stripped of natural flavor and nutrition. Your tastes will have to become less exotic in order to survive economically. Comments and thoughts such as "ick! vegetables," will have to be totally eradicated from your mouth and mind.

Of course, there will be a few things you simply will never be able to stomach. Let's say you dislike beans and asparagus. You can still live economically and avoid them, but if you are strictly a meat and potato person, you will soon discover that the meat part of your diet makes you too expensive to support.

But you can always change. Chances are you never gave yourself the chance to discover what good, fresh vegetables and various fresh and frozen fish taste like. I have a friend who always thought she hated vegetables until she tasted fresh ones. She was pleasantly amazed at the difference between fresh and canned.

By now you may be thinking that it's going to be nearly impossible to change your eating habits. Give yourself a chance. You're not quite as single-minded as you think. For one thing, you'll discover that when money for food is coming out of your own pocket, even bread, milk, and margarine will become very dear to you. I've discovered that all food seems to taste better when I scrounge around to get it. I actually enjoy a soup made out of leftover bones or cheap meat more than I do an expensive steak. There is something very indulgent about an expensive cut of meat—especially if I paid for it.

Nobody loves the idea of slaving over a hot stove, but cooking meals is not as formidable or difficult as you might expect. And even if you do consider food preparation a chore, think of it as one of those necessities of life which you must do in order to keep your body (and mind) in order. Haphazard cooking, to me, is like not washing your back and your feet when you take a shower. It doesn't take a lot of effort to wash your back and feet, and once you've done it you should be glad you did. It makes you feel clean and healthy. A good meal should make you feel the same way.

Learning to control the temperature, the taste, and the quantities of foods you prepare are the important keys to becoming a successful cook. Anyone with a certain degree of patience can do these things. After awhile, cooking becomes as natural as taking a shower. Eventually you won't have to rely on recipes for everything you cook because you'll learn what foods taste good together.

TEMPERATURE

Temperature is a relatively important determining factor in the success or failure of food. Most recipes tell you at which temperature to set your stove or oven. Probably the most important thing to remember is simply not to set your heat very high unless you are boiling water or using a recipe that specifically calls for a high temperature. Most gas stove burners I've used cannot be set low enough to satisfactorily simmer foods. The gas usually flickers out somewhere between low and simmer. But you can set the gas as low as you can without it flickering out and then place a burner you are not using (they're usually removable) right on top of the burner you are using. This way the pot will be farther away from the heat and you'll have a lower cooking temperature. If the two burners do not stack in a stable manner, then you'll have to try to figure out some other method of simmering. A plate made out of cast iron, such as the round disk top to an old wood-burning stove would be good, and some stoves come equipped with simmering plates. Or, as a last resort, you can buy a simmering plate at most discount stores.

If you are cooking something in the oven, the highest temperature your oven can be set is usually 500° F. or broil. Some ovens can be set as high as 550° F. Most ovens must be left open slightly when broiling so as to prevent extreme heat buildup in the oven which can lead to an explosion or grease fire. A temperature of 400° F. is sometimes used for foods such as baked potatoes and home fries. The most common temperature seems to be 350° F. or "medium" or "moderate." A "low" oven setting is about 200° F. to 250° F.

If you are impatient and you set your heat too high, you can burn or char your food outside, while leaving it raw inside, make it lumpy or dry it out. Not only can this detract from the flavor, it takes out some nutrients.

So how hot should your stove or oven be? If you think about what has to be accomplished you can usually come up with the right formula to make something taste good. Suppose you are cooking broccoli. Think about how you would like it to taste. Would you like it burnt, watery, mushy, or a combination of all three, or would you like it to be tender—but not soft and falling apart? I prefer the latter and there's a way to insure that you get that type of broccoli. First, put a little water (a quarter to half an inch of water per two to four servings) in a pot. Boil your water (you can turn your heat up full blast for that). Second, add your broccoli, turn down your heat and cover the pot. Let the vegetable *gently* steam until you can poke it with a fork and the prongs go through with some effort. Do not stab the vegetable to death—just carefully test it. You can also taste it to see if it's done—that's a real foolproof method. An even better way to not overcook broccoli, or most any other vegetable, is to steam it—whereby it never comes directly into contact with the water. You can do this by filling the pot about a quarter to a third full with water, letting it boil and then setting the vegetable in a colander or strainer above the water (if your colander or strainer fits into any of your pots). Cover the pot and cook until tender. Less water gets into the vegetable, fewer vitamins are lost, and you don't have to strain the vegetable. This is just one example of how not to destroy your food. For more hints on vegetable cooking, see Chapter 21 and its section on vegetable meals.

TASTE

Taste is related to temperature—but, of course, it also depends on the ingredients you use and combine with one another. Seasonings such as salt, herbs, and spices really add to food but should not be used lavishly as their taste may permeate the food in a very unpleasant way. It is easy to add more of something but it is extremely difficult to remove, say, too much salt, pepper, or oregano. (For more information on herbs and spices see Chapter 13.)

Probably the best way to gauge taste if you are not an experienced cook is to begin by following recipes. After a while you will want to add your favorite ingredients and, before you know it, you won't be as dependent upon other people's recipes. The easiest way to tell if something will taste right is, of course, to taste it. Just taste a little— don't get carried away. Otherwise, the more experienced you become as a cook, the more you'll begin to resemble a house. Also note that herbs and spices take a while to soak into foods. So if you taste the seasoned food immediately you may get *some* idea as to how it will taste, but it will not be too accurate. You'll have to learn to gauge those taste differences between raw and done.

QUANTITY

Sometimes people find it difficult to estimate how much food to prepare. Most of my recipes for two people will be enough for people with average appetites. If you have a big appetite, you'll have to increase the amounts, or if your appetite is small, you can decrease amounts or count on having leftovers.

I really don't intend to lecture about people who overeat, but let me just mention the following: Some people eat what's there—they don't seem to know when their stomachs are full. They simply know that there is food on the table—so they eat it. That can be an expensive and unhealthy habit. If you are one of those people, the best thing to do is to estimate how much would be reasonable for you to cook for the number of people you intend to feed by referring to recipes or using your eyes. Cook that amount—your stomach will probably never know the difference. If you want leftovers, estimate the amount of extra food you'll need and never bring to the table what is intended for another day.

Sometimes it's hard to estimate how much food to prepare because some foods expand and others shrink when they're cooked. Some foods end up lighter or heavier than you would expect. After a while you'll be able to judge which foods do what and you won't miscalculate quite so often. For instance, fresh spinach, either steamed or fried, shrinks down to one-fourth of its previous volume. Pancakes expand and are heavier than one might expect. You probably can't comfortably eat as many pancakes as you might think. Similarly, noodles and rice expand because they absorb the water they are cooked in.

Lighter foods, of course, are a lot easier to eat and to digest. You'll probably want to eat a small piece of meat and a small amount of rice or potato in comparison to what seems like a large amount of salad. With heavier foods, your eyes are often "bigger than your stomach" and with lighter foods you might underestimate how much to prepare.

11

UTENSILS

I've read cookbooks in which the author emphatically states that the reader should use very specific types of utensils, for example: "Use *only* a black cast iron pot" or "Use a Teflon II frying pan." I am intimidated by statements like those because I can only use what I've got or what is easily accessible to me. Some of us haven't got the money to blow on an object which, in someone else's opinion (or fantasy), is superior or the *only* answer. My general philosophy is that there is no one answer to anything. That should be simple to accept.

Basically, you should try to pick up used pots, pans, spoons, forks, and knives from a Salvation Army, Goodwill, rummage sale (even though these places are not as cheap as they should be), or from parents. I haven't had much success with cheap, new utensils since they often rust, break, burn through or wear out in a matter of weeks. Sturdy, well-made, used utensils will far outlast flimsy, inexpensive, new ones.

You might want to acquire the following for your kitchen:

Frying Pan—with a cover, if possible (or use a large plate which is not made of plastic as a cover).

Medium and Small Pots (also known as saucepans)—some with covers and as sturdy (thick) as you can find. Small pots are good for sauces, medium pots for vegetables.

Large Pot—a sturdy five-quart (or more) pot for spaghetti and soups. A cover would be a great help.

Old Pressure Cooker—or a sturdy, medium-large pot, preferably with a cover, for tomato sauce.

Knives—paring knives, serrated knives, carving knives. One good knife will suffice for all jobs if absolutely necessary.

Soup/Gravy Ladle—or handled cup.

Spoons—wooden and metal, for stirring and serving.

Strainer and/or Colander—plastic or metal, and large enough to strain spaghetti. A strainer (but not a colander) can double as a flour sifter. A metal colander, if the right size and shape, can be inserted into a pot and vegetables may be steamed there.

Spatula—for eggs and other fried things.

Grater—convenient for grating cheese, vegetables, and whole nutmeg.

Measuring Cup—or a good eye or an eight-ounce glass.

Measuring Spoons—or one tablespoon and one teaspoon.

Containers for Storing Food—glass and plastic jars and containers from food purchased like mayonnaise, and ice cream which come in plastic containers.

Mixing Bowls—a pot will do, but bowls are nice to have around.

Bread Board-Chopping Block—an old board (without splinters) is fine.

Bread Pans, Cake Pans, Pie Pans—if you plan on doing loaf breads, cakes, and pies, you'll find them more convenient than any substitute.

Oven Dishes—casseroles of different sizes, or anything oven proof. If you're desperate, use your bread pan.

Egg Beater or Electric Mixer—necessary for beating egg whites stiff, blending eggnogs, and whipping cream. A beater is convenient in many cases but a fork will blend most things sufficiently.

12
STAPLES AND COMMON INGREDIENTS

It's a hassle to run out of something like potatoes or flour when you're in the midst of preparing a meal, and it's a drag to have to run out to the store every evening before you can get started on supper. If you can keep some staple foods around in reasonable quantities, you'll always have "the makings" for nutritious meals, and you'll be able to stretch foods farther when company shows up or you run short of money.

Some of those often-used foods you might want to keep in constant supply are: flour, onions, sugar, honey, oats, cornmeal, baking powder, baking soda, rice, potatoes, noodles, spaghetti or macaroni, herbs, spices, and cornstarch. Extras you might pick up on sale or when you have a little more grocery money are canned tomato products, such as tomato paste, tomato sauce, whole tomatoes, and tomato puree. Other condiments which might be essential to you are oil, vinegar, dry milk, soy sauce, bouillon cubes, margarine, lemons, mayonnaise and, of course, salt.

In this chapter I want to explain to you a little about the storage of these staples and common ingredients and describe some of their many uses.

Because the bug population seems to be steadily increasing in cities, it's very important that you store things properly. Your dry ingredients such as flour, cornmeal and sugar should be stored in containers which have tight lids or covers. The typical cookie jar cover is no good. Ants stealthily slither up the tops of such jars and then wedge their ways through the tiny spaces between the jar and lid. Bugs, in fact, can even get into oatmeal boxes even though the lids may seem secure. Putting a sealed plastic bag over the box should prevent such invasions, and there's always the refrigerator as a final barricade.

White flour does not have to be refrigerated. I've heard it said that white flour is so lacking in natural ingredients that the bugs don't even want it. However, you had better cover it and keep it dry as a precaution. You might want to refrigerate whole wheat, graham and rye flours, though you may not find it necessary. I've kept rye and whole wheat flours up to about six months unrefrigerated, stored in a cool place in well-sealed containers to prevent mildew and pests.

Salt, which is left in a salt shaker, can often turn very moist during the summer months. Pour a layer of rice on the bottom of the salt shaker. This should prevent some sticking.

Onions and potatoes should be stored in the coolest and darkest place you can find in your kitchen. A warm environment will start them sprouting. Cover them well (to prevent bugs, again) and keep them as dry as possible. Some city folks store potatoes and onions in the refrigerator which is probably the most foolproof method against sprouts.

Canned goods are, of course, most easily stored. But, if you open a can and do not finish the contents, do not keep the remainder in the can —put it in a jar or plastic container. Cans exposed to the air can oxidize and the can taste will penetrate your food.

Some staples and common ingredients are mentioned or described elsewhere in this book. The others are discussed here.

FLOUR

Flour comes in many varieties and usually is made from a grain such as wheat, rye or barley. White flour is the most commonly used flour in the United States. It is a by-product of wheat and it has been highly refined. The least expensive white flour is most always bleached. Most of these flours are then enriched—in other words, vitamins that were lost during refinement are put back in, in chemical form. A naturally white flour is becoming more popular and available, even though you must pay a little more for it. This flour turns white through a natural process—aging. Instead of speeding up the whitening process with chlorine, the flour ages into whiteness. White flour in my opinion is practically tasteless. Those other ingredients that are mixed with white flour in cooking create the taste of your bread, cake, or sauce.

Whole wheat and graham flours are also derived from wheat. They are basically, as far as I can see, the same type of flour. Both are ground from the whole wheat kernel. Graham flour is just coarser, because it wasn't sifted a final time. Both whole wheat and graham flours have a distinctive flavor, and coarsely ground whole wheat and all graham flours also have a definite texture. Whole wheat and graham tend to taste mildly nutty and the coarse ground flours even have a slight crunch to them. If you have teeth, you should enjoy this texture. North

Americans seem to want all their food, with the exception of meat, cut into little pieces or pulverized into mush. This is why these whole grain flours are not as popular as white flour. By now, you are probably wondering why graham flour is called graham flour instead of something like coarse ground whole wheat flour. Graham flour was named after someone named Graham who developed the flour. The graham cracker was also named for him.

Rye flour comes from rye and comes either smoothly or coarsely ground. It has a pleasant taste which I've been trying to describe, but can't. Sometimes people associate its flavor with caraway seed—but that's only because rye bread often contains caraway seed. Rye flour has a sharper taste than any of the wheat flours.

Other flours which can be purchased, but usually at higher cost and with difficulty are brown and white rice flours, oat flour, buckwheat, bran flour, and soy flour. Things such as sesame seeds and sunflower (not flour) seeds are sometimes ground up into meal and used with flour. Cornmeal is, of course, your most common meal. It is used both with flours and alone.

White flour is a good all-purpose flour if you just want something that will bind or thicken a food. But unlike other flours, it often has to be sifted. It also is good in combination with other flours. For instance, pizza or pie crust made with half white flour and half graham flour makes a more pleasant consistency than do either of the two alone. White flour can, of course, be used exclusively in any recipe which calls for flour. It also costs less than other flours.

Whole wheat, graham, rye and other grain flours are most often used in bread, pastry, and biscuit recipes. But if you add one of these flours to a casserole such as scalloped potatoes, you'll find it to be a pleasant addition.

Because I bake my own bread, I find that the money I save by not buying store bread makes up for the extra money I spend on whole grains. Of course, if you buy the large store brand white loaves you *might* be spending less than I do. But I somehow suspect that besides being tasteless these loaves are filled with air.

OATS

Rolled oats make a nutritious and very filling cooked breakfast cereal, are good for making granola, and can be added to meat loaf and casseroles. I prefer the old-fashioned oats over quick oats or instant oats. They seem to have more substance to them. When cooked, they are chewier and when roasted for granola they are crunchier.

CORNMEAL

Cornmeal can be used with flours in making breads, muffins, and pastries. It can also be used to coat various foods such as fish, chicken, vegetables, and meat before frying. It adds flavor and texture while white flour simply adds a standard breading.

BAKING POWDER

Baking powder is used to make things like muffins, biscuits, cakes, and dessert breads rise.

BAKING SODA

See baking soda under Household Hints, Chapter 5.

CORNSTARCH

Cornstarch is good as a thickener for Chinese vegetable meals (page 242). It also may be used instead of flour for thickening sauces and gravies and is a major ingredient in blanc mange, a very nice cornstarch pudding. The recipe for blanc mange is often on the label of the cornstarch box.

RICE

See the rice section of Chapter 21.

POTATOES

See the potato section of Chapter 21.

NOODLES, SPAGHETTI, AND MACARONI

See the pasta section of Chapter 21.

ONIONS

Onions are used in so many recipes to add flavor and texture that a list would probably be endless. But to name a few, onions flavor salads, can be used with margarine as a plain vegetable, can be fried, added to casseroles, stews, and soups.

There are five varieties of onions which are usually found in the supermarket. The most commonly used onions are the yellow-skinned, globe-shaped bulbs. They generally come in a package. When cut, they are white on the inside. These can be used for almost all recipes which call for onions, including boiled onions, soups, stews, and salads. Some people claim (and complain) that these onions, when used raw, tend to repeat (cause burping and other gastronomic discomforts). When these onions are cooked or used in recipes such as soup or stew, they generally do not cause repeating. Repeating is not a problem to most people, and these onions are the cheapest variety of the globe-shaped onions.

The fruit and vegetable section of the store may also sell large, yellow-skinned, bulb onions, which are called Bermuda onions. These also have white hearts, but they are called sweet onions, because they are milder than the common onion and are not likely to repeat on the user. Bermuda onions can likewise be used in almost all recipes calling for onions. Occasionally, you will see red onions in the store. These are Italian onions, even though more than half the population calls them Spanish or Bermuda onions. These onions are imported from Italy in handwoven baskets. Italian onions are also sweet onions which do not generally cause repeating. These have a very pleasing taste which is most apparent in salads and on sandwiches and hamburgers.

Leeks and scallions (green onions) are onions that do not have the usual onion shape. They have white stalks, a small bulb at the bottom, and green tops. All parts are edible and are milder than the common onions. The green tops are especially good when cut up into omelettes, salads, dips, and herb rice. The white stalks can be used in salads, omelettes, and even eaten raw, if you do not have an overly sensitive stomach. Both leeks and scallions are decorative and can be served with raw vegetables such as carrots and celery.

All of the varieties of onions are acceptable vegetables that can be served with a meal as you would any other vegetable.

SUGAR

White sugar is another one of the overly refined foods. It used to be the least expensive of all sweeteners, but its price has more than tripled recently. However, the human body does not digest it as well as it does honey. Sugar can be used in practically anything that requires a sweetener and can also be dissolved in a little warm water when a liquid sweetener is desired.

HONEY

Honey, the most digestible of all sweeteners, comes in different varieties. The name given to the particular honey you buy, such as clover honey or basswood honey, indicates the type of flower from which the bees predominantly got their pollen and nectar to make the honey. Often, a honey is not labeled specifically with a name such as alfalfa, loosestrife, or another specific flower, because the bees used many different varieties of flowers to make the honey and the jar label usually contains a list of those flowers. Beekeepers can never really be sure exactly what flowers were used. They can only guess by the types of flowers which were dominant in the area at the time the bees gathered the pollen and nectar for the honey.

Some honeys are dark and almost overpoweringly strong when used in large quantities. Others are very mild, light, and rather weak. The ideal honey, in my opinion, is in between these two. Dark honey is usually end-of-the-season honey and is thought to be inferior by many honey connoisseurs. However, some health food stores will sell this honey at higher prices than a light clover honey and will deceive the purchaser into believing that it's an exotically rare honey.

Honey can be used in cooking in place of sugar, and in drinks, on toast, and on pancakes. Generally you would use less honey than sugar and less of a dark honey than of a light. Since you use less, you may find that honey is more desirable than the very expensive sugar.

TOMATO PASTE

Tomato paste is a major ingredient in some tomato sauce recipes. It comes in small- to large-size cans, usually ranging from six to twelve to eighteen ounces. It may be added sparingly to homemade soup, as it will really add flavor to the broth.

TOMATO SAUCE

The term "tomato sauce" might be confusing. There are three basic types of "tomato sauce." One is the canned, mildly-seasoned sauce that is often added to other ingredients to make homemade tomato sauce. It comes in small and large cans, the most common being fifteen ounces. This sauce can be used in casseroles, soups, on pizza, and in lots of other ways.

Homemade tomato sauce, which you'll find in this book under the Pasta section of Chapter 21, could also be called spaghetti sauce. But I like to avoid that term because it seems to limit the uses of this versatile sauce. Not only can it be used as spaghetti sauce, but also on other pastas as well as on rice and potatoes.

Jarred tomato sauce, known as "spaghetti sauce," "marinara sauce," or by other descriptive terms is already seasoned and can simply be put in a saucepan, heated, and then used. You'll most likely get a lot more satisfaction and flavor if you do not use the preseasoned sauce from the jar.

WHOLE TOMATOES

Whole tomatoes usually come in a relatively large can that is most often twenty-eight ounces. They are simply whole tomatoes in the thin broth (or juice) of the tomato. They are good with poached fish, in chicken cacciatora and are a major ingredient in some tomato sauce recipes. They can also be added to a score of vegetable dishes, soups, stews, and to eggs.

TOMATO PUREE

Tomato puree is a combination of whole tomatoes and a sauce. It is used in some tomato sauce recipes. It comes in cans of varied sizes, the most common being twenty-eight ounces.

HERBS AND SPICES

See Chapter 13.

OIL

Common oils come in many different grades and qualities. Unfortunately, plain vegetable oil, the cheapest of all oils, contains little nutritional value and has many more polysaturates than corn oil, sunflower oil, and safflower oil. The oil that is supposed to be the lowest in polysaturates and also seems to have the most unobtrusive flavor is safflower oil. It's also outrageously expensive.

Chances are all this saturated-polyunsaturated-cholesterol garbage has you confused. Basically, saturated fats are predominantly solid fats such as lard, meat fat, and butterfats. Unsaturated or polyunsaturated fats are predominantly liquid fats such as vegetable oil. Unsaturated fats do not promote high cholesterol as do saturated fats. High cholesterol in the body can lead to arteriosclerosis (hardening of the arteries) and other complications, such as heart disease.

If you do not use a great deal of oil, you can probably use plain vegetable oil without significantly contributing to future heart disease. If you use a lot of oil, you are probably better off to buy corn oil, which is polyunsaturated and in the mid-price range.

Although you probably thought I was finished with the evils or controversies of oil, I have just one more thing to say. Unfortunately, it's quite difficult to find an inexpensive or mid-priced oil that does not contain preservatives. Wesson oil is the only common brand I know of that does not contain preservatives, besides expensive "natural" or "health food" brands. Maybe I'm missing the point somewhere, but it seems to me that you should have to pay more when an ingredient is added—such as a preservative—and you should pay less when it's not added.

Oil can be used a great deal when frying or steaming foods though some people prefer to use margarine. A frying pan lightly coated with oil prevents food from sticking. Vegetables, fish, meat, and eggs can be cooked above a light surface of oil. If you don't overdo it with the oil, nothing will taste greasy. Fried, breaded foods require more oil, as do fried potatoes. These foods might have to be placed on a paper bag or towel after frying. The greasy effect is removed in this way. Oil used for deep-fat frying, if not burned or overflavored, can be saved and reused with the same or similar ingredients.

Oil is often called for in baking and is used in many types of salad dressings.

VINEGAR

Vinegar is made from several different sources. The most commonly used vinegars are white grain, apple cider, and wine. White grain vinegar is usually the least expensive and is the best all-purpose vinegar. It is the type one would prefer to use when deliberately souring milk or adding to sweet ingredients. Apple cider vinegar and wine vinegar have more distinctive tastes. They are both good as a flavoring.

A few teaspoons of vinegar per cup of milk will sour milk. Some recipes such as chocolate cake call for sour milk. When you add the vinegar to milk, very soon you will see it curdle. It's really an amazing process to watch.

Vinegar can be sprinkled on meats before or during cooking. This helps a bit to tenderize the meat and also adds a faint and pleasant tangy flavor. Because most of the vinegar steams off you are not left with the characteristic acidic vinegary taste.

If your stews or other vegetable and meat combinations seem to need something like wine, but you don't have any wine, add a little vinegar. Again, the acidic taste will not pervade your food, providing that you don't overdo it with the vinegar. Wine vinegar is usually the best type of vinegar to use as a wine substitute.

Vinegar is a valuable ingredient in marinades and barbecue sauces unless lemon is used. It also is used in various types of salad dressings. Wine vinegar on a salad adds a really nice zip.

DRY MILK

Any type of dry milk can be used in cooking in place of whole milk, unless a very rich flavor is essential to the success of the recipe. You probably won't be able to tell the difference if you prepare cream sauces, soups, biscuits, cakes, and yogurt with dry milk. Pudding might taste a little different, but it is still very palatable.

Whole milk used as drinking milk can be stretched out with dry milk and water. Use one part whole milk to one part dry milk and water and save a fortune if you're a big milk drinker.

When you use dry milk, in most cases, it is best to mix it with water according to package instructions before you add it to whatever you're making. If you add the dry milk powder to the dish you are preparing before you mix it with water, there's a good chance the powder will lump together on you. For things such as biscuits and cakes, if you make sure everything is mixed well, it is not necessary to premix the powder with the water.

SOY SAUCE

Not all soy sauces taste the same, so you may have to experiment before finding the brand you like best. For instance, Kikkoman's soy sauce has a very strong flavor while La Choy's is more mellow. All soy sauce is supposed to be made from soybeans. If you find a brand that isn't, then you're not getting soy sauce.

Soy sauce is a convenient ingredient because in a lot of cases it is a good substitute for meat gravy. Soy sauce can be used in sauces, soups, broiled meat, fried rice, meat and vegetable combinations, fried spinach, for marinading, and a host of other things.

Do not add salt to something you've added soy sauce to before tasting the combination. Often the salt in the soy sauce is sufficient.

BOUILLON CUBES

I do not enjoy admitting I've put a bouillon cube in a recipe. Somehow it seems like cheating. I do use bouillon cubes occasionally in soups, stews, gravies, and rice. As unpioneer-like as the bouillon cube may seem, it enhances the flavors of things which are dull and creates flavor in those things which have no taste at all. The bouillon cube also saves time. Soups and stews eventually make it on their own with the proper amount of cooking time and doctoring with herbs. But I find it more convenient and less frustrating to cop out at times and resort to the cube.

Bouillon cubes dissolve well in a boiling liquid or can be crushed with a spoon and dissolved in a somewhat cooler liquid. The cubes come in two meat flavors that I know of—beef and chicken. Chicken bouillon cubes go well with pork and fish as well as with chicken and turkey. Beef bouillon cubes may be used with beef and lamb.

MAYONNAISE AND SALAD DRESSING

There is a distinctive difference between mayonnaise and salad dressing, though their purposes are quite similar. Mayonnaise has a bland taste while salad dressing has a sweeter taste. Both can be used on sandwiches, in potato and macaroni salads, and in dressings for salads. Whether you decide to use mayonnaise or salad dressing will be up to your individual taste. I prefer mayonnaise simply because I dislike the sweet taste of salad dressing. Also mayonnaise when mixed with lemon tastes very much like sour cream and is delicious in potato and macaroni salads and in baked fish dishes. Lemon will also slightly tone down the taste of salad dressing. If you like the taste of salad dressing but don't want it to overpower your salads, the addition of lemon will be very pleasing.

SALT

Salt, believe it or not, comes in several different varieties. Common table salt remains one of the few bargains in the supermarket. Iodized salt is probably your best bet for an all-purpose salt. It's your most commonly sold salt and it's a good salt to buy simply because the human body, which needs iodine, has few other sources of the mineral.

Kosher salt has a pleasant consistency and flavors meats very nicely while they cook. It also does not soak into salad greens as rapidly as fine salt—thus it does not wilt them. (The kosher salt box makes this claim, and it's true.) However, kosher salt, as far as I know, is not iodized. If the box label does not mention iodine in some place, assume that it has none. If you use kosher salt, it should be supplemented with iodized salt, unless your particular brand is iodized.

Salt is, of course, used commonly as a seasoning, but it also acts as a preservative for many foods. Salt is a major ingredient in canning. Also, if you read the 1974 *Farmer's Almanac,* you'll find many different household uses for salt. For instance, they suggest that one use salt for removal of stains in utensils and clothing, on wicker furniture and in jars and vases. Salt is effective, they say, in laundering and as a fire extinguisher. Salt, the almanac also informs us, prevents cracked boiling eggs from running and enhances the flavor of cocoa. Their list goes on for three pages.

MARGARINE

Gourmet cooks use butter. I am not a gourmet cook because my pocketbook does not allow it. Butter is outrageously expensive and supposedly not good for you. I no longer remember what butter tastes like and I don't miss it. Some other people's recipes even have the audacity to call for fresh sweet creamery butter. My recipes call for margarine. You are not committing a sin by using margarine.

Some store brand margarines taste really greasy on toast but are O.K. to use in my recipes so long as you don't burn them. Store brand margarines are most often less expensive than name brands. If you want, you can buy the cheaper stuff for cooking and use some better margarine, such as corn oil margarine, for spreading on your bread.

LEMON

Ah—a seemingly simple form
The lemon takes.
Plump yellow oval,
Lethargically perching near the celery
Concealing the secret of your existence.

But what labyrinthian wonders lie within you.
Your latticed cells emit life's essence
To languid broccoli, lackluster sea food
And a latent leaf of spinach.

So evil yet so pure are you
O Citrus Passion,
That one who's tasted
Your sweet lips,
Forever a prisoner
Of your power is made.

And were you not that licentious fruit,
O Golden Lemon,
Who into the banquet room
Threw yourself
Announcing, "For the Fairest"
Causing the goddesses to feud,
Creating the Judgment of Paris
And the Trojan War?
(While you rolled back
Emitting enticing odors
Which clouded the reason
Of the multitudes.)

Yes—the torture, trauma, destruction
You have caused
Would call for a lemonectomy,
Were it not that kitchen life
Would soon be ceased without you.

The lemon is one of those versatile food items that saves or adds to many conglomerations which I prepare. I have grown dependent upon the lemon. It has become sort of a crutch for me.

You will notice that a moderate number of recipes in this book suggest the use of lemons. The lemon may also be used in proportions of a squirt here and a squirt there on numerous things. For instance, squirt various green vegetables with lemon. Broccoli, asparagus, and green beans taste great with it. Just about any fish I can think of has a vastly improved taste when lemon is added to it. Broiled chicken sprinkled with lemon before or after cooking brings out an interesting flavor. And mayonnaise (but not "salad dressing") tastes a lot like sour cream when mixed with lemon. Mayonnaise and lemon is a good combination in potato salad, cole slaw, tuna, and chicken salad, and also when baked with fish. Also, a cup of bouillon with a swig of lemon and a sprinkle of a few herbs, makes a decent drink. Tea, liver, baked turkey parts, fruit salad, and green salads are considerably perked up when lemon is added to them.

Lemons in the kitchen bring with them the illusion that everything is clean and fresh. Lemon rubbed on an onion or garlic-stained cutting board saves one's nose from a very nasty odor. Stale onion on a cutting board smells like bad underarms—(I wouldn't suggest the use of lemon under your arms).

The juice of the lemon can most easily be brought forth by rolling the lemon with the flat of your palm on a hard surface, like a table. The lemon can then be cut open and squeezed. The use of this process allows more juice to come from the fruit.

If you have a choice (meaning that the lemons are not prepackaged and sealed), *gently* feel and caress your lemons before buying them. You can do this without totally molesting the fruit. After all, someone else may want to buy the ones you reject. My favorite lemons are firm, not soft, and do not have brown spots. Old lemons can be detected by their dull skins; they do not shine in comparison to a fresher lemon —their pores look as if oil would not come out of them—and their skins cannot really be used for anything. I prefer the thick skinned lemons. You can sometimes detect them by a large bump on top of the lemon. However, if the skin is too thick, you could end up with mostly skin and a peewee lemon inside. Good lemons are pregnant with potential, so it's best to choose them carefully.

My husband and his sister are such lemon-in-iced-tea fanatics that you'd have to see it to believe it. When they are together drinking iced tea, the house is inevitably sheer havoc. If Mary Ann doesn't have her fingers in Michael's glass about to grab his last piece of lemon, Michael has already stolen her lemons or eaten half a piece and returned the other half to her glass. Mary Ann would think nothing of pouring the iced tea and "forgetting" to put lemon in Michael's glass while putting five or six pieces in her own. She loves to deprive him immediately while he would prefer to give her the lemons and then take them away.

Occasionally, the lemon encounter becomes fairly physical. Lemon peels are thrown down shirts, discovered behind ears or in between toe nails, and Mary Ann's dog starts jumping around, yapping, screaming, and slipping on lemon peels.

So you see, the lemon is evil. It can temporarily transform beautiful people into raving yellow kleptomaniacs.

For directions on how to make this nasty drink, see page 112.

13
HERBS AND SPICES

Herbs and spices can make ordinary food into something quite provocative. For instance, parsley mixed with margarine can turn an anemic boiled potato into an object worthy of eating. Sweet basil on a hamburger creates a not-so-common great taste, and dill in tuna fish brings out all its nonfishy assets.

A distinction must be made between herbs and spices. People with ulcers or sensitive digestive tracts should stay away from hot seasonings (generally called spices) such as black pepper, chili powder, white pepper, and cayenne. These people should also avoid the tangy herbs such as thyme, but mild herbs can be used by almost everyone. Parsley, sweet basil, dill, and sweet paprika can be used in almost any quantity within reason, and oregano and bay leaves can be used in moderation. With this approach to herbs and spices, everyone can savor the aroma and taste of most herbs.

Being poverty stricken and eating food that tastes blah should have no direct correlation. I once knew some penniless students who in a martyr-like fashion ate boiled potatoes and frozen vegetables or plain rice and frozen vegetables for dinner every night. When delegated to cook one night, I discovered several cans of spices and herbs on their dusty shelves. By adding some of these seasonings to their potatoes and vegetables, a fairly decent meal was created. I was, of course, declared a miracle worker and was exploited many more times. But the point is that anyone can make a potato taste palatable, and at no real extra cost. Most herbs and spices that you will probably want to use can be purchased quite economically. For a very few dollars you can supply yourself for months with spices and herbs, thereby preventing your tastebuds from undergoing atrophy.

Experimenting with seasonings is fun even though occasionally one comes up with something quite atrocious. When I am unsure of the possible compatibility of a food with an herb or spice, I either smell or taste a little of the herb and imagine how it would taste when combined or cooked, or I throw it in and pray.

When using herbs and spices, do not overseason. Add small

amounts at first and allow the flavor of the ingredient to permeate through the food. You can always add more. You might want to try some of these herbs and spices in the following combinations.

BAY LEAF

In homemade soups, sauces, gravies, spaghetti sauce.

CINNAMON

In fruit salads, cookies, on oatmeal, cooked fruits, hot chocolate, hot white milk, eggnogs.

CURRY

In a few spicy dishes such as bean soup and some stews.

DILLWEED

In tuna, other fish, chicken soup, on broiled chicken, in green salads.

NUTMEG

In fruit salads, cookies, Swedish meatballs, cooked fruits, eggnogs, eggs, fish, in tomato sauce.

OREGANO

On fowl, beef, pork, lamb, fish, in green salads, tomato salad, soups, spaghetti sauce, meatballs, meat loaf, and on omelettes.

PARSLEY

In green salads, omelettes, on fish, on potatoes, on noodles, in soups, and in bean salads.

PAPRIKA

On fowl, green salads, cream cheese and celery, eggs, cottage cheese, tuna.

SWEET BASIL

Its uses are similar to that of oregano, but it has its own distinctive taste. Use in combination with oregano or separately. Sweet basil is really great on lamb and in cooked rice.

THYME

On lima and kidney beans, pork or lamb, fish, and in soup.

As I have mentioned, these common herbs and spices will not cost you much. If you cannot afford the extra few dollars at one time, build up your supply gradually. Also, look for the local store brand name, as it is usually a bargain in comparison to a well-known name product.

If you are interested in growing your own potted herbs, see Chapter 24 on A Few Country Things.

CHART 3[1]
HERBS AND SPICES

Beef	basil, nutmeg, oregano, curry
Fish	basil, dillweed, nutmeg, oregano, paprika, parsley, thyme
Fowl	basil, dillweed, oregano, paprika
Lamb	basil, oregano, thyme, curry
Pork	basil, oregano, thyme
Eggs	basil, nutmeg, oregano, paprika, parsley
Green Salads	basil, dillweed, oregano, parsley, thyme, curry
Soups	basil, bay leaf, dillweed, oregano, parsley, thyme, curry
Vegetables	basil, oregano, parsley, thyme
Fruits and Sweets	cinnamon, nutmeg

[1] This chart is meant to be a general guide; it is not an absolute.

14

CREATIVITY IN COOKING

Most main recipes do not really have to be followed to the letter. Although you might want to follow recipes for breads and cakes fairly closely, the success of other recipes does not depend upon following all the rules in the cookbook you use. For the most part, use your own judgment. If a procedure sounds logical, follow the directions; if it sounds superfluous, you might take a chance and skip it. Also, the more you use one particular recipe, the more it will develop your special touches as you try different methods and change some ingredients. In some cases it will become so altered that the person who invented the recipe would no longer recognize it.

Recipes are not mysterious secret formulas—that's why by using reasonable judgment you can experiment. Think about it—isn't it rather strange that recipes are always calling for ingredients in proportions of wholes, halves, quarters, and eighths? Why not 1-1/16 cups of flour? Because it would look weird if a recipe called for 1-1/16 cups of flour and also it would be hard to measure it in a standard measuring cup. Some recipes do work out better if 1-1/16 cups of flour are used instead of the one cup that the recipe calls for. This is where you must take over and realize that an inanimate book must not run your life in the kitchen or elsewhere. Cooking requires a human factor—and you are that factor in this case.

Think of innovation in the kitchen as an art. Suppose you were painting a picture. Occasionally you would stop, look at the picture, and figure out what it needed to make it more appealing. You can do that with your cooking too—only you have to use some different parts of your imagination—something that is a little less tangible. You have to rely a bit on memory, say, the memory of what lemon and paprika taste like and what they might taste like together. After a while you'll begin to enjoy the challenge.

Your imagination and innovation can be useful when you run into a bargain at the supermarket. Let's suppose you see turnips at a low price at the store, but you have never made turnips. You don't have a book which has a recipe for turnips and to call your mother is a toll call. (If you were to call your mother, the turnips would no longer be a bargain.) Just think about turnips and the way you remember them. Perhaps you remember them mashed and buttery with sprinkles of something on them that tasted good. To mash and butter them is simple enough—do it the same way you mash potatoes—by boiling them in water until tender, straining, and then mashing them with a fork and adding margarine. Then think about the seasoning on top. Try to remember the taste and maybe you'll be able to figure out that it was nutmeg—and even if it wasn't, maybe nutmeg would taste fine on turnips. You now have a turnip recipe and a vegetable at a bargain price.

Or, maybe you love mushrooms but you can never afford them. Finally you see a bargain for nice, fresh mushrooms. Even if the only recipes you know of that call for mushrooms are very expensive and exotic, do not despair. You can put mushrooms in practically anything: eggs, cream sauce, spaghetti sauce, fried plain or with onions, in soups, stews, and stuffed. It would be foolish to pass up the mushrooms because you didn't know immediately how to use them. If you think before you panic while cooking, you can usually think of something that turns out very well.

Even stream of consciousness may be responsible for the invention of a creative recipe. You're lying in bed trying to get to sleep. Whenever you have trouble getting to sleep you begin itching. Why am I itching? If I lie still and I don't think about it, I won't itch. Ho hum. I itch. Must have dry skin or a fungus—except I only get dry skin in the winter and I never get a fungus. Wonder what fungus feels like? Like poison ivy? I don't have poison ivy! Haven't had poison ivy since I was in the fourth grade and Timmy Laskrinski pushed me into a patch of it. Can see myself falling into shiny green leaves. Cover my face. Feel it tickling my hands and ears. Itched for weeks—worse than now. Fourth grade. See rows and rows of wooden chairs and desks with old ink wells—never used them—didn't even know what they were for except to carve around. Many children sitting there, coughing, whispering, passing notes. Heater in the room is rumbling. The teacher, Miss Hoolihan, tall and skinny. Wonder how tall and skinny she really was. Horrible year. That was the year I weighed 84 pounds and everyone else weighed about 60, except Lester Schnipple, who weighed 100 pounds in kindergarten, so he really didn't count. Why did they always weigh and measure you in front of everyone else? In a loud booming voice Miss Hoolihan used to say:

"Susan Stanley, 54 inches, 62 pounds . . . Arthur Morrissey, 53-1/2 inches, 60 pounds. . . ."

Then she got to me. Her voice boomed louder.

". . . 56 inches, 84 pounds. . . ."

Man, what a drag. If I hadn't stopped growing, I would have shot myself. Between that and pimples. . . . Being a child is a horrible thing. Makes me cringe to think about it. The time we were jumping rope on the black top. My turn. I jumped in expertly. Had little cleats on my shoes that clicked on the pavement:

"Down in the valley where they don't wear pants . . ." I sang. I thought that's how the song went—I *really* did. I wasn't trying to be wise. Must have gotten it mixed up with,

"I see Boston, I see France . . ."

Mrs. Finley, the first grade teacher, cut me off. Oh, I can't stand it, why do I have to think about this?

"Young lady, you know very well those aren't the words to that song. What's the meaning of this? . . ."

Can feel my face turn red as a beet, even now. People say, "red as a beet," but beets aren't really red, they're more maroon or wine color. Tomatoes are red. If I put beets with tomatoes, they'd be sort of red . . . If I don't stop itching . . . even my teeth itch . . . oregano, beets, tomatoes, cheese, onion, maybe in a casserole . . .

Ho hum.

Whether you plan your menus in advance or on the spur of the moment is, of course, up to you, but sometimes you can invent meals from what you were able to find at the store. If you are unable to find any inexpensive meat a particular week, you might have to cut down on your meat intake. Perhaps that same week, cauliflower, mushrooms, and spinach aren't too expensive. While at the supermarket you can make the decision to have creamed cauliflower, mushrooms and spinach with eggs. You can think about the seasonings later. Or, if you can't come up with recipes in the store, you can buy the more reasonably priced items and promise yourself that you'll think of a use for all those things before they rot.

Previously, when you were well-to-do and wasteful while living with your parents, you may have looked down upon the possibilities of having string beans twice in one week. Well, you may not have much of a choice now, if the string beans are sold prepackaged or are one of the few reasonably priced vegetables in the store. You will want to use them before they go bad. You will not grow tired of them if you can cook them in different ways. Eat them plain one day, in stew or soup the next. By preparing them differently each time, you will barely be able to tell you are using the same vegetable.

Eventually, you will find that your taste buds are not as spoiled as you think they are. Through different cooking methods and a variety of seasonings, you will find that you will be able to tolerate and enjoy a more limited variety of foods while learning to discover and appreciate the more subtle tastes of the foods you prepare.

15
SUBSTITUTION

Many people are really caught up in using only particular ingredients. In fact, some folks even make every salad they prepare with the same ingredients—let's say escarole and tomatoes. Those people might become quite upset if someone snuck some celery and peppers in their salad and took out the tomato. They'd be still more disturbed if you were to suggest to them that a salad doesn't even need lettuce or escarole if you don't happen to have it or want it.

It's really not that hard to open your mind to the varied substitution possibilities for many different foods, and you may have to. It is quite likely that you will not always be able to get your first choice because it costs too much, you can't get it, or it's too hard to use. Chances are you may substitute one thing for another and then discover that, for you, it is a more desirable ingredient.

See Chart 4 for a list of possible substitutions. These are just suggestions which should help you get the idea of the whole thing.

One type of substitution which I think is a bad practice is substituting a starch for a nonstarch. You do not want to overload your diet with bulk in the form of starch. Take mock apple pie: In this recipe crackers are substituted for apples. True, because of the other ingredients such as nutmeg and cinnamon, the pie gives you the impression you're eating apples, but the whole combination is nothing but starch and spices. If you don't plan on eating any other starch at a meal, then a substitution such as this is O.K. so long as you make sure that sometime during the day, you're getting the vitamins you lost by not having the apples.

Some mothers always seem to have great recipes that they pass on to their children as they leave home. That's just great—but I usually can't afford many of these recipes. (My mother's an exception. She usually gives me cheap recipes these days.) Most mothers are enough beyond the point of poverty that they might figure that a meal which costs a little more will do no harm. But you'll discover that more expensive meals can really put a hole in your budget.

Suppose your mother gave you a recipe for beef Stroganoff that called for top round (a choice cut of beef), onions, sour cream, mushrooms, vermouth (high class wine), poppy seeds, butter, garlic, oregano, salt, and pepper. In most cases, you can't afford or don't have top round, sour cream, mushrooms, vermouth, butter, and poppy seeds. Instead of top round you could use a lower quality meat, and less of it, well trimmed of fat and maybe soaked in vinegar and soy sauce for a while to make it tender. The sour cream and poppy seeds could be eliminated, but you may decide that you can afford the sour cream anyway because you've cut out all of the other expensive ingredients. Celery or more onions will take the place of mushrooms, and the vermouth may be substituted by any rotgut wine or a dash of vinegar. Margarine can of course take the place of butter. Your mother will probably cry when she hears about this but she may have a reasonable income to afford more expensive food—you don't.

The following substitution chart is to be used to avoid buying the higher priced foods and to use what you have on hand in your kitchen rather than going out to buy something special. Substitution in cooking, besides being challenging and fun, is also meant to save you money. Frequently, recipes will call for ingredients that you do not have. Suppose a potato salad recipe calls for sour cream, and it's expensive. The high price you spend on it would be wasted. This type of situation can easily unbalance your budget. All you need to do in many cases is to use mayonnaise and lemon instead of sour cream. When recipes call for ingredients which you do not have, check the substitution chart for those things which can be used in place of the called-for ingredient. You may already have the other ingredient around.

Also, suppose you are going to make a barbecue sauce which calls for brown sugar. If you don't have brown sugar, which is an expensive ingredient anyway, check the substitution chart and you find that honey or molasses are the substitutions, but you don't have those ingredients either. Your first reaction may be to buy brown sugar, since that's what the recipe calls for. But, that may not be the best thing to do. You should consider all three ingredients—brown sugar, honey, and molasses—and decide which one would be most generally useful. You may only have use for the brown sugar in this barbecue sauce. Molasses can be used for this recipe, in some breads, and in baked beans. You may use honey on toast, in tea, in bread, in hot milk, and in barbecue sauce. So honey seems to be the one ingredient of the three that most assuredly will not sit on your shelf unused. So honey looks like your most prudent choice.

In the chart below, substitutions may be interchanged as well as substituted, unless marked with an asterisk (*). For instance, lemon can usually be used in place of dillweed; but dillweed cannot always be used in place of lemon. In, say, ice tea or cake, dillweed substituted for lemon would certainly not be an appetizing choice.

CHART 4
SUBSTITUTIONS

INGREDIENT	SUBSTITUTION
Herbs	
black pepper, white pepper	paprika
caraway seed	dillseed
dillweed	lemon*
oregano	basil
Meats, Poultry and Fish	
whole chicken or turkey	chicken or turkey parts
turkey	chicken
sausage	chopped meat with herbs and spices
leg of lamb	lamb shank
sirloin steak	chuck steak (make sure fat is white)[1]
pork	chicken
pot roast	stew meat, chuck, shanks
veal	pork
fillet of perch and sole	any type of fish fillet, such as turbot, flounder, pollock, haddock
tuna	any type of boned fish
Vegetables (most vegetables can be interchanged)	
spinach	escarole (endive)
mushrooms	broccoli stems, celery, black olives
pimento	red or green pepper
tomato paste	can of tomato puree or sauce—with less water

97

Fruit

currants	raisins
strawberries	black or red raspberries, blackberries, dewberries, blueberries
pineapple (e.g. when cooked with ham or pork or put in coleslaw)	peaches, apples, many other fruits

Sweeteners

honey	brown sugar, white sugar
molasses	honey, brown sugar
turbinado	brown sugar, white sugar, honey

Dairy

sour cream (in cold dishes and baked fish)	lemon and mayonnaise together (do not use salad dressing)
mozzarella cheese	brick or Muenster cheese
ricotta cheese	cottage or yogurt cheese
whole milk	In cooking, cold meals, and drinking: skim, 1%, 2% or nonfat dry milk. For cooking only: whey (from yogurt cheese or other source)
cream (when whipping is not required)	milk, buttermilk, sour cream, evaporated milk, condensed milk (may not taste good in every combination)
evaporated milk	buttermilk, whole milk, nonfat dry milk, skim milk or 1% or 2% milk
butter	margarine, vegetable, corn or seed oil

Miscellaneous

wine	beer, vinegar, lemon
soy sauce	bouillon cube with water (to taste)
almonds	walnuts, peanuts, sunflower seeds and others

---

[1] My grandmother says that if the fat on a steak is white and not yellow, there's more of a chance that the meat will be tender. She says that yellow fat is from on old cow.

16
BIG APPETITE
OR UNEXPECTED COMPANY

A lot of people seem to think that the way to increase the size of a meal is to add more meat. People tend to focus on the meat part of the meal as the nutritional, filling, or main ingredient of dinner. This does not have to be true. In fact, it had better not be true if you intend to stick to a food budget within your means.

Usually meat is the most expensive ingredient of the meal. Though at times foods such as cheese can cost more per pound, people tend to eat less cheese because it is not considered to be the main part of the meal. Once you begin to realize that you can cut down your meat intake without becoming unhealthy, you will notice all the other good foods around you that can take the place of meat or can supplement a smaller portion of meat.

Let's suppose you are cutting down on the meat portion of your meal anyway and someone shows up unexpectedly, or maybe you're just very hungry. If you are making a stew, pot pie, or vegetable and meat casserole, simply add the meat you have and increase your vegetables. Try not to increase your starches. If you made two small pork chops and four people are eating, cut the chops in half, surround them with vegetables, and serve a salad, and whatever you do, don't apologize.

Other foods which can be used to compensate for small meat portions are cheese, sunflower seeds (if you can get them cheaply), and eggs. (Eggs might be used sparingly as some doctors say people should not eat too many eggs a week because of the high cholesterol level.) Carrots, beets, soy, or lima beans and other nonfibrous vegetables tend to aid in one's appetite.

Before long you will begin to discover a new meal concept. Your meals will cost less and they will no longer consist of one piece of meat, one blop of starch, and one vegetable. Instead, you will have a little less of some things but more of a variety. You'll discover that it's great to have several vegetables at a meal and also to have little things you can keep picking at such as sunflower seeds, celery, and carrots.

17
MEASUREMENTS

Measurements in a recipe are usually given simply as a guide to the cook. Old time recipes sometimes call for things as "a handful of flour" or "oil three times around the pot." Now most measurements are standardized—I suppose, because everyone's handful is not nearly the same and three times around the pot depends upon the size of the pot and the speed at which you're pouring the oil. Just the same, a lot of folks cook successfully by feel, using only approximate measurements. If you are unsure of what you're doing, or you are making something like a soufflé, cake, Jell-O, or pudding, follow the directions as accurately as you can. Otherwise, you can use measurement guides casually.

Most of the recipes in this book either have no measurements, or the measurements that are given are intended to be interpreted approximately. Quantities of ingredients for things such as soups, stews, and vegetable dishes usually depend upon the amount of a particular ingredient you have around the house.

Chart 5 should familiarize you with standard measurements and their abbreviations.

CHART 5
MEASUREMENTS

MEASURE	EQUIVALENT	ABBREVIATION(S)
cup[1]	8 oz., 1/2 pt., 1/4 qt.	c.
egg	1 medium egg	
gallon	4 qt.	gal.
ounce	dry ounce = 1/16 lb.	oz.
	fluid ounce = 1/8 c.	
peck (dry measure)	2 gal.	
pint	1/2 qt.	pt.
pound	16 oz. (dry measure)	lb. #
quart	1/2 gal., 2 pt.	qt.
tablespoon	4 tbsp. = 1/4 c.	Tb., Tbs., tbsp., T
teaspoon	3 tsp. = 1 tbsp.	ts., tsp., t

[1] Measures are usually level rather than heaping—such as a level cup—unless otherwise specified in a recipe.

18
PRESERVATIVES

B.H.T., polysorbate 80, sodium nitrite, sodium nitrate, and other mysterious-sounding things are not just weird words written on your food labels—they're really in your food. The worst thing about this situation is that few, if any of us, know which of these additives are harmful to our bodies and which are not. It is rumored that even researchers do not know what effects—both long range and immediate—these additives can have on our systems.

I can personally testify that two out of the three times I bought a particular, supposedly reputable, brand of dried apricots, which contained sulfur dioxide as a preservative, I had bad experiences. The first time, the fruit had a strong chemical taste. I assumed that the packers had made a rare mistake and had overloaded the fruit with the chemical preservative. The second time, all I had to do was to open the package. The smell which came from within was enough to knock me out. In a way, this experience was fortunate because the taste and smell warded me away from the chemicals. But things you cannot taste or smell in your food tend to give you the feeling that they're not really there, or that they are O.K. for you.

For all anybody knows, sodium benzoate and sorbic acid may be perfectly benign and even healthful chemicals, but nobody and nothing has given me any reason to believe this. As far as I'm concerned, these preservatives have not been adequately explained to the public. One of the most offensive ambiguities is the term "flavorings" which is so often seen on food labels. These things could be delicately "flavored" with arsenic for all we know—and that's not meant as a joke.

Many of our packaged, canned, jarred, and bottled foods contain these mysterious preservatives. Many cold cereals contain B.H.T.; tuna in water often has chemicals in it; Coca Cola contains benzoate of soda; maple syrup contains sorbic acid and sodium benzoate. The list goes on. Buy oils and shortening and you will most likely come face to face with something strange on the label. One of the ironies of the situation is this: You can avoid chemically inseminated foods by paying more for something which has not been loaded with chemicals. Those pure, untampered-with foods can cost you as much as double for something that tastes about the same. You can get ripped off and spend the extra money, or you can do what I do and read the labels and avoid chemicaled foods as often as possible.

But we don't even know everything that's in the foods which do list their ingredients on their labels. Just for example, "natural" cereals do not claim to have been grown without the use of chemical insecticides and herbicides—which is to say that chances are we're getting all that stuff through the "pure" vegetables and grains we eat. And to make things more mind-boggling, no one really seems to know just how harmful chemical insecticides and herbicides are. We do know that under certain conditions they can be very dangerous. Barely a year goes by without a report of deaths to farm laborers caused by too much exposure to an insecticide or herbicide. The people who favor the use of these insecticides and herbicides claim that the consumer does not ingest as much of these chemicals as did the farm laborers who died. But over a period of maybe twenty to forty years we may eat enough foods which were grown in fields sprayed with these chemicals to kill us. And our deaths will be reported as being from some unknown disease. The public must realize that even sprays are washed into the soil by rain and then taken into the plants through their root systems.

One study of artificial flavorings, colorings, and preservatives reported in *Newsweek* several years ago focused on a group of twenty-five hyperactive children. By normal standards, these children were incapable of concentrating, or "sitting still" as old-time teachers would say, for even a very short time. They were considered disciplinary problems by their schools, when, in fact, they were just uncontrollably hyperactive (hyperkinetic). When one doctor had all of these children placed on a diet of foods that contained no preservatives or artificial flavorings or colorings twenty of these twenty-five children were no longer hyperactive. And, if any of them were given foods which contained preservatives or artificial flavorings or colorings, within hours these children would begin to exhibit characteristics of hyperactivity. The point is, if preservatives, artificial flavorings, and artificial colorings can cause hyperactivity in some people, it's possible they could cause neuroses in others, depression in some, heart disease to still others, headaches to another group of people, and countless physical or emotional problems to the balance of the population.

The federal government does not know if these preservatives, artificial flavorings, or colorings are harmful to us. Many people say, "If the Food and Drug Administration allows the manufacturers to put these preservatives into our food, then they must be O.K." Consider though, the cyclamate/saccharin dilemma. First, cyclamates were banned from use because tests showed they caused cancer when given to rats. Saccharin was repopularized as the replacement for cyclamates. Now tests have shown that saccharin causes cancer in rats even faster than cyclamates. Knowing this, how can anyone dare to say that the Food and Drug Administration knows that preservatives, artificial flavorings and colorings are not harmful to people? For our own health and serenity, all of us must try with conviction to stay away from preservatives, artificial flavorings and artificial colorings as often as possible.

It's a terrible thing, in my opinion, to live in ignorance like this and to be fairly-well trapped into consuming something we may not care to. But many people are going to have to drop an awfully big bomb of protest before the government will begin to do anything about the situation. And we can all fairly-well guess that this will never happen.

19

LEFTOVERS

CHINATOWN

We were sitting in a park in Chinatown one day resting after an excursion. The day was supposed to be a treat. We had figured out how much money we were going to spend down to the last seventy cents which was for an out-of-the-way subway ride to visit my grandmother. Part of our treat, though we were too poor to buy a dinner, was to try something new to eat—something we had never tasted, or anything like it, before. So we decided to try some Chinese pastries. We decided on one of the many pastry shops in the area and walked in. The shelves were loaded with colorful pastries which had been masterfully designed to represent little people and houses and buddhas and other Chinese symbols. After pondering many minutes, we chose several kinds of little pastries.

There we sat in the park sampling the mysterious sweets. We felt like two evil little kids because we so rarely bought ourselves anything sweet. Most of the pastries we sampled were very nutty and sugary. Though they were distinctively different from anything we had ever had before, we liked them. Then we bit into one yellow pastry that did not taste good to us at all. It was one of those rare foods that I'd probably have to spend a lifetime developing a taste for. We sat there and wondered what to do with the thing.

People sat in the park alone or in couples, eating their lunches, conversing with their neighbors, or relaxing before returning to work. Two men sat there methodically playing a game of chess. A man dressed in a long, holey, tweed coat and in shoes much too large for him walked from one trash can to the next looking for scraps that someone might have left from lunch. We sat on our bench and watched, holding our yellow cake. Occasionally, the man found the crusts of a sandwich and quickly devoured them. My thoughts made me nervous. I wondered if I should offer the yellow pastry to the man, because if he wasn't hungry he certainly wouldn't be picking in trash cans. I imagined walking up to him and offering it to him. Various images of how he would reject it went through my head. Even though he was scrounging through trash cans, I believed that he had some sort of pride. The most vivid image I had ran parallel to a poster I once saw. It was of a very skinny man, presumably in India or Pakistan, with wooden C.A.R.E. packages that had apparently been airlifted to him. The boxes contained Baby Ruth candy bars. The man sat there with a what-the-hell-am-I-supposed-to-do-with-these look on his face. So, I rationalized, the crust of a tuna sandwich is probably a lot more substantial to this man than a delicate yellow pastry with a weird taste.

We packed up our yellow pastry and put it in my purse. Weeks later, while cleaning the refrigerator I removed a mysterious waxed paper-wrapped package from the darkest corner of the refrigerator. I opened it. Inside was a yellow mass with brilliant red and green furry tentacles protruding from its body.

There's nothing wrong with leftovers—if you get to them on time. Quite a few foods actually improve in flavor the second or third time around. Spaghetti, for instance, tastes great reheated. However, if you wait too long to get to a leftover, when you open the container it's stored in, you'll be confronted with unrecognizable, icky, moldy gunk. Most foods should be reused within the week, although some foods, such as fish, will spoil in a few days.

Leftover meats, fish, and vegetables can be converted into pot pies or thrown into soups. They can also be reheated in a pot or frying pan. If you want foods to be on the crisp side, fry them in oil. Otherwise, cover foods and steam them with a few tablespoons of water.

Almost any vegetable can be combined with another or with many others. There is no reason why you can't combine green beans, peas, carrots, and corn. If you have small portions of starches leftover, such as rice and noodles, reheat them together. Just be sure that it's not the bulk of your meal. Sometimes recombined things need some new zip. For instance, you may have a lot of spaghetti leftover but just a little sauce. Mix the sauce and spaghetti together, add milk, cheese, and a vegetable, if you want, and bake it in a greased baking dish. If you leave the cover off for all or part of the time, you'll get nice crunchy spaghetti on the top.

Your leftover gravies, vegetable water, yogurt, cheese whey, and juice from canned tomatoes can be mixed with powdered milk when a recipe calls for milk. Or, they can be used instead of water in a recipe, or, simply added to soups.

Some things may not be particularly palatable when in combination with one another. For instance, I may hesitate to combine fish with most meat. Sausage, however, tastes interesting with fish in soup.

If you're not sure of how some things might taste all glopped up together but you have several little dishes of leftovers, reheat them in different pots. If there are two people eating, maybe one person will eat the drumstick and carrots and another will eat the meat loaf and stewed tomatoes.

The following is a chart of leftovers that is meant as a guide and certainly should not be followed faithfully. Use your imagination. Some recipes in Chapter 21 will refer you to other recipes in which leftovers from the first recipe may be used.

CHART 6

LEFTOVERS	NEW MEAL CREATED FROM LEFTOVERS	METHOD OF PREPARATION
chicken	pot pie, creamed chicken, chicken salad	see recipes in Part 4
	reheated with vegetables	steam or fry in pan
meat	soup	throw meat into soup
	pot pie	see recipe in Part 4
	reheated with vegetables	steam or fry in pan
	sliced with gravy	put in pot, cover with gravy
fish	fish and vegetable soup	if enough fish, make a new soup, or add to an all-vegetable or fish soup
	fish salad	mix like tuna, add relish, if desired
	pot pie	substitute fish for meat—use chicken stock or bouillon

spaghetti	reheated	heat in baking dish in oven or heat in pot on stove with a little water
rice	fried rice	see recipe in Part 4
baked or boiled potato	fried	fry in margarine or oil, season with salt, paprika, pepper
stuffing	fried	fry in margarine or oil and season with salt, paprika, pepper
salad	soup	throw in soup
	cooked vegetables	steam or fry alone or with other vegetables
vegetable	soup reheated	throw in soup steam, fry, or add to casseroles

20
HOW TO SAVE TIME

People who feel like slaves in their own kitchens put that upon themselves. If you learn to plan your time well, you can spend a day working, going to school, or browsing through museums, the planetarium, looking at the river, admiring the Clarence J. Farnsworth memorial fountain and trekking on home to an almost-made dinner.

Quick meals that you prepare on the spot include such things as omelettes, hamburgers on toast, oven-top macaroni and cheese, spaghetti and clam sauce, scrambled vegetables, poached fish, vegetables and a salad, and any reheated leftovers. These meals can usually be prepared within ten minutes to half an hour.

Other meals can be quick if you prepare a few things in advance. Creamed eggs with vegetables, vegetables and fried rice, pasta fagiole, frozen or reheated pizza, soup made with premade soup stock, and premade meat loaf or stuffed peppers take a little planning. Also, anything prepared in a fairly flat dish can be covered and heated at 350° F. to 375° F. in a short time.

Or, if you are tired but can wait forty-five minutes to an hour to eat, pot pies and casseroles which have been prepared ahead of time can be popped into the oven.

Stop a minute and think about all the time you waste by using your eyes, ears or mouth, but not your hands. You can watch TV or talk to a friend while you are cutting meat off bones in preparation for a pot pie. Or you can call your mother on the phone and chat with her while you're making meat loaf. People eat while they're talking, so there's no reason why you can't prepare meals and talk, too. It really doesn't take that much concentration.

Some people who work all week and also must cook meals for their families, cook all the meals, except the quick ones, on their days off, store them in the refrigerator, and then just reheat them when they get home. Of course, I don't like spending all of my days off cooking, but it sure is nice to come home to a meal that's ready to go.

Chapter 19 explains how to reheat leftovers. Foods that can be made quickly are indicated as such in Chapter 21 recipes. Look also for hints on advance preparation of some recipes in Chapter 21.

part 3
BOUNTIFUL RECIPES
FOR THE POOR
AND HUNGRY

This section contains enough recipes for you to break into the whole cooking thing and adjust to it before developing your own recipes or going on to various cookbooks. It should also teach you the basics about certain foods and their general method of preparation. Once you know the basics about potatoes, rice, eggs, chicken, and other inexpensive foods mentioned in this chapter, there is no reason why you can't feel confident in the kitchen and become a competent, imaginative, and relaxed cook.

Before beginning to prepare a recipe, read it all. You have to know what you're getting yourself into and you will want to make sure that you have the proper utensils and ingredients or that they can be reasonably substituted and that you have allowed yourself enough time. If you skim the recipe and note that it must be baked for thirty minutes, you may miss the point that the recipe could take thirty minutes to prepare, and you may not have that much time. You may also discover that you really don't feel like doing all the things a recipe requires. For instance, you may assume that a biscuit recipe requires that you drop the batter onto a baking sheet. If you read further, you may discover that the biscuits must be cut out. You might not feel like doing it; so it's best to find out before you begin. There is also a possibility that no matter how open-minded you are trying to be, you just can't stomach the idea of some particular ingredient or method of preparation. This is just another reason why you should read the whole recipe before getting started.

This chapter will end with a sample menu for two weeks. I do not expect, of course, that you will religiously follow it. Its purpose is to give you some idea of which recipes might be considered with one another, or which ones might be served on alternate days.

You will notice that some recipes claim to serve two people, others two to three people, and still others, more than three people. The number of servings is meant as a guide for what I think is the average portion, but you may find that my two servings will be enough for only one or for three or four. It may seem rather erratic to include recipes serving various numbers of people, but it's nice to have leftovers once in a while and sometimes it's easier to cook larger portions. Cans or jars of ingredients such as spaghetti sauce or sauerkraut come in quantities which when combined with other ingredients, will serve more than two people. I find it convenient to make the larger portion instead of saving part of the contents of the can or jar. In the case of something like lasagna or Inés's Fish Dinner, I felt that you might want to serve these things when you have a crowd over.

Of course, if you don't want leftovers or you're only one person and the recipes are just providing too many leftovers, divide the recipes in half, or thirds or whatever fraction will provide for your needs. "Half an egg," you may say, "is ridiculous." "If a recipe calls for one egg, and I'm going to divide the recipe in half, what am I supposed to do?" The answer is that if you know you can use the other half egg within a few days, *divide* the egg in half—it's not quite that ridiculous. Then again, many recipes will just taste a little richer if you add the extra half egg. In the case of fried rice, for instance, it makes no difference at all how many eggs you add. Of course, if you have more than two people in your household, you will have to proportionately increase the ingredients for most recipes. If there are three people and you want to make a recipe that supposedly serves two, use a little high school math and increase the recipe by one-half, or double it and have leftovers.

The recipes are followed by suggestions for how to recycle unfinished portions into reheated leftovers or into part of a soup or casserole. Leftovers can most often be reheated at a medium stove heat or at a medium (350° F.) oven heat. If watched carefully, foods can be reheated at higher temperatures. Some leftovers will aid in creating recipes that are listed elsewhere in this chapter. Following many recipes are suggestions for using leftovers. This may sound very confusing but it will all become clear when you glance over the recipes.

Some recipes require that food be placed in a greased pan or baking dish. In all cases, this "grease" is shortening or margarine. If you do not have either of these ingredients, oil will also prevent food from sticking excessively to a dish.

Also, many recipes in this book are not intricate or precise. You should feel free to innovate and change these recipes. You should also not feel as if you have to cut, chop or slice ingredients in any particular manner unless a recipe for some reason specifies a particular manner of cutting, chopping or slicing. My thought is that a one-half-inch piece of celery tastes the same as a "finely chopped" piece of celery and that you —the cook—should have the freedom to cut your vegetables in any manner you desire. Smaller pieces of food will cook faster than larger ones, but it makes little if any difference whether those pieces are long thin slices or finely chopped ones.

21

THE RECIPES

BEVERAGES

While you're wondering where all your grocery money goes, you may not be accounting for the fact that people seem to run out of beverages several times a week and end up having to replenish those supplies. We drink a lot more liquid than we realize. For instance, if you drink as much milk a day as a lot of milk advocates recommend, you'll go through a quart of milk by yourself. And the price of milk is probably soaring as I write this section.

Of course you can go to extremes, too. On a bet, I once went on a diet (for a day and a half) that required at least eight glasses of water a day in addition to other liquids. I spent practically my entire day on the john.

If you drink a lot of milk, cut it with powdered milk and water as suggested in Chapter 12. None of your vitamins will be destroyed, as powdered milk is fortified with vitamins A and D, the same as whole milk, one percent, two percent, and skim milk.

The following beverage recipes should help you avoid excessive expenditures for expensive thirst quenchers such as soda and bottled juices.

Quick Preparation

Lemonade

Suggested Ingredients

3 lemons
1-3/4 qt. cold water
enough ice to bring level to 2 quarts
(if you don't have ice, use more water)
1 c. sugar

Utensil
    A pitcher

Squeeze lemons into the pitcher. Pour in sugar and melt it with *a little* hot water. Add cold water and ice. Cut up lemon peels into the ade if you wish but wash the skin beforehand.

Commercial, canned, frozen lemonade might be cheaper to make. Though it doesn't taste as fresh, it might be worth buying.

Quick Preparation

Orangeade

Suggested Ingredients

1 can frozen orange juice
a little less than twice the amount of water called for
ice cubes (if you don't have ice, use more water)
sugar, to taste

Utensil

A pitcher

Make orange juice using almost twice the amount of water called for. Dilute sugar in *a little* hot water and add it to the ade according to taste. Fill the container with ice cubes.

Quick Preparation

Bouillon Cube Drink

Suggested Ingredients

1 c. boiling water
1 bouillon cube
a squeeze of lemon
sprinkles of basil

Utensil

Something to boil your water in

Combine all ingredients. Allow bouillon cube to dissolve. Help it along with a spoon. If you really want an exotic drink, add sprinkles of grated cheese and have fun chewing it off your spoon.

Iced Tea
(makes 1-1/2 to 2 qt.)

Suggested Ingredients

1 or 2 tea bags
water
1/2 lemon
2/3 c. sugar or, to taste

Utensils

Something to boil your water in, a teakettle or equivalent for steeping the tea, and a container to store your iced tea in

Bring about 3 cups of water to a boil. Pour it into a teapot with the tea bags and let it steep for at least 15 minutes. Add sugar, to taste. Add 6 or 8 cups of cold water, depending upon the size of your pitcher. Add steeped tea. Refrigerate until cold. When the tea is cold, squeeze in the juice of the lemon. Cut up the peel into the liquid if desired—but make sure it has been washed.

Cheap Recycled Tea

The full potential never seems to be gotten out of a tea bag. Somehow, when you're throwing away a tea bag, it seems as if it should no longer look like the sound, healthy tea bag it is. But often it does. Therefore, in my opinion, tea bags should be used until they can no longer produce a single drop of tea. Hot tea can be made with several used tea bags per cup of tea. You can also use about ten to twelve old bags for iced tea. Just follow the directions as in the previous recipe—only use your old tea bags instead of the two called for in the Iced Tea recipe.

If you do not plan on using the bags within a day or two, allow the tea bags to dry (don't bunch them all together). They will become moldy or musty if they stay damp too long. Or, you can refrigerate the used bags until you plan on using them.

Quick Preparation

Sweet Hot Milk

Suggested Ingredients

1 c. milk
cinnamon (optional)
1 tsp. sugar or honey

Utensil

Something to heat the milk in

Heat the milk until it steams; do not boil it. Put your finger quickly into it. You'll know if it's hot enough. Pour into a cup and add sugar or honey. Sprinkle the top with cinnamon, if desired.

Anybody remember the Fizzies craze? I wonder what was in *them*?

BREAKFAST

If you don't eat breakfast, you'll most likely make up for it by snacking sometime during the day. So if you think you can keep your weight down by eliminating breakfast, you're probably wrong.

Actually, North Americans are pretty illogical when it comes to the size and sequence of meals. We usually have a small breakfast, a medium-sized lunch, and a large dinner. We then go to bed with all that food still gurgling in our bellies. It then, most likely, turns into fat. It would be more logical to eat a larger breakfast and a smaller dinner. But it's hard to change age-old habits.

Possible breakfast recipes are scattered throughout this chapter and in Chapter 23. Of course, you can eat cereals or toast for breakfast or you can even reheat soup from the night before. Believe it or not (and I didn't believe it until coerced to try it) soup is a really nice breakfast—especially when your apartment is very cold at dawn. The soup is a great body warmer. Recipes for pancakes and French toast can be found in this chapter in the section under Biscuits, Breads, Pizza, and Pancakes.

Cold rice with milk and honey or sugar makes a substantial breakfast (see this chapter under Rice). All kinds of eggs, including omelettes, start a morning well (see this chapter under Eggs). Finally, various combinations of yogurt, fruit, and granola should definitely be tried for breakfast, or any other meal.

CASSEROLES

With potatoes, rice, noodles, or beans as a base, you can invent endless casseroles. The old standby seems to be tuna-noodle casserole, but you won't have to get sick of it because you have so many other combinations to choose from.

When making a casserole with noodles or rice, cook your noodles or rice according to package directions until slightly underdone and then add them to the casserole. Beans should be partially cooked, unless a recipe specifies otherwise. Although potatoes may be precooked, it is not always necessary. If potatoes are cut into thin slices for something like scalloped potatoes, they will be done in an hour or so.

Casseroles require a greased baking dish (or a reasonable substitute), ingredients such as a starch, vegetables, meat, cheese, or just about anything you have, and enough liquid so that the combination will cook but not burn, remain moist, but not runny or mushy. The amount of liquid depends upon the casserole.

Many different liquids may be used for casseroles. The juice from a can of whole tomatoes, milk, cream sauce, yogurt whey, soup stock, and gravies are a few things you might consider.

Casseroles require from fifteen minutes to an hour of baking time on the average. If all of your ingredients have been recently precooked and are still hot, then your casserole will take the minimum amount of time. Refrigerated or raw ingredients will require near the maximum time.

The casserole recipes in this section may be specifically followed if desired. However, these should be used also as a guide for the development of your own imaginative casserole combinations.

Chicken, Vegetables, and Rice Casserole
(serves 4)

Suggested Ingredients

3 c. cooked brown or white rice
about 2 c. thin cream sauce or other liquid, seasoned with herbs
1/2 to 1 c. leftover cut up chicken
1 c. or more vegetables such as
carrots, tomatoes, peas,
celery, onion (precook
the vegetables if you mind the crunch)
any kind of cheese

Utensils
    A casserole or baking dish

Preheat the over to 350° F. to 375° F. Grease the casserole. Add and mix all ingredients, topping the mixture with cheese. The casserole will be fairly loose. Cook covered until bubbly but fairly well solidified. If the casserole seems to be burning or is dry but does not appear to be done, add some milk or other liquid to it. Uncover the casserole during the last 5 to 10 minutes to brown the top.

Leftovers You Can Use
    Chicken, vegetables, and rice.

Suggested Use of Leftovers
    Add liquid and reheat.

Tuna Casserole
(serves 3 to 4)

Suggested Ingredients
    a can of tuna (6 to 7 oz.)
    3 cups cooked rice
    or 3-1/2 c. cooked noodles
    (6 oz. when dry)
    about 2 c. cream sauce or other liquid
    celery, onion, or other vegetables
    desired seasonings

Utensils
    Covered casserole or baking dish

Preheat the oven to 350° F. to 375° F. Mix all ingredients in a greased casserole. Follow directions for Chicken, Vegetable, and Rice Casserole.

Leftovers You Can Use
    Rice.

Suggested Use of Leftovers
    Add liquid and reheat.

Vegetable Casserole

Follow directions for Chicken, Vegetable, and Rice Casserole omitting the chicken and substituting more vegetables. Or, use 6 ounces of noodles instead of rice and use more vegetables.

Leftovers You Can Use
>Rice and vegetables.

Suggested Use of Leftovers
>Add extra liquid and reheat.

Scalloped Potatoes

Suggested Ingredients

>**potatoes**
>**onion**
>**flour**
>**cheese**
>**bits of ham (or ham-flavored protein precooked according to package directions—optional)**
>**salt, pepper, paprika, nutmeg**
>**margarine**
>**milk**

Utensils
>A baking dish or casserole with cover

Estimate the number of potatoes you'll need. You might want to use enough along with other ingredients to fill your baking dish. Wash potatoes or peel them if you want. Preheat your oven to 375° F. to 400° F. Grease your baking dish and cut thin slices of potato which will make a layer that covers the bottom of the dish. Next, sprinkle a little onion, ham, a tablespoon or so of flour, cheese, seasonings, a few pats of margarine, and enough milk to make the combination wet. Begin the layers again starting with potatoes until the casserole is filled. Make sure you have enough liquid; the mixture should be saturated but not floating.

>Cook covered until the potatoes are done, for approximately an hour. If the mixture seems to be burning, add more liquid. If there seems to be too much liquid, during the last 15 minutes or so, remove the cover and let some of the liquid evaporate. Remove the cover anyway during the last 5 minutes to brown the top.

Leftovers You Can Use
    Ham.

Suggested Use of Leftovers
    Reheat in the baking dish adding more milk, if necessary, or steam in a saucepan at a medium-low heat on the stove.

Pot Pie
(serves 2 or more)

Suggested Ingredients

    1/2 to 3/4 c. leftover cut up and cooked beef,
    lamb, pork, or fowl
    1 carrot
    1 stalk celery
    a small onion
    a large handful of green beans, peas, broccoli, spinach,
    or other vegetables
    1 potato or a handful of noodles
    2 to 2-1/2 c. soup stock (see Soup
    section for Soup Stock)
    or the same amount of water
    seasoned with 2 bouillon cubes,
    bay leaf, basil, and parsley

Pie Crust

    1 c. flour
    1/2 c. shortening
    1/2 tsp. salt
    enough milk to make a paste

Utensils
    Saucepan for cooking vegetables; bowl for mixing pie crust dough, a casserole or baking dish

Cook the vegetables and the potato or noodles in the stock until tender. Spoon or drain out the vegetables into a greased casserole with the meat. Do not throw away the stock. Add water to the stock to bring it back up to 2 cups. Take out a cup of stock and gradually add 2 tablespoons of flour to it. Pour it into the remaining stock and cook for a few minutes until it begins to thicken. Pour the stock over the meat-vegetable combination.

Preheat your oven to 375° F. Next, make the pastry. With a fork, combine the flour, salt, and shortening. Gradually mix in the milk. Spread the pastry over the meat-vegetable-stock combination. The pastry will be gloppy and will not spread exactly evenly. Bake covered for a while and then uncovered so the pastry will brown on top. Cooking time should be 30 to 45 minutes depending upon your oven.

Leftovers You Can Use
    Vegetables, meat.

Suggested Use of Leftovers
    Put pot pie in a soup or reheat it in the same casserole.

DESSERTS

I'm very fond of eating desserts, but not very fond of making them. For me, they seem to be more of a bother to prepare than most main dishes. This section contains enough desserts to keep you going for a while. Note that the section under Biscuits, Breads, Pizza, and Pancakes contains a biscuit and corn bread recipe which, when topped with fruit or fruit salad (see the salad section of this chapter), make fine desserts. The fruit salads without the biscuit or corn bread also make good desserts. In Chapter 23, you'll find pumpkin pie, banana bread, orange cake, and granola and yogurt. Granola and yogurt, combined with fruits, help to end your meal pleasantly.

Pudding Float

Suggested Ingredients
    **1 pkg. pudding, plus the amount of milk
    the recipe calls for or 1 recipe for blanc mange
    (usually on the cornstarch box)
    1 egg white, room temperature
    a pinch of salt
    1 tbsp. sugar**

Utensils
    Pot for cooking the pudding, bowl for beating the egg white, a hand or electric beater

Make the pudding and allow it to cool. Put the egg white, salt, and sugar in a bowl. Beat until the white is stiff. Add to the top of pudding instead of whipped cream.

Sambayon
(1 serving)

The following is a pudding recipe from Argentina given to me by my friend Inés. You'll probably find this recipe very interesting as it does not have your characteristically desserty taste. The predominant taste will be that of the wine you use. Sambayon is the answer to what to do with the yolk of the egg from Pudding Float.

Suggested Ingredients

> 1 egg yolk
> 1 tbsp. sugar
> 1 tbsp. sweet wine

Utensils

> 2 pots—one which will fit inside the other for a double boiler effect

Beat the egg. Combine the ingredients in the small pot. Put a little water in the larger pot and then set the small pot in the larger pot. Put the two pots on a burner at a medium heat. Hold on to the handle of the small pot and constantly stir the mixture until it thickens. Eat the pudding warm or cool.

Nicholas's
Banana-Graham Cracker
Ice Box Cake

This recipe was given to me by my 12-year-old brother Andrew who was visiting Nicholas when they cooked it together. The only thing I know about Nicholas is that he'd say "right arm" for "right on" and "out of state" for "out of sight," and then everyone would laugh. You probably have to be in a ridiculous mood to make this recipe.

Suggested Ingredients

> about 12 square graham crackers, or 6 long ones
> a box of banana pudding (or vanilla if you can't get banana)
> a box of butterscotch pudding
> 1 or 2 bananas
> enough milk to make the pudding

Utensils

> 2 saucepans for puddings

A square or rectangular cake pan or other dish with a flat bottom

Make the puddings in separate saucepans according to package directions. Line the bottom of the cake pan with graham crackers. Pour the butterscotch pudding about 1/3 of the way up the cake pan. Then put some graham crackers on top of the butterscotch pudding. Pour the banana pudding over the crackers to about 2/3 of the way up the pan. Put graham crackers on top of the banana pudding and top with a layer of sliced bananas. Refrigerate until the mixture is cold. In case you're confused:

bananas
graham crackers
banana pudding
graham crackers
butterscotch pudding
graham crackers
pan

Work from bottom up.

Bruised Fruit Cobbler
(serves 2 to 3)

While doing your grocery shopping, you might have noticed that near the produce section of some stores, bruised, old or not-so-great-looking fruit or vegetables are offered for sale at much reduced prices. If, after examining the fruit offered in this section, you discover it to be bruised but not moldy or oozing, you may find it worth purchasing. Bruised apples, bananas, pears, peaches and other fruits, in combination or separately, make great cobblers. Just remove the sections of the fruit which you feel are inedible. Minor spots or bruises do not have to be removed. Although fruit does not have to be bruised to make a great cobbler, lower quality fruit can mean a savings—you may be able to afford a dessert at a time when you thought you couldn't.

Although some people might prefer to make the pastry topping of a cobbler with Bisquick or some other commercial pastry, I don't. Bisquick, as far as I'm concerned (aside from the fact that it contains a preservative), is an expensive gimmick. Your own pastry can be prepared less expensively in about the same amount of time.

Suggested Ingredients

1 c. sliced fruit
honey or sugar
cinnamon
lemon juice (optional)

Pastry

1 c. flour (1/2 whole wheat and 1/2 white or all white)
1/4 tsp. salt
2 tsp. baking powder
1 tsp. honey or sugar
2-1/2 tbsp. shortening
1/2 to 1 egg
1/4 to 1/2 c. milk

Utensils

Bowls for mixing, a greased baking dish

Slice fruit and combine it with desired proportions of honey or sugar, cinnamon and lemon. Set the fruit combination aside.

Combine the dry ingredients in a bowl and the wet ones in another. If you use 1 egg instead of half an egg, you'll probably end up using the minimum amount of milk. Mix the dry ingredients with the wet to get a moist but stiff dough.

Spread the fruit onto the bottom of the greased baking dish and top the fruit with generous spoonfuls of pastry. Bake at 400° F. for 30 minutes or until the pastry is done.

Baked Apples

I would loosely categorize apples into two different types: juicy and nonjuicy. Delicious, golden delicious, and mackintosh are juicy and can be successfully baked using many methods. Other apples such as winesaps, baldwins, and cortlands are not as juicy and need to be baked with some additional liquid in order to make them into tasty baked apples.

If you have a juicy variety of apples, you can simply put them in a greased pan, and bake them at 350° F. until they become soft (between 20 and 45 minutes). Serve them plain or with honey, sugar and milk, ice cream or anything else you like.

Or, you can cook them with sweetener. Wash and core the apples, removing stems and seeds, but be sure to leave some of the apple at the bottom to hold the sweetener. Do not peel the apple. Pour the honey or brown sugar mixed with raisins and cinnamon into the core opening of each apple. Then bake them the same as above.

Mom's Baked Apples

Suggested Ingredients
>4 cortland or other nonjuicy apples
>1/2 c. water
>1/2 c. sugar
>4 tsp. honey
>about 4 tsp. raisins

Utensils
>A small saucepan, a baking dish

With a vegetable peeler, peel the top fifth of each apple, keeping the skin intact. It will be a spiral.

Place the peel in a solution of water and sugar and boil it gently until the sugar dissolves and the liquid is pink.

Set your oven to 350° F. Core the apples, leaving a thin layer at the bottom. Stuff the opening with raisins and honey. Put the apples in a greased baking dish. Pour some of the sugar-water over the apples. Put the apples in the oven and baste them often with the syrup. In other words, keep pouring syrup over the apples. Cook 20 to 45 minutes or until apples are tender but not falling apart. Serve plain or with milk.

Suggested Use of Leftovers
>Reheat in the oven or eat cold.

Chunky Applesauce

Applesauce, though good as a dessert, can also be used with meats such as chicken and pork. In fact, applesauce is said to help digest the fat in pork.

Suggested Ingredients
>**apples**
>**cinnamon**
>**nutmeg**
>**sugar**

Utensils
>A saucepan with cover

Wash and core apples. Do not peel them unless you want to. Cut them into chunks and put them in a pot with just enough water to prevent them from sticking to the bottom of the pan. Cover the pot and allow the apples to cook at a medium heat.

Lower the heat as it becomes too hot. Cook the apples to the desired consistency. If you want small chunks in your applesauce, it will be done a lot sooner than if you are looking for a smooth sauce. Cooking time also depends largely upon how much applesauce you are cooking. Count on 10 minutes as a minimum time and 45 as a maximum. Season the sauce to taste with cinnamon and/or nutmeg and sugar. Serve hot or cold.

Suggested Use of Leftovers
    Refrigerate and use until you finish it.

EGGS

What may seem obvious to you is not always that simple to others. If you know how to buy, boil, fry, scramble, and separate an egg, skip this section. If not, read on.

When you buy eggs, check the cartons and make sure the eggs aren't cracked. If one of the eggs sticks to the carton, chances are it's cracked. Cold eggs placed in boiling water often crack. If you want a nice boiled egg, put your eggs under warm water until they are at room temperature, before putting them into a pot of boiling water.

Quick Preparation

Soft-boiled Eggs

Ingredients

eggs (at room temperature)
water

Utensil
    A saucepan

Put enough water in the pot so that when the eggs are eventually added, they will be covered by the water. Bring the water to a boil. With a spoon place eggs in the pot and let them boil for 3 to 4 minutes depending upon the desired consistency.

Put the eggs under cold water before opening so you can handle them.

Suggested Use of Leftovers
    Put eggs in the pot and boil for about 10 minutes until they become hard-boiled eggs.

Quick Preparation

Hard-boiled Eggs

Ingredients

eggs
water

Utensil

A saucepan

Make sure eggs are at room temperature. Spoon them into boiling water which will cover the eggs, and boil the eggs for 15 to 20 minutes.

Or, place cold eggs into warm water and bring them to a boil together. Cook eggs 10 to 15 minutes after the water begins to boil.

Cool eggs by running them under cold water. Refrigerate them if you want them cold.

Suggested Use of Leftovers

Hard-boiled eggs will keep in the refrigerator as long as your raw eggs do (about three weeks). Many recipes call for hard-boiled eggs.

SEPARATING EGGS

Some recipes call for egg yolks or whites but not for the entire egg. Set out two dishes. Crack your egg open and hold it so nothing spills. Keep the filled shell in one hand and the empty one in the other hand. Hold the full egg over the dish you intend to use for whites. Dump the contents of the shell which does not contain the yolk, into the dish. Pour the contents of the one shell into the other, alternately, over the dish, gradually spilling the white into the dish, until you have nothing but yolk in the shell. Dump the yolk into the yolk dish. Do not expect every speck of white to go into its proper dish. Often it's hard to get every bit of it out of the shell.

Quick Preparation

Fried Eggs

Suggested Ingredients

**eggs
margarine, oil or grease
salt, pepper, paprika**

Utensil

A frying pan

Put the frying pan on a burner at a medium heat. Add enough margarine to coat the pan well and let it melt. When the margarine bubbles just a little, crack your eggs into the pan, being careful not to break the yolks. Allow the eggs to solidify and bubble. Let this happen gently—if the heat is too high, lower it. As the egg whites solidify, with your spatula, cut between each egg so that the eggs are separate from each other. Cook until the white is not runny. Season at any time, and spatula out the eggs.

If you want sunny-side down eggs, flip them over for 15 seconds or so, before you take them out of the pan. Or, do not flip them, but cover the frying pan and let a thin layer of yolk cook for 15 seconds to half a minute.

Suggested Use of Leftovers

Break the yolk and fry until the yolk solidifies. Put the egg on a sandwich, hot or cold.

Quick Preparation

Scrambled Eggs
(serves 1)

Suggested Ingredients

**2 eggs
1 tbsp. or so water or milk
salt, pepper, paprika
margarine, oil or grease**

Utensil

A frying pan

In a bowl, beat together all ingredients except margarine. Heat a frying pan to a medium heat and add a tablespoon or so of margarine. When the margarine bubbles slightly, add the egg mixture. As soon as the eggs begin to steam, start stirring them almost continually until you've reached the desired consistency. The eggs will begin sticking to the pan. Just keep scraping and turning them, keeping as much off the bottom of the pan as possible. All kinds of things can be cooked with scrambled eggs. If you use bacon, you won't need margarine. Just cook the bacon first, drain off the excess fat, and add the eggs. Or, try cooking sliced onion and peppers together in a little bit of margarine (cover the pan and let them sauté until barely cooked), then add the eggs and scramble.

Suggested Use of Leftovers
    Put on a sandwich hot or cold.

Quick Preparation

Frambled Eggs
(1 serving)

Suggested Ingredients

    2 eggs
1-1/2 to 2 tbsp. margarine
salt, pepper, paprika

Utensil
    A frying pan

Heat a frying pan to a medium heat. Add margarine. When it melts, crack your eggs into the pan. Break the yolks and scramble the yolks into the whites with a fork or wooden spoon. Continue to stir the eggs until a desired consistency is reached.

Suggested Use of Leftovers
    Put on a sandwich, hot or cold.

Quick Preparation

Fried Spinach Omelette
(serves 2)

Suggested Ingredients

4 eggs
1 or 2 tbsp. of onion
1/4 stalk celery
1 tbsp. soy sauce
1 c. fresh spinach with stems
vegetable oil
sprinkles of paprika, salt, oregano
2 slices American cheese (optional)

Utensils

A frying pan with cover, a bowl for mixing

Gently fry the cut-up spinach, chopped celery and chopped onion in a frying pan with enough oil to lightly coat the bottom. Add soy sauce. Fry for a few minutes or until onion and celery are slightly cooked but still crunchy. Take this mixture out of the pan and put it in a dish. With a fork or egg beater, beat together the eggs and seasonings and pour into a lightly oiled frying pan. (If you did not burn the spinach, celery, and onion, use the same frying pan without washing it.) Let the eggs bubble and fry at a medium- to medium-low heat. When the eggs begin to congeal—especially around the edges—pour the vegetables onto one side of the eggs. In other words, half the frying pan full of eggs will have vegetables. When the side without vegetables seems congealed but not dry, gently flip it with a spatula onto the side with vegetables. Cover the pan and let it simmer for a few minutes allowing the center of the omelette to become less runny. If desired, melt a slice of cheese on top during the last minute or so.

If you do not like the idea of flipping one side of egg over another, beat your eggs as suggested in the recipe but only put half of the egg and seasoning in the pan. When it congeals slightly, put spinach over the eggs in the entire pan—not just half of it. Allow the spinach and eggs to cook a bit longer, and then cover the spinach with the remaining egg batter. Cover the pan and let it simmer as with the first method. Your omelette will be a full circle but thinner than in the original recipe. To remove it from the pan, cut it into halves or quarters and take it out with a spatula.

Suggested Use of Leftovers

Reheat by steaming in a lightly-greased, covered frying pan.

Quick Preparation

Broccoli Omelette
(serves 2)

4 eggs
1 or 2 tbsp. onion
1 tbsp. soy sauce
2 large stalks fresh, raw broccoli
vegetable oil
sprinkles of salt,
nutmeg, paprika, oregano,
parsley, or other seasonings

Utensils
    A frying pan with cover

Follow directions for Spinach Omelette. Broccoli and onion may be fried at a medium-high heat in a covered pan. Just be sure it does not burn.

Suggested Use of Leftovers
    Same as Fried Spinach Omelette.

Quick Preparation

Anything Omelette

Add anything you have to an omelette. Cooked meat and vegetables can be added directly to an omelette. If you use bacon, fry it until fairly crisp. Drain off some grease, and use the rest instead of oil.

Creamed Eggs

Suggested Ingredients

hard-boiled eggs
cream sauce (see Cream Sauce on page 199)
seasonings

Utensil
    A saucepan

Add sliced, hard-boiled eggs to cream sauce. For vegetable and egg in cream sauce recipes, see the section under vegetable dishes in this chapter.

Advance Preparation
  Hard boil eggs in advance to create a quick meal.

Suggested Use of Leftovers
  Reheat in a saucepan gradually adding more milk, if necessary.

Eggs Benedict
(1 serving)

Suggested Ingredients

**1 hard-boiled egg
1 piece of toast or English Muffin,
with margarine, if desired
1 slice of ham, Canadian bacon
or bacon (a little margarine
if you use ham or Canadian bacon)
1/4 c. cream sauce (see page 199)
salt, pepper, paprika**

Utensils
  A frying pan, saucepan

Fry your ham or bacon. Use margarine to fry ham or Canadian bacon. Make the cream sauce and toast the bread. Put sliced egg on the toast, then the ham or bacon. Top the meat with cream sauce and season. Serve warm.

Advance Preparation
  Hard boil eggs in advance to create a quick meal.

Leftovers You Can Use
  Bacon or ham.

Suggested Use of Leftovers
  Reheat in a warm oven.

FISH

The most economical cut of fish, generally, is a fillet or any boned fish. Though whole fish can be purchased at a lower price per pound, it generally costs you more by the time you scale it, bone it, and cut off its head and tail. Because those parts that you end up throwing away were originally included in the cost per pound, the price you paid for the whole fish is deceptive. With boned fish, you can assume that at least ninety-nine percent of the fish is edible.

Fillets are fish cut into slices which usually contain few or no bones. Frozen fillets are often cut thicker than the ones you buy fresh. They are generally too thick for Inés's Fish Dinner (see this section), but would suffice for any of the other recipes. If the frozen fillets or boned fish are too thick and you want them thinner for a recipe such as Inés's, slice them with a sharp knife while they are slightly frozen.

Fresh fish is always a treat, but fish markets do not even exist in some parts of this country. I have friends from Milwaukee who have never seen a fish market. Frozen fish is usually less expensive and is generally of good quality. Just be sure when you buy frozen fish that it's a fillet or is boned, unless you want to see if it's economical to scale and bone your fish.

Most fish recipes take a short time to cook. Also, fish can be baked plain when frozen if you have forgotten to plan something for dinner, and can be cooked in any fashion as soon as it has thawed enough for you to separate the fillets. Fish should be washed or soaked a few minutes in salted water before preparing.

Fish is extremely perishable. If you thaw out frozen fish or you don't freeze fish within twelve hours, you should plan on using it very soon. If you don't, it will begin to smell "fishy" and will become inferior in taste and quality.

Quick Preparation

Poached Fish
(flounder, perch, pollock,
turbot, haddock, cod, etc.)

Suggested Ingredients

any type of fish fillets
onion (chopped)
celery (chopped)
vegetable oil
lemon
salt, pepper, nutmeg, paprika

Utensils
>Frying pan with cover

Soak fillets with a little salt in a shallow pan of cold water for a few minutes. Remove fish from pan and water and season each fillet with sprinkles of salt, pepper, nutmeg, and paprika. Put a little oil—enough to lightly cover the bottom—in a frying pan. Gently fry a small amount of onion and celery for a few minutes. Add the fish and cook gently. When one side is done, you may either flip it over or cover the pan and let the steam cook the fish. Lemon may be squeezed on the fish at any time during the cooking process or after. The fish is done if it separates when poked with a fork or if you can see that it does not look raw. Over a medium-low heat, the fish should take no more than 15 minutes to cook.

Suggested Use of Leftovers
>Break up the cold fish and mix it with mayonnaise, relish, and other seasonings as a salad—or put it on a sandwich.

Quick Preparation

Poached Fish and Tomato
(serves 4)

Suggested Ingredients
>1 lb. fish fillets, washed
>1/2 onion
>1/2 green pepper (optional)
>mushrooms (optional)
>bay leaf, oregano, basil,
>salt, pepper, nutmeg
>oil
>1/2 to 1 large can (28 oz.) whole tomatoes

Utensils
>Frying pan with cover

In a frying pan coated with a little oil, gently fry the onion, green pepper and mushrooms. Add the fish, tomatoes, and seasonings. Carefully break up the tomatoes. Cover the pan and allow fish to gently bubble until done, or about 20 minutes. Serve with rice or noodles and top with grated cheese.

Suggested Use of Leftovers
   Reheat in a saucepan within two days or add to a fish soup.

Quick Preparation

Plain Baked Fish

Suggested Ingredients
   fish fillets—frozen, thawed, or fresh
   salt and pepper

Tartar Sauce
   mayonnaise
   relish

Utensil
   Baking dish or pan

Rinse fish. Put fish in the oven at 400° F. in a dish or pan and bake for 20 minutes or until fish is tender. Serve with tartar sauce or with a squeeze of lemon.

Suggested Use of Leftovers
   Same as for Poached Fish.

Quick Preparation

Fried Fish
(serves 3 to 4)

Suggested Ingredients
   1 lb. fish fillet, washed and dried
   about 3/4 c. flour, bread crumbs,
   or a combination of both
   seasonings such as salt, pepper,
   parsley, basil, paprika, cheese, nutmeg
   1 egg beaten with 1 tbsp. water
   oil or combination of margarine and oil

Tartar Sauce
   mayonnaise
   relish

Utensils

A frying pan, a bowl for the egg, and one for the flour or bread crumbs

Set a frying pan coated with oil at a medium heat. Dunk each fillet in egg and then in the flour and seasoning mixture. Fry the fillets until brown on both sides. Take out the done fish and put it on a dish in an oven set at a low heat if there is not enough room in your frying pan for all the fish. Serve with tartar sauce or lemon.

Suggested Use of Leftovers

Reheat in the oven within two days. Or, serve on sandwiches or plain.

Ines's Fish Dinner
(serves 8)

Suggested Ingredients

8 thin fish fillets
1-1/2 c. grated cheese, or 3/4 c. bread crumbs
and 3/4 c. cheese
1 to 2 tbsp. parsley, chopped, dried, or fresh
2 to 4 sections garlic, finely chopped
3 eggs, beaten
nutmeg, salt

Sauce

28-oz. can whole tomatoes (or tomato sauce)
1/2 medium-size onion
a little oil
oregano
basil
salt
1/2 to 1 tsp. sugar
1 to 2 bay leaves

Utensils

A large (5 qt. or more) saucepan, a bowl for combining cheese mixture, wooden toothpicks

Put the fish in salted water for a few minutes. Mix the grated cheese, parsley, garlic, and egg together in a bowl. Take the fish out of the water and let each piece dry well on a towel or paper bag. Season the fish lightly with nutmeg on one side and salt on the other. Lay each fillet flat on your counter and spread 1/8 of the cheese and egg mixture on each fillet. Roll each fillet (like a bed roll) and hold it together with wooden toothpicks.

Meanwhile, prepare the tomato sauce in the large saucepan. Fry the onion in the oil, add tomatoes and seasonings. Allow the sauce to cook over a medium heat for 10 minutes. Then gently place the fillets into the sauce, cover the pan, and let the sauce gently bubble for about 20 minutes or until the fish looks done.

Suggested Use of Leftovers
Reheat in a saucepan within two days, or add to a fish soup.

Fish Soufflé
(serves 3 to 4)

For lack of a better name, the following recipe is a fish soufflé. But don't get all excited if you've heard that soufflés are very delicate things which flatten into pancakes if someone sneezes. This soufflé doesn't puff up very high to begin with and it doesn't fall either. This is a good recipe for those times when you don't have enough fish for all the people who come for dinner.

Suggested Ingredients
1/2 to 3/4 lb. cod fillets, or any other boned fish
salt, parsley, garlic, bay leaves, and other seasonings
2 or 3 eggs
2/3 c. wheat germ or bread crumbs
2 tbsp. milk

Utensils
Baking dish—no cover needed

Preheat oven to 350° F. Wash fish in salted water. Slice it into bite-size pieces into a greased baking dish. Beat eggs into fish and add all other ingredients except bay leaves. All mixing can be done in the baking dish. When all ingredients have been added, top them with several bay leaves. Bake at 350° F. for 20 minutes or until the fish is tender and the egg has solidified.

Suggested Use of Leftovers
Moisten with tomato sauce or other liquid and rebake.

Quick Preparation

Mackerel
(serves 4)

Jim and Char, people I know who were with the Peace Corps in Micronesia, have traveled through Europe and even taught for a short time in Tanzania, East Africa. The last I heard of them was from friends of mine in Argentina, who said that Jim and Char are expected to visit them in Buenos Aires in a few months. It's hard to imagine them moving back to New Jersey after having lived in so many "exotic" places.

While they were in Tanzania, I wrote to Char and asked her if she had any interesting recipes. She said that she was making a lot of items from scratch that she had always taken for granted that you had to buy in a store such as mayonnaise, sauerkraut, cheese, dressings, yogurt, pickles, noodles, and breads. ". . . but all these things come from my littl' Fannie Farmer cookbook, so that's not much help for you, is it?" she wrote. Of course, I was a little disappointed. I had expected that they would have experienced some really different food tastes. One thing Char said was that it was difficult to modify food from Tanzania to suit American tastes—for instance—Africans use a lot of milk and like to drink it slightly curdled. With all the protein and milk products they consume, they do not seem to suffer from cholesterol problems as we Americans do. The American Dairy Association claims it's because they drink their milk curdled.

Char came up with one recipe for me which she and Jim had devised while in Micronesia. Because there was a meat shortage there, they bought cans of mackerel which were packed in Japan and mixed the fish with lots of onions which helped to kill the overpowering fishy taste that mackerel has. Mackerel packed in Japan can also be purchased here for almost half the price of grated tuna. Following is a recipe which I have devised from Char and Jim's idea.

Suggested Ingredients
a can of mackerel
oil
14-oz. or so canned whole tomatoes or tomato sauce
lemon
1 or 2 onions
cheese, any kind
seasonings such as oregano and basil

Utensils

    Saucepan or frying pan

Drain the mackerel. Fry a liberal supply of onions in the pan which is coated with oil. Add all other ingredients according to taste. Allow the mixture to simmer for about 10 minutes. If the mixture when tasted is too fishy, add more lemon or cheese. Serve over rice, macaroni, or noodles.

Suggested Use of Leftovers

    Reheat within two days in a saucepan.

MEATS

If you think that you can miraculously whip up a sirloin steak or roast beef dinner at budget prices, as far as I know, you're wrong. When I first began to write this book, prices were bad, but they are even worse now. There used to be a time when you could "splurge" once in a while—that time was not too long ago. Now, you really have to use all your mental resources to make ends meet. Part of doing this does not include sirloin steak or roast beef unless you can find a terrific bargain. But you still can get the flavor, consistency and satisfaction of eating meat without devouring a tremendous chunk. If a large cut of meat is more economical than a smaller one, you might buy it. But don't eat it all at once—save it for many meals. Meat, unless more economical than any other part of the meal, should not be the main part of the meal. It should share equally with vegetables, grains, and salads.

    All meat bones can be saved and used for soup, thereby creating another meal. If meat is used resourcefully, it can be an economical grocery item.

CHUCK STEAK AND CHUCK ROAST

Chuck is a cut of beef which comes from the upper thigh region of the cow. Although many people favor this cut, it is not what is known as one of the finest cuts of beef—but actually it tastes quite good and can be used in many more ways than most steaks and roasts. During the saner periods of this insane price increase, blade chuck cost about the same as chopped meat. With chuck, you get bones, fat, and meat—so actually you are paying more than for chopped meat per pound, but these supposed waste parts can be very useful. A reasonable amount of fat, for instance, can be left on steaks or roasts while cooking. This will tend to make the meat juicier. If there is excess fat, which you would like to trim off, save it for the birds, if you live in a place where you can hang a feeder. If the meat contains a lot of fat,

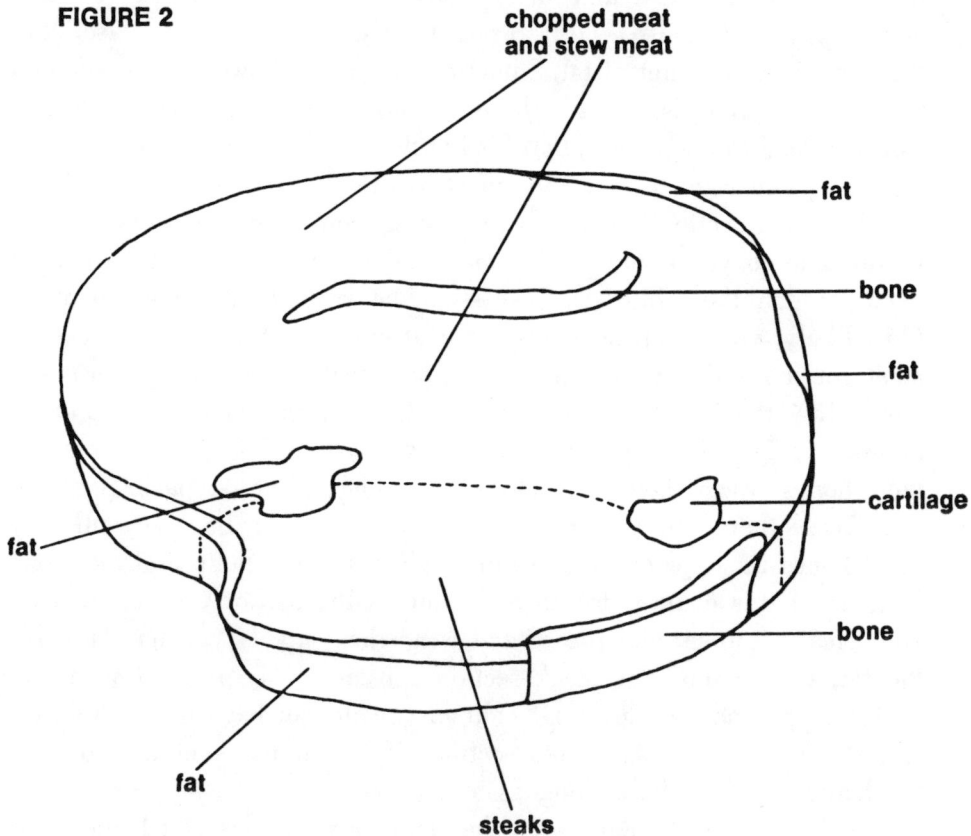

FIGURE 2

then it's not worth buying. Bones can be used for making soups, or they can be used to flavor tomato sauce. When bones are used in soups or sauces, it is not necessary to add meat to them.

The basic difference between your blade chuck steak and blade chuck roast, is thickness. The roast, of course, is thicker. Basically, your chuck should look like Figure 2, unless the steak or roast was cut in half or a third and then packaged. In addition to fat, as labeled in the figure, your meat will have grains of fat, known as marbleized fat, throughout the meat. These small grains will keep the meat moist while it cooks. There are a few ways of telling on sight whether or not you are looking at a good cut of meat. If the fat is white, the meat is good. If it is yellow—according to my grandmother—you are looking at an old cow. If there is little meat in the lower section which is labeled "steaks" in the diagram, you are being chiselled out of the finest part of the meat and chances are the cut is not worth the price you're paying because you'll probably also notice in this case, that there is a large amount of fat. Sometimes in roasts, however, even though the lower section is sparse, there is enough meat to make the cost worthwhile. Just remember, that it's not the best chuck in that case.

If you want to make the most of the chuck steak you purchase, cut the upper section into bite size pieces, trim them of excess fat, but leave some so you'll have juicy meat. If you have some sort of hand meat grinder, these bite size pieces can be ground into chopped meat. Most likely, you don't have this piece of equipment so you can use the meat for a regular meat stew or pepper steaks (see the stew section, page 215). Package the stew meat into dinner portions and freeze them, unless you intend to use some within twenty-four hours. Next, cut out your bones, wash them to remove any bone splinters, package them, and freeze them—or use them soon. The bones can be used with any other bones in soups or tomato sauce. (Refer to the Soup and the Pasta sections of this chapter for information on the use of the bones.) Cut your steaks into serving pieces and wrap them up. If you have use for the fat, save it too. The steak section can simply be broiled with seasonings. (See next recipe.) Of course, you do not have to cut up your chuck steak into the suggested sections if you don't want to. You can broil and eat the whole thing as a steak.

Roasts can be cut up as the steaks are, as described above, or they can be pot roasted as in the recipe in this section.

Quick Preparation

Broiled Steak

Chances are, the only type of steak you'll ever be able to afford, is chuck, which happens to be a very good steak. If by chance I'm wrong and you manage to get something else, just follow the directions as below. However, if you purchase thin boneless steaks, usually known as minute steaks, you should probably quick fry them, as they will be tough and rubbery if broiled. Other thin steaks, if broiled, should be watched carefully and cooked for a short time. One-inch-thick steaks should be cooked a total of about 10 to 15 minutes. One and one-half inch steaks should be cooked about 15 to 20 minutes. If you like your steaks rare, cook them the minimum time, and if you like them well done, cook them the maximum time. Set your oven rack on the next to the highest rung from the stove heat. Set the oven on broil, and when cooking the steak leave the door opened a crack unless you know it is not necessary in your oven. Season the first side of your steak with any thing you like, such as salt, pepper, Worcestershire sauce, soy sauce, parsley, oregano, or other herbs. Set the steak on a broiling rack or other pan and cook the first side of the steak. Then open the oven, flip the steak over and season the second side. Return the steak to the oven. Test it for doneness by putting a knife through the meat. If it's the color you like, consider it done.

Suggested Use of Leftovers

Cold, thinly sliced steak is good in sandwiches with lettuce and mayonnaise.

Potted Chuck Roast

Suggested Ingredients

1 chuck roast
water
a dash of vinegar or cheap wine (optional)
seasonings such as oregano,
basil, salt, pepper
onion
bay leaf
a clove (section) of garlic

Utensil

A covered pot large enough for the roast

Put the roast in the pot. Set the heat at medium and brown the roast on all sides, quickly. Then add enough water to half cover the roast. Cut the onion in quarters and add it with the other seasonings. Cut the garlic in little pieces and add that. Cook the meat for one hour and a half or until tender. Add the vinegar or wine during the last few minutes.

Suggested Use of Leftovers

Reheat in a pot in the gravy (see Meat in Gravy recipe) or use in pot pie.

MEAT LOAF

Meat loaf may certainly sound like one of those old standbys which becomes very dull after a while. But aside from the fact that you now have many recipes to choose from which are just as cheap as meat loaf, you also can cook meat loaf in a variety of ways with different condiments, thereby creating a new flavor every time you make it. Vegetables such as onions, green peppers, celery stalks with greens, can be added to your meat loaf. Meat loaf can be left plain on top, or can be topped with tomato sauce or a combination of catsup and brown sugar. If you like solid meat loaf you can add a liberal amount of rolled oats or bread crumbs to your chopped meat. If you like loose meat loaf, do not add a lot of filler. You can even make meat loaf without eggs. It falls apart, but it tastes good. Your most common chopped meat is beef, but you can also, at times, get chopped pork or lamb which can be mixed with chopped beef or used separately to create a slightly different flavor. Meat can also be supplemented with vegetable protein which can be purchased in most food stores. Vegetable protein is usually made from soy flour, hydrolyzed vegetable protein, salt and spices, and some have U.S. certified color (which is not necessarily a harmless ingredient).

Given below are two meat loaf recipes. Increase or decrease ingredients in this section to create different consistencies.

Meat Loaf
(serves 3 or more)

This recipe will make a meat loaf of average consistency, though your meat will be a large determining factor in exactly how it turns out. Feel free to vary proportions of any ingredients and see what you get.

Suggested Ingredients
>about 1 lb., 5 oz. to 1-1/2 lb. chopped meat
>1 c. rolled oats or 3/4 c. bread crumbs
>a few tbsp. or chunks of cheese
>seasonings such as oregano,
>dill, basil, salt, and pepper
>1/2 onion, sliced or chopped
>1 stalk of celery with leaves, sliced or chopped
>1 egg
>2 tbsp. catsup

Other Options
>topping of tomato sauce, or
>topping of 2 parts catsup to 1 part brown sugar

Utensils
>Baking dish or bread pan, mixing bowl

Preheat your oven to 375° F. Mix all ingredients together. Put them in a baking dish or bread pan. Top with tomato sauce or catsup and brown sugar, if desired. Cook for 45 minutes or until done inside when poked with a knife. The size of your pan will be a determining factor in the length of time the loaf will need to cook.

Advance Preparation
>Prepare meat loaf in advance to create a quick meal. Cook until almost done, and then refrigerate until ready to reheat another day.

Suggested Use of Leftovers
>Slice and serve cold on sandwiches.

Meat Loaf and Vegetable Protein
(serves 5 to 6)

This recipe will create a very solid meat loaf which will slice evenly and will be good cold for sandwiches. If you want to make it somewhat looser, use the minimum measurement of oats or bread crumbs.

Suggested Ingredients
**about 1 lb., 5 oz. to 1-1/2 lb. chopped meat
1 to 2 eggs
1 3-oz. package vegetable protein,
prepared according
to package directions
4 tbsp. catsup
seasonings such as
oregano, dill, basil,
salt or pepper
1/2 to 1 onion, sliced or chopped
1 stalk celery with leaves, sliced or chopped
1 to 1-1/2 c. rolled oats,
or 3/4 to 1 c. bread crumbs
a few tbsp. or chunks of cheese**

Other Options
**topping of tomato sauce, or
2 parts catsup to 1 part brown sugar**

Utensils
Baking dish or bread pan, mixing bowl

Preheat oven to 375° F. Mix all ingredients together. Put them in the baking dish. Bake for 45 minutes or until done.

Suggested Use of Leftovers
Same as Meat Loaf recipe.

Stuffed Peppers

Suggested Ingredients
**a meatball or
meat loaf recipe
(see Meatballs in Pasta section
of this chapter,
or see Meat Loaf
in Meat section)
fresh green peppers, halved and cleaned**

Utensils
    A mixing bowl, a flat baking dish

Preheat the oven to 375° F. Estimate the amount of chopped meat and other ingredients you'll need to fill the desired number of peppers. Mix your meatball or meat loaf recipe and then stuff the peppers. If desired, top each pepper with sauce or cheese. Put them in a greased dish and bake for 30 minutes or until done.

Advance Preparation
    If desired, prepare the peppers a few days in advance. Bake them in a greased dish for about 25 minutes at 375° F. and then refrigerate them. When you want to serve them, stick them back in the oven until bubbling and hot.

Leftovers You Can Use
    Leftover raw meatball or meat loaf mixture.

Suggested Use of Leftovers
    Reheat in the oven and slice onto sandwiches.

Quick Preparation

Basil Burgers (Hamburgers)

Suggested Ingredients
**enough chopped meat to make the desired number of hamburgers
salt, pepper, and basil
a little rolled oats or bread crumbs, if desired
about 1 tsp. of catsup to each hamburger (optional)
cheese (optional)**

Utensils
    Mixing bowl, frying pan with cover, or broiling pan

Mix all ingredients together. Shape the mixture into hamburgers. Either broil them, setting the rack high but not so it touches the top of the oven, or fry them in a frying pan at a medium heat, with a cover until done. If desired, put a piece of cheese on top of the burgers for the last minute or so of frying for Basil Cheeseburgers.

Suggested Use of Leftovers
    Add to soup or refry.

Quick Preparation

Hortense's Burgers on Toast

Suggested Ingredients
>same as in Basil Burgers
>1 chopped onion, to taste
>1 piece of bread for every hamburger

Utensils
>Mixing bowl and broiling pan

Mix together all ingredients except bread. Toast one side of the slices of bread under the broiler. Then remove the toast from the broiler and spread the meat mixture on the side which was not toasted. Make sure you spread the meat as close to the crust as possible to prevent too much of the crust from burning. Put the hamburgers under the broiler until they are cooked through.

Suggested Use of Leftovers
>Use the meat for soup. Feed the toast to the birds. (I hate to be wasteful, but I really can't think of any constructive way of recycling soggy toast. If you can think of something, I'd surely like to know about it.)

Swedish Meatballs

Suggested Ingredients
>a recipe for meatballs
>(see Pasta section of this chapter),
>minus the usual seasonings
>1 tsp. nutmeg
>oil
>salt and pepper
>sour cream (optional)

Utensils
>Mixing bowl, frying pan

Cook meatballs as in Meatball recipe. Leave the meatballs in the pan and drain out the grease and oil. Add a little sour cream to the warm meatballs, if desired. Serve as the meat course of the meal. These meatballs do not have to be thrown in a sauce.

Suggested Use of Leftovers
   Reheat in a covered frying pan or make a cold meatball sandwich.

HAM

Quite often you can get pretty good buys on smoked, whole or half hams, or picnic hams. These buys are on hams which are not in a can. Though you'll spend a few more dollars than you normally would for a piece of meat, you'll actually be spending much less because it will last for quite a few meals. If the ham costs between twenty and thirty cents less than you normally pay for chopped meat, you've probably got yourself a good buy. As best you can, check out the meat to make sure it's not all bone or all fat and if it looks good, buy it.

   If you don't have a meat thermometer it's best to buy a ham which has been fully cooked. I really am not sure whether people can still get trichinosis from partially cooked ham which has been infected by trichinae, or if it's just a medieval disease. I always buy fully cooked hams because they're easier and I don't have a meat thermometer, nor do I want to take any chances with trichinosis. If I ever were to find a good buy on a partially cooked ham, I might change my mind.

   There are two types of half hams you'll commonly find at the store. One is the half ham shank end, which has a bone, and the other is a half ham butt end which is boneless. Put them together and you have a whole ham, which you'll also see at the supermarket. Picnic ham is a roast from the shoulder of the pig. It, in my experience, is the least expensive ham per pound, though you have to remove the skin and more fat than on other hams.

   You can roast or boil your ham one night, use it for sandwiches the next day and then use it in scalloped potatoes, or a casserole of your own invention, and then make a pea or lentil soup with the bone. After you've cooked the soup, if you have a dog, give him the bone, which he'll devour in no time at all because it will have gone through so much at that point, that it will fall apart.

   Ham is easy to cook but it takes a few hours. Actually it's perfectly safe to eat hams which you've bought fully cooked without cooking them additionally, but their flavor seems to be much improved when you cook them. Fully cooked half or whole hams which are shank or butt end are usually very good baked. They should be baked an average of fifteen minutes per pound, fat side up. Set them in a baking pan, or, if you don't have one which is large enough, a large rectangular cake pan or on a cookie sheet which has sides.

Picnic hams are good boiled about twenty-five to thirty minutes for every pound and then baked for about fifteen minutes. Because picnics usually come with a large layer of skin on them, they should be skinned before boiling.

All varieties can be "scored" during the last fifteen minutes to half an hour of baking. Scoring is those crisscross lines you see in artistic pictures of hams. Just slice with a knife on the top of the ham about a quarter inch deep. The purpose of this is so that if you intend to baste the ham with a sauce, the gravy will soak into the meat. However, I only score when I feel like it.

Many different condiments may be added to a ham. Whole cloves can be poked into the meat every few inches, sliced pineapple can be toothpicked onto the top of the ham. Little pieces of garlic can be shoved into tiny slices made in the meat. Also, a little vinegar can be added to cooking water when boiling a ham. By the way, hams are presalted, so don't add any salt to the water. Basting sauces can be made with fresh orange juice and pulp and brown sugar or honey. Other fruit juices such as apricot or lemon can also be used. Apples can be baked along side of hams and basted along with the meat. The possibilities are practically endless. You can also just put a ham in the pot or oven and not add anything to it. It will taste just fine.

Following are two recipes—one for shank, butt or whole ham, and one for picnic. Add your own condiments for variety.

Baked Ham
(use whole ham, shank or butt)

Suggested Ingredients

a ham
whole cloves
1 orange
1/4 c. honey or brown sugar

Utensils

A baking or roasting pan, a small bowl for orange-honey sauce

If your ham is over 6 pounds you may want to use more orange and honey or sugar. Put your ham fat side up in a baking dish. Poke some cloves into the top of the meat, every few inches, or however you care to do it. Bake the meat at 350° F. about 15 minutes per pound. During the last half hour or so, squeeze the juice from your orange and add the pulp to the juice. Combine it with the honey or sugar. If desired, crisscross ("score") your meat as described under the general ham instructions in this section. Pour the sauce on the meat and put the ham back in the oven for 30 minutes. If a lot of juice drips down onto the pan, every few minutes open the oven and pour the juice onto the meat. This is what is known as basting. Remove the ham from the oven, allow it to cool for a few minutes and then slice it. To slice the ham, make slices one after another, half way through the meat. Then put the knife on its side and cut the bottom of each slice. The rest of the meat can be sliced in a random fashion. If this all sounds very impeccable and intimidating to you, just hack the meat in whatever manner you wish.

Suggested Use of Leftovers

Sliced cold in sandwiches, put in casseroles or pot pies, soups, or fried in a little margarine. If you used a ham with a bone, the bone can be used for pea or lentil soup.

Picnic Ham

Suggested Ingredients

a picnic ham
water
whole cloves
1 orange
1/4 c. honey or brown sugar

Utensils

A large kettle or pot with cover, a baking pan, a small bowl for orange-honey sauce

Peel the skin off the picnic. Poke cloves every few inches into the ham. Put the ham into the pot and cover it with water. If the very top cannot be covered with water, don't worry. Cover the pot and let the water come to a boil and then simmer the meat for 25 to 30 minutes for every pound of meat. (After you've removed the skin and its attached fat, you can probably assume you've removed a pound or more off the meat.) Squeeze the juice from the orange, add the pulp, and combine it with the honey or sugar. If your picnic is over 6 pounds you may want to add more orange and sweetener. Put the ham on a baking pan. Score the meat as in general ham directions in this section, if desired. Then add the sauce and put the meat in the oven at 350° F. for about 15 minutes. Every so often, baste (pour the sauce back on the meat). Follow carving directions as in the Baked Ham recipe.

Suggested Use of Leftovers
　　Same as for Baked Ham

Lamb Shank Marinade

A lamb shank is part of the leg of lamb but it costs much less than the leg because most of the meat has been cut off leaving only the meat closest to the bone. This meat may not be quite as tender as most of the leg, but it is good meat.

Suggested Ingredients
　　lamb shank

Marinade

2 tsp. brown sugar, honey or molasses
2 tsp. soy or Worcestershire sauce
2 tsp. catsup
(or see marinade recipe p. 202)

Utensils
　　Baking dish with cover or aluminum foil, dish for mixing marinade

Place the shank in a baking dish, mix all ingredients for the marinade, and pour the marinade over the meat. As the sauce drips down, every so often pour the sauce back on the meat until you feel as if some of the sauce has soaked into the meat. (Baste it.) Let the meat sit and soak up the sauce while you baste at intervals, for at least 30 minutes. Put the meat in the oven, cover it and bake it at 375° F. for an hour or until it looks done when cut with a knife.

Suggested Use of Leftovers
　　See Meat in Gravy recipe on page 154 and Lamb Curry on page 218. Or add to casseroles, pot pies or soups.

FRIED LIVER

Beef or pork liver (and calf's liver, if you can afford it) can be fried up simply and quickly. If the pieces are partially frozen, you can begin frying them just as soon as you are able to separate the pieces. Liver can be cooked in different ways. Fried liver can be breaded, floured, fried in margarine or oil with onions, or just fried alone with seasonings. You'll probably be able to invent a few others —especially if liver ends up being the cheapest meat available.

Quick Preparation

Once Over Lightly Liver

I know that's a ridiculous title for a recipe. This title has a rather ambiguous history—no one is willing to take the credit for it. Every so often when I prepare a meal, my husband will say, "Is that in your book?" or "Don't forget to put that in your book." One of us will usually make a note of it then and there so I won't forget it. Needless to say, there are scraps of paper with recipes on them all over our apartment. Some of these papers are also decorated with tomato sauce, oil and other condiments, because the notes were taken while I was cooking. Anyway, I just found one of these little pieces of paper. On it is written "Once Over Lightly Liver." That certainly is not my handwriting (and if you ask me, it certainly is Michael's), but neither of us have any recollection of the invention of the title. The recipe I'm familiar with. You really can't imagine what it's like trying to invent names for recipes which is one reason why so many recipes have intriguing names like Vegetable Soup, Soft-boiled Eggs, Poached Fish and the like. Somehow "Once Over Lightly Liver" grows on me like a wart.

Suggested Ingredients

sliced beef or pork liver
lemon
seasonings such as salt and basil
oil or margarine or a combination of both

Utensils

Frying pan with cover

Shake excess blood off the liver. Coat a frying pan with oil and add more oil as needed. Keep the burner heat between medium-low and medium. Season the liver and fry it lightly on both sides. Squeeze a liberal amount of lemon on the liver, cover the pan and steam the liver until it is cooked inside—about 15 minutes or more. Liver can simmer for over an hour, if needed. This also means that you can cook liver before your company comes and, if they are late, the liver can just simmer in the pan. Just be sure that it is at a low enough heat so that it does not become dry.

Suggested Use of Leftovers

Reheat in a frying pan, adding a little water, if necessary, or add to a casserole.

Quick Preparation

Milk and Egg Fried Liver

Suggested Ingredients

**sliced beef or pork liver
egg (start with one,
no matter how much liver you have)
whole wheat or white flour or bread crumbs
(all) seasoned with salt,
pepper, oregano, basil, grated cheese,
or other ingredients
milk
oil**

Utensils

Frying pan with cover, if desired, several dishes for dunking

The amount of milk, egg and flour you use depends upon how much liver you are cooking. Start with a little of those ingredients and then add more, if needed.

Coat your frying pan with oil, adding more as needed. Put the pan at a medium heat and lower it, if it becomes too hot. Put beaten egg and milk in a dish in any proportion desired—a half cup of milk to one egg is a good proportion. Put flour with seasonings in another dish. Shake excess blood off the liver and dunk each piece first in the milk and egg combination and then through the flour. If some sections of the liver are not coated with flour, as desired, put it through the egg and milk and flour a second time. This will give you a thick breading. Place the breaded liver in the heated frying pan and fry each side until it is golden brown. If all the liver does not fit in your pan at once, stack browned liver on top of other liver or put the cooked liver in a dish in a low (200° to 250°F.) oven while the rest of the liver fries. To make sure the liver is done, allow it to simmer for a while after it is browned. Cover the pan, if desired. If the pan is left uncovered, the breading will most likely remain crunchier. Leftover egg, milk and flour can be mixed together (along with a little liver blood for flavoring) and fried along with the liver. This makes good mock fried liver.

Suggested Use of Leftovers
    Same as in Once Over Lightly Liver.

Quick Preparation

Flour Fried Liver

Graham flour or rough ground whole wheat flour taste especially good in this recipe. The crunch, which is created by the flour, really adds to the liver.

Suggested Ingredients
    sliced beef or pork liver
    graham, whole wheat, or white flour
    oil
    seasonings such as oregano,
    basil, dill, salt, and pepper

Utensils
    Frying pan with cover, if desired, and a bowl for flour

Set frying pan at a medium heat and coat the bottom of the pan with oil. Add more oil and lower the heat as needed. Shake excess blood off the liver and press the liver onto the flour which has been mixed with the seasonings. Follow frying directions as in Milk and Egg Fried Liver.

Suggested Use of Leftovers
    Same as the previous liver recipes.

Liver and Onions

Follow directions for Once Over Lightly Liver or any of the breaded livers. Add a liberal amount of sliced onions to the liver in the frying pan and add more oil or margarine if needed. If you use oil, make sure you don't use too much, or the combination will be greasy. Lemon squeezed on the liver and onions while it cooks makes the combination especially good.

Suggested Use of Leftovers
   Same as for other recipes.

Meat In Gravy

Leftover meats such as turkey, lamb, and chuck roast can be sliced and reheated in gravy, if you've saved the gravy which was created while you were cooking the meat. Drippings collected from the bottom of the pan can be turned into a gravy to be used in this recipe by following the recipe for Bottom of the Pan Gravy on page 200. If there is not enough of this gravy, add bouillon cubes and water. The gravy which you made in the pot roast can be thickened or left unthickened and used in this recipe.

Suggested Ingredients
   **sliced, cooked turkey, chicken, lamb, chuck roast,
   or other meat, well trimmed
   of fat and gristle
   enough gravy to cover all the meat
   seasonings such as parsley, basil, oregano,
   if the gravy is not already seasoned**

Utensils
   Frying pan with cover

Put all ingredients in the frying pan and heat until bubbling. Allow it to simmer for a few minutes. Serve over macaroni, noodles, rice, or bread.

Leftovers You Can Use
   Meat and gravy.

Suggested Use of Leftovers
   Heat again in the same manner.

Fried Pork Chops and Apples

It's about time I gave my mother some credit for the creation of this book. When I was a kid, I always wanted to be in the kitchen to find out what was going on. I also liked to eat and knew that if I hung around, I could be my mother's "official taster," as she would say.

Even when I go home for visits now, she looks at me and says, "Who wants to be my official taster?" She also used to say, "Who wants to do the dishes?" My sisters and brother were no fools. They didn't want to do the dishes, so they never said anything. "I do," I'd say, because I thought if my mother asked the question that way, she must think there was something special about the job. So I did the dishes and also spent many pleasant hours tasting and learning how to cook. Eventually my mother and I became quite a team. I'd throw one thing into the pot, she'd throw in another. We never seemed to worry about what the other person had just thrown in. As I remember, our meals were always a success. At least we thought so. A few of the recipes in this book are from my mother. Some are variations of hers, and many have some hidden origin. The following is one of her recipes.

Suggested Ingredients

pork chops
a little margarine, if necessary
onion (about 1/2 for every 4 chops)
mushrooms (optional)
apples (about 1 for every 4 chops)
seasonings such as salt, pepper,
a little crushed garlic, paprika, oregano

Utensils
Frying pan with cover

Put the flame under the frying pan at a medium heat. Season the pork chops on both sides. Put the chops in the pan and fry each on both sides until the meat turns white. If all chops do not fit in one layer, stack one on top of the other as you fry them. Switch the positions of the chops so each is browned. If not enough fat is given off during this quick frying to prevent the chops from sticking to the pan, add a little margarine. When all chops are fried, core and slice the apples and add them and the onion and mushrooms to the pan. Cover the pan and let the chops steam and bubble at a medium-low heat for about 30 minutes or until the pork is cooked through. You may shift the positions of the chops every so often so each chop gets a turn at the bottom and will be allowed to brown a bit.

Suggested Use of Leftovers
Reheat in a frying pan, or cut pork into small chunks and fry with fried rice. (See Fried Rice recipe on page 187.)

Baked Turkey Parts

Frequently, you can find prepackaged frozen turkey parts (legs or wings) at the supermarket. You can follow the directions for cooking which are often on the packaging, or you can use this recipe.

Suggested Ingredients
**turkey legs or wings, thoroughly washed in cool water
salt, pepper, and basil or other herbs
lemon (optional)**

Utensils
Baking dish with cover or aluminum foil cover, or 2 bread pans, 1 on top of another for a Dutch oven effect

Season the turkey, place it in the baking dish, and bake at 375° to 400° F. A good cover will insure fast baking (about 1 hour).

Suggested Use of Leftovers
Put in casseroles or see Meat in Gravy recipe on page 154.

CHICKEN

Chicken is usually one of the most economical meats around. Most of the time it doesn't cost as much as other meats, and all of its parts can be used. It can be cooked in a variety of ways and is good hot or cold. You can spend many minutes over a chicken or you can just throw it in the oven.

Chicken livers, gizzards and necks, collectively known as giblets, can be cooked, chopped up and then put in gravy. For a giblet recipe, see page 201. These parts can also be added to soups, and livers can be fried for various recipes.

Chicken bones can be made into delicious soups, and according to a subscriber to *The Mother Earth News* magazine, the bones, after creating the soup become so soft, you can safely feed them to your dog. For a chicken stock and soup recipe see the section under Soups.

The following should give you the basic information you should know about chickens.

TYPES OF BIRDS

The types of chickens you'll see at the supermarket are broiling, frying, roasting and stewing chickens. You're probably wondering what could possibly be the difference between these four birds. The differences are age and weight which create different consistencies and make each bird better for a specific method of cooking. Broilers are eight to twelve-week-old chickens which weigh two to three pounds. Fryers are twelve to fourteen weeks old and weigh three to four pounds. Roasters, fourteen-week to six-month-old birds, weigh four pounds or more. When the bird is over six months old, it becomes a stewing bird. Fryers can be used any time for broiling, and broilers in turn can be fried. Fryers can also be roasted, but they will not be as juicy as a roaster will be. Anything can be stewed, but it will fall apart sooner than a stewing bird, which is pretty tough. Stewing birds are not very good fried, broiled, or roasted.

CLEANING THE CHICKEN

Sometimes chickens straight from the store have a rather nasty smell about them. When you bring them home, if you want you can wash them, put them in a clean plastic bag, and then freeze them. If you do not wash a chicken before it is frozen, by all means wash it as you prepare it for cooking. A chicken's odor can really spoil a potentially good meal.

If a chicken has an excessive number of feather stubs still on it, and if you have a gas stove, holding the chicken by the legs, run the bird quickly through the burner flame to singe off the feathers.

THAWING THE CHICKEN

Chickens should be pretty well thawed before preparing so that they will cook evenly. Depending upon the time of year and the temperature of your apartment, thawing should take anywhere from a few hours to about five hours. A chicken also will usually thaw in a refrigerator in eight to twelve hours.

HOW TO CUT UP A CHICKEN

A chicken basically has the same parts to its body that you have to yours. It might be rather repulsive to you to look at things that way, but if you are aware of certain joints in your body, it will be easier for you to cut up a chicken.

I find that the most convenient way is to begin by removing the wings and legs from the body. Wings are connected to the body much like your shoulders are hinged to your body. Once you find the ball and socket-like joint by stretching out the wing and feeling the connecting area with your knife, you should be able to slice it easily. Legs are connected to the thighs in much the same way. Find the joint and cut through it. Now put the chicken on its back and slice the cartilage-like breast down the center from the neck cavity to the tail cavity. Take both sides of the bird and flatten them to the table. Now cut the back—either straight down the middle (if you want it to be part of the breasts and thighs) or along either side of the column. With either method when cutting the back, you must cut through bone. If you go through the back, you cut the column. If you cut along the sides you must go through the ribs. Next, look at the two remaining sections (breasts and thighs together). You will see a fold which delineates the two sections. Follow this line with your knife. You will have to cut through some bone again, but if you do it correctly the bone should be cut through the joint which connects the two sections.

Precut chickens usually cost more per pound; so it's worth cutting them yourself. The above method can be utilized before or after cooking the chicken.

COOKING METHODS

Chickens can be broiled, baked, fried, potted, or roasted. When prepared by any of the above methods, they can be used as leftovers for casseroles, creamed chicken, chicken salads, just eaten cold, reheated or made into sandwiches.

Broiled Chicken

Suggested Ingredients
**Chicken broiler or fryer cut and thoroughly washed in cool water
salt, oregano, paprika, and other herbs
lemon (optional)**

Utensils

Broiling pan (usually comes with the oven); or several layers of aluminum foil on a cookie sheet, edges of foil turned up.

Cut up the chicken. Then season the underside of the breasts, second joints, wings and backs, and either side of the legs. Put the chicken pieces skin down on the broiling pan. Set the oven rack in the next to highest position or in a position where the chicken will be close to the heat but no parts will touch the coil. Turn the oven on broil, leave the door opened a crack unless you specifically know you don't have to in your oven, and cook until the skin on the legs is golden brown. If you have an oven instruction chart, follow the time indicated by the chart. Otherwise, cook the first side for 25 minutes and the second side for 15 to 20 minutes or use your own judgment. When the first side is done, season the second side and broil until the skin is golden brown. Pour the drippings over the chicken, if desired, or serve with various sauces listed in the sauce and gravy section of this chapter.

Suggested Use of Leftovers

Sliced plain on sandwiches, chicken salad, creamed chicken, or reheated in a baking dish in the oven. See recipe for Creamed Chicken, page 164.

Baked Chicken

Suggested Ingredients

**cut-up, washed, broiling or frying chicken
desired seasonings such as
salt, pepper, oregano, basil**

Optional

**1 c. or more flour
onion, celery**

Utensils

A large flat baking dish or cake pan

Chicken can be baked all by itself, can be breaded, or baked with vegetables. For good old plain baked chicken, preheat your oven at 375° F. Place the chicken pieces side by side, skin side up in a baking dish or long sheet cake pan. Season chicken to taste. Set the oven rack at approximately the middle of the oven. Bake for about an hour, or until the leg is tender when poked with a fork.

For breaded chicken, combine flour and herbs in a bag. Shake the excess water off the chicken and place the pieces in the bag, one at a time. Shake until the flour coats the pieces. (You guessed it, it's like Shake 'n Bake). Place the pieces on a baking dish and bake at 375° to 400° F. for about an hour.

You can also add onions, celery and other vegetables to baked chicken, simply putting them around the chicken when you put it in to bake.

Suggested Use of Leftovers

You can do the same things with leftover baked chicken that you can do with leftover broiled chicken.

FRIED CHICKEN

Fried chicken, as most any chicken dish, tastes great hot or cold. After you fry the chicken in oil or shortening, the grease can be poured into a covered jar and stored in the refrigerator for frying at some other time. Refrigerated oil will become cloudy, but this is no indication that it has spoiled. The deepest and sturdiest frying pan you have, or a large sturdy pot are best for frying chicken.

Jessie's
Southern Fried Chicken

Suggested Ingredients

cut-up, washed, frying chicken
flour (start with 1 c.)
salt
pepper
oil or shortening

Utensils

A paper or plastic bag, a deep fat fryer or a 5 qt. or larger pot, or a deep frying pan

Shake excess water off the pieces of chicken. Put pieces, one at a time, into a bag with the flour and seasonings. When the pieces are coated, take them out of the bag and put them on a plate. Place enough oil in the pan or pot so that when you're ready to put the chicken in, it will cover your average-sized piece of chicken half way. Do not put the chicken in the pot yet. Heat the oil to a temperature which will be hot but will not cause the oil to burn or spatter too much as you fry. When the oil begins to form light bubbles and seems to be on the verge of boiling, put in some chicken parts. Do not crowd all of them into the pot. They should have enough room to cook on all sides. Fry each side until crispy and brown. If you are not sure if they are done, make a small slice into a piece of dark meat with a knife to check it out. If it is pink or red, put it back in. Drain done pieces on a torn open paper bag. To keep the chicken warm as you cook other pieces, place pieces on a dish in a warm (200° to 250° F.) oven. You can probably fry two whole chickens within an hour.

Suggested Use of Leftovers
Reheat in the oven in a dish, or serve cold on sandwiches.

POTTED CHICKEN

Chicken can be potted in various ways using different types of birds.

Chicken which is stewed in a pot with water, herbs, and vegetables for several hours or more forms a broth which can be used as soup or stock. The chicken can be used as one meal, and the soup or stock can be saved for another. Most often, stewing birds are used for stewing, because as mentioned before, most other birds will fall apart if they are cooked for such a long time.

Other potted chicken recipes call for fryers or broilers. Chicken Cacciatora, which was supposedly a great favorite of my Sicilian ancestors, is one of those recipes. This recipe calls for a shorter length of cooking time than does stewed chicken as the broth for cacciatora is made from tomatoes and other seasonings, while stewed chicken has to form its own broth with water and seasonings. Also, broilers and fryers cook in a much shorter length of time than stewing chickens.

Chicken and Soup
and Chicken Stew
(2 meals in 1)

Suggested Ingredients
1 whole, washed, stewing chicken
enough water to barely cover the chicken
2 bay leaves
2 stalks celery
salt and other seasonings to taste
2 tbsp. flour (if making stew)

Optional
wine or wine vinegar

Utensils
    A 5 qt. or larger pot with cover

Put the bird in the pot. Cover with water, add other ingredients and let the water come to a boil. Turn the heat down so that the water gently rolls but does not boil vigorously. Cook until the chicken is tender. Taste the broth. If it is too weak add more seasonings. Save the broth as soup or stock. Remove chicken and serve.

    For chicken stew, add a little less water and a few more vegetables such as broccoli, beans and potatoes. Thicken the broth with a few tablespoons of flour when everything is done. To do this, take out a little liquid, mix it with the flour, and then pour it back into the pot. Turn up the heat so the broth gently boils and stir until the mixture thickens. You can add a little wine or wine vinegar to this if you like.

Suggested Use of Leftovers
    The chicken can be creamed (see page 164), made into chicken salad, or reheated any way you like.

Chicken Cacciatora

Suggested Ingredients
1 washed, cut-up, frying chicken
1 whole onion
1 green pepper (optional)
5 or 6 large, washed or peeled,
sliced mushrooms (optional)
may be substituted with broccoli or celery
1 bay leaf
oregano, basil, salt, pepper
oil
1 large (28-oz. can) whole tomatoes

Utensils
    A 5 qt. or larger pot with cover

Sparingly coat the bottom of the pot with oil. Gently brown each piece of chicken just for a few minutes. Add all other ingredients. Allow mixture to boil and then turn down the heat so the combination will gently roll. Check your pot from time to time to make sure the heat is not too high. When the chicken is tender, your meal is done. Serve with noodles or rice and grated cheese.

Roasted Chicken

Suggested Ingredients

**a whole roasting chicken
seasonings
1 stuffing recipe (optional)
oil (optional)**

Utensils
    A baking dish or long cake pan

Roasted chicken can be made stuffed or unstuffed. As with other things, the accuracy of your oven determines how long the chicken will take to cook. As an average gauge allow 20 to 30 minutes of cooking time per pound of chicken roasted at 375° to 400° F.

If you do not want to stuff the bird, simply put it in a baking dish, sprinkle with salt and other seasonings, if desired, and brush with oil (optional). Bake the bird on its back (breast side up). The chicken is done when the leg, when jiggled, is crisp and moves freely at the joint.

To stuff the bird, follow recipe for stuffing on page 219. Pack the bird well. If desired, fill both the neck cavity and the "larger" cavity. (I don't know what to call the "larger" cavity.) Close the neck cavity by folding the loose skin under the bird. Close the "larger" cavity by wedging a crust of bread in the opening, pinning it with a poultry skewer, sewing it, or just leaving it open. I usually leave it open. During the cooking process, the stuffing puffs out and sometimes oozes onto the pan, but you get a nice glob of crusty, brown stuffing. The stuffing which remains inside the bird, stays moist. Follow directions for unstuffed bird as in the previous paragraph.

With the drippings from the bottom of the pan, make a gravy as described on page 200 under Sauces and Gravies in this chapter. Or, make a Giblet Gravy as given on page 201.

Suggested Use of Leftovers
    Same as for Broiled Chicken.

Creamed Chicken

Suggested Ingredients

    leftover, cooked chicken
    cut into chunks or slices
    celery
    onion
    salt, pepper, oregano,
    basil, paprika, or other seasonings, to taste
    precooked or leftover beans,
    peas, carrots, or other vegetables
    a little margarine
    cream sauce
    (see the section on Sauces and Gravies in this chapter)

Utensil
    Saucepan

Fry the onion and celery at a medium heat in the saucepan in a little margarine. Make the cream sauce in the same saucepan (about 1-1/2 cups cream sauce for every cup of chicken and vegetables). Add chicken and vegetables and seasonings and cook at a medium heat until everything is hot. Serve on rice or biscuits.

Leftovers You Can Use
    Chicken and vegetables.

Suggested Use of Leftovers
    Thin with extra milk and reheat on the stove.

PASTA, SAUCES, AND MEATBALLS AND THEIR CONDIMENTS

Pasta is the Italian word for the general category into which spaghetti, lasagna, macaroni, and noodles fall. Spaghetti (fondly known as scabetti and piscetti by gourmet pasta eaters) is something you can get most kids to eat. Another type of pasta which you may have heard of and even tasted, but possibly have never seen spelled out, is pasta y fagiole (pronounced pasta fazool in American). The first time I saw it,

I pronounced it pasta ē fa gē olē. My mother, who grew up in an Italian home, cracked right up. It's one of the things she's been bringing up for the past ten years now: "You know how Nancy pronounces pasta y fagiole?" she'll say. Pasta y fagiole is beans and pasta. You'll find the recipe in this section.

Pasta is great stuff which can be used in many different ways. It's a good thing to boil up quickly when four friends arrive unexpectedly and tell you they're not hungry while you listen to their stomachs roar. Just keep in mind the fact that pasta is very starchy—translated into calories that means a lot. Because I don't like to overload meals with starch, I don't make spaghetti and lasagna too often. Most of the time, I use pasta as a side dish mixed with cheese, eggs, onions, and margarine. Some simple pasta side dishes are listed in this section.

Pasta condiments such as meatballs and tomato sauce are also listed in this section. Of course, these condiments may also be used with rice or anything instead of pasta.

Pasta is most successfully prepared when one follows the directions on the noodle, spaghetti, lasagna, or macaroni package for the amount of water to be used and the length of cooking time. With some types of pasta, especially macaroni and lasagna, you might want to add a little oil to the cooking water to prevent them from sticking to the bottom of the pot. A big pot of water should certainly require no more than a tablespoon of oil. When your water boils, stir in your pasta. Stir it often until you are sure that the pasta is not sticking together. Spaghetti tends to do this most readily—especially when it is first put in the pot.

Pasta should not be cooked to a mush. Italians prefer pasta cooked *el dente* or enough so that it has a bit of a chew left in it. Some people claim that to test the doneness of pasta, you should throw a piece up against the wall. If it's done, it will stick to the wall. This may be true, but I also think it's ridiculous. If you're going to waste a good piece of pasta, you might as well just taste it to see if it's done. I was in one apartment where the wall above the stove was literally crawling with dried up spaghetti. The residents of the same apartment (one of whom made his acting debut in *Marat Sade*) had a rather macabre sense of humor. They dyed their spaghetti with food coloring until they were forced to give up the practice when they claimed the colorful pasta gave them stomachaches.

There are several ways to prevent drained pasta from sticking together. The reason pasta does stick is because the starch has a tendency to do this when cooked. The most effective way to prevent sticking, is by loosening or removing excess starch. To do this, cook the pasta until done. Turn off the heat and add some cold water to the undrained pasta. About one cup for every six cups of pasta water should do. You don't have to measure, really. Just add enough water so that the pot water is still hot, but not near boiling. Now drain your pasta through a colander. Another method of preventing sticking is to add a little sauce (several ladles full per half pound of pasta). Mix it in after draining. Or, add some margarine to your drained pasta to loosen the starch.

Pasta that is to be used in a casserole should not be cooked thoroughly. It should only be cooked three quarters of the way. Otherwise, you'll get mush. For casseroles using pasta, see the casserole section of this chapter.

Sarah's Broccoli Macaroni

This recipe was given to me by my aunt Sarah who kept raving about the flavor combination so often that I finally had to try it. Broccoli Macaroni can be used as a side dish or as the main dish of the meal. Use a lot of broccoli or a little—it all depends upon your taste. Remember when cooking the desired amount of pasta that six ounces of dry pasta will make about three and one-half cups of cooked pasta.

Suggested Ingredients
> **tomato sauce recipe with or without meat (page 172)**
> **broccoli**
> **onion**
> **garlic**
> **shell, elbow, ditalli, or other macaroni**
> **grated cheese**
> **bread crumbs, for the top of the dish (optional)**

Utensils
Large pot, medium-sized pot, colander, frying pan, baking dish

Begin cooking the pasta according to package directions. Cook it until it's 3/4 of the way done. Drain it and set it aside. Brown a small amount of bread crumbs by quickly frying them in an ungreased frying pan for a minute or so. Meanwhile, wash your broccoli and remove hard or scaly sections of the stem. Parboil it in lightly salted water for about 3 minutes. Drain it and slice it into small pieces into an oiled or margarined frying pan set at a medium heat. Add also, onion and crushed garlic. Add seasonings such as oregano and basil to this mixture if you want—or rely on the seasonings in the sauce. Fry this combination until the onions are golden and the broccoli is fairly tender.

Set your oven at 350° F. *Thinly* coat the bottom of your baking dish with sauce. You will be adding the next ingredients in layers, so when I say to add something, do not add all of that something. After coating the dish with sauce, add a layer of macaroni, and top it with some sauce. Next, add a layer of the broccoli-onion combination and then a sprinkling of cheese. Repeat all layers and top them with the browned bread crumbs. Bake it for 20 minutes or until hot and bubbling.

Leftovers You Can Use
Sauce, broccoli, onion, macaroni.

Suggested Use of Leftovers
Reheat in the oven or on the stove. Add more liquid (sauce or water) if needed to prevent sticking.

Lasagna
(serves 12 or more)

I don't consider lasagna to be very economical, though it is less expensive than many meat meals. But it's fun to make and I think it's a very convenient thing to serve if you should ever have a lot of friends over for dinner. People are known to make pigs of themselves over lasagna.

Lasagna may be made with or without meat. Meatballs cooked in the same sauce are a nice side dish as are salad and Italian bread. No human being, except someone with a stomach disorder, could complain about this meal. Your friends will think you're a gourmet cook.

If you don't have a large pot (say eight quarts) for tomato sauce and at least the same size pot for cooking the lasagna noodles, try to borrow them. You'll also need two lasagna pans which are none other than rectangular sheet cake pans.

This particular lasagna recipe is very generous and very rich. If you're cheap (or can't afford it), create your own proportions by cutting down on the ricotta, parmesan, and mozzarella cheeses. I do that all the time.

Suggested Ingredients

>**2 tomato sauce recipes (see tomato sauce page 172 in this section) with or without meat**
>**1-1/2 lbs. (when uncooked) lasagna noodles**
>**1 tbsp. or so salt (for cooking noodles)**
>**1-1/2 lbs. ricotta cheese**
>**1 or 2 eggs**
>**a little parsley and salt (optional)**
>**1-1/2 c. grated parmesan cheese**
>**1 ball (about 8 to 10-1/2 oz.) mozzarella cheese**
>**2 tbsp. oil**

Other Options

>**1 or 2 meatball recipes (see Meatballs page 174)**
>**salad and salad dressing recipes (see pages 189–195)**
>**Italian bread (page 248)**

Utensils

1 small mixing bowl, two 8 qt. (or larger) pots with covers, 2 rectangular sheet pans, approximately 11 × 8 × 2 inch or a little smaller

Make a tomato sauce recipe following Tomato Sauce #1, page 172, as usual except double the proportions. If desired, make meatballs according to the recipe on page 174. When the sauce is done, remove the meatballs from the sauce and set them aside in a warm place or reheat them later. If you don't use meatballs, cook the sauce using as little or as much chopped meat as you can afford, or just flavor the sauce with bones.

Next, cook your lasagna noodles, carefully following package directions. Even if the package does not suggest it, add some oil and salt to the cooking water. Add the amounts they suggest, or if they do not specify, add a tablespoon of salt and the amount of oil suggested previously in this section.

When the noodles are done, pour some cold water in the pot to prevent the noodles from sticking. Then drain the noodles. If they do not immediately separate, leave them in your colander in the sink and run cold water over them. If you have a counter near your sink, it will be convenient for you to leave the noodles in the colander in the sink while you do the recipe. If you have no counter there, you might want to put a bowl under the colander and bring the colander and bowl over to your counter. This may all sound superfluously ridiculous, but you want to prevent your noodles from sticking together or getting mushy and falling apart. If all the noodles do not fit in the colander, drain them all, but then put them back in the pot and take them from the pot as needed. If some of the noodles break while cooking or drainng, just place them in their rows as best you can.

While the noodles are cooking, mix the ricotta with a beaten egg or two. If you wish, you may also add parsley and salt to this combination. Slice your mozzarella cheese into thin slices and set it aside.

You are now ready to begin placing all your ingredients in layers in the pan:

1. Ladle a thin layer of sauce onto the bottom of the pan.
2. Spread out one layer of noodles, side by side. If the noodles are too long for the pan, let them slope up the edge of the pan or fold the excess under alternating the side each noodle is folded over on. In other words, fold the first noodle over on the north side of the pan, the second on the south side, third on the north, etc.
3. Spread out a layer of ricotta, about half an inch to one inch thick.
4. Cover the ricotta with slices of mozzarella cheese.
5. Cover the mozzarella with sauce.
6. Sprinkle the sauce with parmesan cheese.
7. Begin again with noodles and repeat the layers.
8. Just before the last layer of sauce, change the pattern and add the mozzarella after the sauce instead of before it and end the pattern with parmesan.

The pattern should look like this:

>
> parmesan
> mozzarella
> sauce
> ricotta
> noodles
>
> •
> •
> •
>
> parmesan
> sauce
> mozzarella
> ricotta
> noodles
> parmesan
> sauce
> mozzarella
> ricotta
> noodles

Start here ⟶ sauce in the bottom of the pan

This is not as confusing as it sounds. Bake the lasagna at 350° F. for 30 to 45 minutes or until it is hot. If you want a crunchy crust, leave it uncovered. Otherwise, cover the pans with aluminum foil. If you make 2 sauce recipes, there should be plenty left over for people who desire more sauce to put on top of the lasagna.

Advance Preparation

Lasagna can be cooked in advance, refrigerated for a day or so, and then heated at 350°F. for as long as it takes for it to get hot. (Be sure it's hot in the center.) It can also be frozen for a number of days or even a few weeks in a fairly good freezer, and then heated. It can be reheated many times until you finish it.

Suggested Use of Leftovers

If you have noodles left over after you've completed putting the lasagna in the pans, they can be cut up or left whole and heated in a casserole or in a pan with a little water. Add cheese or other ingredients to them.

Poor Man's Lasagna

If you really like the taste of lasagna, but you can't afford to spend money on all of the condiments, begin substituting less expensive but good ingredients for the more expensive ingredients. This recipe gives suggestions on what you may want to substitute. Substitute all or some of these things, using the previous recipe as a guide, and you'll have yourself a very pleasant meal. This recipe is also simpler to prepare than the regular lasagna recipe if you use shell macaroni in place of lasagna strips.

Suggested Ingredients

shell macaroni (or other macaroni) instead of lasagna
yogurt cheese mixed with egg
and a little milk and parmesan cheese,
to get 1-1/2 lbs., instead of ricotta,
brick or muenster cheese instead of mozzarella
all other ingredients the same as in Lasagna recipe

Utensils
>Same as for Lasagna recipe

Place your ingredients in the pans in the same way as in the Lasagna recipe:

>>parmesan
>>brick or muenster
>>sauce
>>yogurt cheese
>>macaroni
>>
>>.
>>
>>.
>>
>>.
>>
>>.
>>
>>.
>>
>>parmesan
>>sauce
>>brick or muenster cheese
>>yogurt cheese
>>macaroni

>Begin here ⟶ a little sauce on the bottom of the pan

>Bake at 350° F. for 30 to 45 minutes (covered or uncovered), or until hot.

Suggested Use of Leftovers
>Same as for Lasagna.

Quick Preparation

Quick Clam Sauce and Macaroni
(serves 2)

Ingredients
>**6-1/2- or 7-oz. can of minced clams**
>**oregano and basil**
>**macaroni**

Utensils
>A small saucepan for clams, a larger pan for macaroni

Put the clams and a little oregano and basil in a saucepan and cook at a low heat for at least 10 minutes. Meanwhile, cook the macaroni according to the box directions, drain, and add margarine. Pour clam sauce over the macaroni. If you can afford it, top with parmesan cheese. Otherwise, top with any cheese (or no cheese).

Suggested Use of Leftovers

Reheat with a little water on the stove, or put in a greased baking dish. Add sauce or water and cheese and put in the oven.

Tomato Sauce #1
(serves 6 with pasta)

Suggested Ingredients

**1 tbsp. oil, more if needed
1 small onion, chopped
1 clove (section) garlic, chopped
2 small (6-oz.) cans tomato paste, plus 1 to 2 cans water,
depending upon the desired consistency of the sauce
1 large (28-oz.) can whole tomatoes
oregano, basil, salt, pepper, to taste
1 tsp. sugar, if desired
nutmeg or allspice, to taste, if desired**

Other Options

**1/2 to 1 lb. chopped meat (if not making meatballs)
mushrooms cleaned or peeled**

Utensils

One thick 5 qt. or more pot with cover (a thick or sturdy pot seems to retain heat and cause less burning and evaporation than thinner pots)

Set the temperature of your burner to a medium heat. Put the oil in the pot and gently fry the onion. Add mushrooms, if you use them. If you do not intend to make meatballs, you may want to add some chopped meat as you are frying the onion for the sauce. For other varieties, try adding other meats, like leftover fowl, pork, or beef, a can of minced clams, or any bones, directly to your sauce after you've added your canned sauce and paste.

Add all other ingredients, break up the whole tomatoes somewhat, cover the pot, and cook the sauce over a medium heat until it begins to boil. Lower the heat and allow the sauce to simmer for at least a few hours, stirring occasionally and turning it down if it boils too hard. Taste the sauce after the first hour to see what it needs. It usually needs more herbs. The longer the sauce cooks, the better it tastes. Add more water if the sauce seems too thick. Add sugar if the sauce seems too acidic.

If you do make meatballs, add them to the sauce at any time you wish after all ingredients have been added to the sauce. Meatballs really add to the flavor of the sauce.

If the sauce seems very greasy—meaning that a thick layer of liquid oil floats on top of the sauce—remove some of the oil with a spoon. A thin layer of oil can be easily stirred into the sauce.

Cook spaghetti, noodles, or macaroni according to package directions and serve them with the sauce.

Leftovers You Can Use
> Bones.

Suggested Use of Leftovers
> Reheat many times. Add water, if necessary. Sauce can even be frozen to be used weeks later. Sauce with spaghetti or macaroni can be reheated together in a saucepan on the stove. Add a little water to prevent sticking. Or, combine sauce and pasta in a greased baking dish, and add a little water and bake either covered or uncovered. Uncovered will give you a crunchy top.

Tomato Sauce #2
(serves 4 with pasta)

Suggested Ingredients
> **2 15-oz.-cans tomato sauce**
> **1/2 to 3/4 lb. chopped meat,**
> **if other meat or meatballs are not used**
> **1 small onion, chopped**
> **1/2 to 1 clove (section) garlic, chopped**
> **oregano, basil, salt, pepper, to taste**
> **1 tsp. sugar, if desired**
> **nutmeg or allspice, to taste, if desired**

Utensils
> One thick 3 to 5 qt. pot with a cover

Follow directions as in Tomato Sauce #1

Suggested Use of Leftovers
> Same as for Tomato Sauce #1.

Meatballs

The following recipe will give you a more than adequate supply of meatballs for six people when served with spaghetti and sauce. It will probably feed four people when served with a vegetable and rice, noodles, or potatoes.

Suggested Ingredients

1 lb. chopped meat
1 egg
1/4 c. or more bread crumbs
1/4 c. parmesan cheese
parsley, oregano, salt, basil, pepper,
a little garlic, to taste
oil

Utensil

A frying pan

All measurements are approximate since the consistency of meats differ. Mix all ingredients together using your hands, if necessary. Add more bread crumbs if the meat does not look as if it will roll into balls. Add a little milk if the mixture seems too thick. Form balls of whatever size you desire, dipping your hands in a little water as you make each ball. The water aids in keeping the meat mixture together. Gently fry them in a frying pan lightly coated with oil. Turn the balls with a fork when they are finished browning on one side. If the meatballs seem to be sticking to the pan and falling apart, roll them around in white flour *before* putting them in the oil. Frying pans vary, and some, because their surfaces are not smooth enough, require that you use flour on the meatballs. When all sides are brown, if you are putting the meatballs in tomato sauce, you may add them at this time. Otherwise, put the browned meatballs on the coolest side of the pan, on top of one another, or in a dish. When all the meatballs are browned, they may simmer together in the frying pan, or they may be added individually to a tomato sauce. Drain off most of the oil to avoid a greasy taste.

Suggested Use of Leftovers

Reheat with sauce and pasta or make cold meatball sandwiches.

Quick Preparation

Pasta y Garlic y Onion
(y mushrooms, if you can afford them)

By now, you should be able to estimate how much noodles, macaroni, or spaghetti you can eat; so estimate all ingredients in this recipe. This can be a side dish or the main course. My mother used to cook it when she came home late or it was the day before she shopped and the only other things left in the house were some dog food and half a bottle of catsup.

Suggested Ingredients

> margarine or oil
> onion, as much as you want
> garlic, chopped, 3/4 to 1 clove (section)
> per 6-1/2-oz. dry pasta
> mushrooms (optional)
> noodles, macaroni, or spaghetti
> 1 egg for up to 1/2 lb. pasta
> salt, pepper, oregano, basil
> grated cheese

Utensils

Saucepan, frying pan

Prepare pasta according to package directions. Meanwhile, fry the onion, garlic, and mushrooms in a frying pan at a medium heat. Drain the pasta and while it's still very hot, add some margarine and the egg to it. Mix in your frying pan ingredients and your seasonings. Top with grated cheese.

Suggested Use of Leftovers

Reheat with a little water in a saucepan, or put in a greased casserole in the oven.

Quick Preparation

Stove-Top Macaroni and Cheese

This is a quick recipe which I often serve as the side dish to a meal.

Suggested Ingredients

macaroni
margarine (optional)
seasonings such as salt, basil, parsley, oregano
any type of cheese
1 egg for up to 1/2 lb. macaroni

Utensil
    Saucepan

Prepare macaroni according to package directions. Drain it when cooked and add all other ingredients, to taste. If the mixture begins to cool before the cheese is melted or the egg is cooked, return it to the stove, turn the heat to low or medium heat, and stir the combination very quickly until it is done.

Suggested Use of Leftovers
    Bake in a greased casserole. Add liquid such as milk, sauce, or water.

Pasta y Fagiole
(serves 4)

Suggested Ingredients

a clove (section) of garlic
1 onion, chopped
leftover bones (pork, chicken, beef—anything)
a little chopped meat (if you have no bones)
1 15-oz.-can tomato sauce
1/2 can (7-1/2-oz.) water
seasonings such as oregano, salt, pepper, parsley
a little (1 tsp. or less) sugar
2/3 c. (when dry) soybeans—or a can of pork and beans
elbow or other small macaroni

Utensils
    Dish for soaking soybeans; 3 qt. pot for sauce, with cover; 2 qt. saucepan for cooking soybeans, with cover; 5 qt. pot for macaroni; and a colander

Soak soybeans for 5 to 7 hours or overnight in three times as much water as beans. Using the same water, bring them to a boil and cook them for about an hour. (If you intend to cook your sauce for 3 or more hours, this additional cooking of soybeans is unnecessary.) If you are using chopped meat, brown it in the sauce pot. If you are using soybeans, drain them, and put them in the sauce pot with the garlic, onion, leftover bones, and tomato sauce. Add the half can of water and the seasonings. If you are using canned beans, do not add them until the end of the cooking process. Bring to a boil, cover, and simmer for at least an hour. Taste it to see if it needs more seasonings. Add more water to the sauce as needed to keep it thin.

Cook your macaroni according to package directions, drain it, and mix the sauce and macaroni together. Or, if you are using pork and beans, add it to the sauce 20 minutes before serving. Serve the pasta y fagiole with cheese on top.

Leftovers You Can Use
Bones.

Suggested Use of Leftovers
Reheat on the stove, adding more water if necessary.

POTATOES

Some people think it's weird to eat potato skins. Every once in a while when I'm eating with certain people, I wonder if I'm supposed to eat the potato skins. It's ridiculous how you can put yourself in stupid situations like that. Anyway, I've decided that I'm going to eat the skins when I feel like it because the skins taste good and to peel the skin of a potato in most cases is unnecessary. Yams and sweet potatoes have tougher skins which you may want to remove unless you're baking them.

Potatoes can be home fried, boiled, baked, roasted, scalloped, and even mashed without the removal of the skin. There are vitamins in the skin which we are letting go to waste when we throw it out. Potato skins, when home fried, boiled, scalloped, or mashed, have a pleasantly faint crunch to them. You'll be amazed by a newly discovered gustatory sensation.

Potatoes should be washed well as you prepare them. If you peel them, wash them after peeling. Put potatoes in a bowl of cold water as you peel them to prevent the meat from turning brown. Unpeeled potatoes should be washed well or scrubbed with a vegetable brush or clean, soapless, plastic scouring ball used for dishes. All sprouting eyes and bruises should be removed. Because unpeeled potatoes do not take as long to prepare, it is usually not necessary to put each potato in cold water as you finish slicing it because you will probably have begun cooking them by the time they have had a chance to turn brown. However, if you are preparing many potatoes you might want to put them in the water.

There are many different varieties of potatoes. The ones you're probably most used to hearing about are Maines and Idahos. The potatoes you see at the store (even though the different types may seem indistinguishable to you) usually are either Maine potatoes or Maine-like potatoes. These are your least expensive and all-purpose potatoes. They are excellent for mashing, frying, baking, or boiling. These potatoes have medium to thick skins and are usually as dark as the dirt which you might find on the potato. Idahos, in difference to your Maine-type of potatoes, are long rather than round. They generally cost more than other potatoes. Idahos are firm and more meaty and are the best baking potatoes, but they do not have the proper texture needed for good results when boiling, frying, and mashing.

In midsummer you will find light-colored, thin-skinned potatoes at the fruit and vegetable counter. These are the first potatoes of the year and are aptly called new potatoes. Some new potatoes have thin red skins. Generally, new potatoes are smaller than your other potatoes. They cook a little faster and are best if not used for baking. New potatoes, red potatoes, and Idahos have an almost vaguely sweet (but not unpleasant) taste to them.

Sweet potatoes and yams are pumpkin or mustard colored on the outside and pumpkin colored on the inside. Both are distinctly sweet.

Home Fries
(frying pan method)

Suggested Ingredients
thinly sliced, peeled or unpeeled potatoes
oil or 1/2 oil, 1/2 margarine to cover the bottom of the pan
salt
other seasonings such as pepper, oregano, paprika, basil, nutmeg

Utensil
A frying pan

Slice potatoes about 1/8- to 1/4-inch thick into an oil-coated pan. Put the burner heat at a temperature which will allow the potatoes to brown but not burn. Medium to medium-high should be a good temperature. Turn the potatoes often as they brown. Scrape the bottom of the pan where the potatoes will begin to crust first. (The crusty stuff is of course good to eat—one of the best parts.) Add more oil as it soaks into potatoes. When the potatoes are tender inside and crunchy or brown on the outside, they're done. Cooking time should be no more than half an hour.

Suggested Use of Leftovers
  Reheat in a greased or oiled frying pan.

Home Fries
(oven method)

Suggested Ingredients
  thinly sliced, peeled, or unpeeled potatoes
  oil
  salt

Utensil
  A cookie sheet or other large, flat, baking pan

Place sliced 1/8- to 1/4-inch thick potatoes on a cookie sheet. Do not pile too many potatoes on top of one another. Spread them evenly in the pan. Pour oil fairly liberally (about 1/2 cup per big pan of potatoes) over potatoes and with your hands mix oil and potatoes together. Season with salt. Put in the oven and with a spatula turn the potatoes infrequently at first and then more often as they begin to brown. Cook 30 to 45 minutes, until crunchy and brown.

Suggested Use of Leftovers
  Reheat slowly in the oven.

Quick Home Fries

Suggested Ingredients
  leftover, cold, boiled or baked potatoes
  with or without skins
  oil or 1/2 oil and 1/2 margarine
  salt
  other seasonings such as pepper,
  oregano, paprika, basil, and nutmeg

Utensil
    A frying pan

Slice cold potatoes into an oiled frying pan and follow directions for frying pan method Home Fries. The outer layer will not be as crunchy as with potatoes which have not been precooked.

Leftovers You Can Use
    Potatoes.

Suggested Use of Leftovers
    Refry.

Deluxe Home Fries

Follow directions for frying pan method for Home Fries. Add other raw vegetables such as onion, pieces of carrot, rutabaga, celery, broccoli.

Leftovers You Can Use
    Potatoes and other vegetables.

Suggested Use of Leftovers
    Refry.

Boiled Potatoes

Potatoes can be boiled whole, if they're small, or in quarters or eighths if they are larger. For reasonable cooking time, pieces should be about the size of a small egg—or smaller.

Suggested Ingredients

        potatoes
        water, salt

Utensil
    A pot with a cover

Cover potatoes with water, salt the water and let the potatoes come to a boil in the covered pot. Cook, still boiling, until tender but not mushy—about 20 minutes or more after they come to a boil. If too much water evaporates before the potatoes are done, add more. Drain and serve.

Suggested Use of Leftovers
    Add to soups, casseroles, use for Quick Home Fries, or add mayonnaise and seasonings and serve cold, or see Potato Salad recipe.

Boiled Potatoes
With Margarine Herb Sauce

Follow directions for Boiled Potatoes. Drain and cover with Margarine Herb Sauce, see recipe on page 202.

Baked Potatoes

Ingredient
well washed potatoes with skins

Utensil
    The oven rack

Put the potatoes on the oven rack near the middle of the oven and bake at 375° F. to 400° F. Cooking time depends upon the size of your potatoes and the temperament of your oven. Half an hour to an hour is a wide range estimate.

Suggested Use of Leftovers
    Add to soups or use them for Quick Home Fries.

Roasted Potatoes

Ingredients
potatoes with skins, well washed
oil

Utensil
    Some sort of baking dish

Preheat the oven to 375° F. Oil a baking dish and place quartered or eighthed potatoes skin down on the pan. Bake uncovered until a potato is tender when poked with a fork. The exposed white of the potatoes will form a crust. Baking time will be 30 minutes or more.

Suggested Use of Leftovers
    Add to soups or reheat in a covered, greased baking dish in the oven.

Roasted Potatoes
in Gravy Drippings

If you are planning to roast chicken, turkey, or any other meat, you can cook your potatoes along side the meat. Prepare the potatoes as in the recipe for Roasted

Potatoes. Thirty minutes to an hour before the meat is done, place the potatoes around the roasting dish in the drippings. Do not add oil unless your meat refuses to drip.

Suggested Use of Leftovers
    Same as for Roasted Potatoes.

Scalloped Potatoes

See the recipe under Casseroles on page 118.

Mashed Potatoes

Suggested Ingredients
    potatoes, peeled or unpeeled
    a little milk
    margarine

Utensils
    A pot with cover

Cook potatoes following directions for boiled potatoes. Drain and while still hot add a *little* milk, but not too much, and some margarine. Mash with a potato masher, fork, or the bottom of a drinking glass.

Suggested Use of Leftovers
    Add to casseroles or fry in margarine.

Potato Pancake

I bet you're imagining something which looks like a pancake. Well, you're wrong. This concoction though misnamed, tastes really good. When I suggested that it be called *"soufflé,"* my suggestion was met with a grimace by my husband, Michael, who got the recipe from his mother who got it from her mother-in-law who got it while a young girl in Lithuania. *Soufflé* sounds too French cheffy, I guess. Michael's grandmother doesn't look like a French chef. She looks more like a country woman. When she talks about Lithuania, she's sure to mention "da leetle piggies" that run in the yard. For some reason that always makes me smile.

Suggested Ingredients
peeled potatoes
1 egg per 2 to 3 c. strained potatoes
salt
2 tbsp. oil per 2 to 3 c. strained potatoes
margarine

Utensils
    A strainer, a baking dish with cover, or a bread pan with an aluminum foil cover

About ten minutes before cooking, turn on the oven to 400° F. Grate the potatoes or put them in small pieces in a blender (if someone has willed one to you). You will notice that the potatoes discolor slightly and the water and pulp separate. Put the potatoes in a strainer (not colander) or on a porous cloth, and strain out all excess water. Put the potatoes in a greased baking dish and mix in the egg, oil, and salt. Top the casserole with pats of margarine. Bake covered for about 30 to 45 minutes and uncovered for 15 minutes, or until done. The potatoes are done when the sides and top are crusty or brown. Poke the center and taste it if you're not sure. The consistency will be the slightest bit pasty. My friends think it's weird. I think it tastes great.

Suggested Use of Leftovers
    Slice into wedges and fry in margarine or oil.

Tortilla de Papas
(Argentine Potato Pancake)
(serves 5 as a side dish)

When I told my friend Inés that I was putting this book together, she began to rack her brains for some good recipes of hers that would fit into the spirit of the book. She came up with quite a few of them, and I am genuinely grateful to her. She invited me over to her house and together we cooked Pizza, Bean Salad, Pudding Float, and Sambayon one day, and another day we made Inés' Fish Dinner, and Tortilla de Papas. Eduardo and Marta, Inés' brother-in-law and sister, were visiting from Argentina and George, Martin and Jeanine (Inés's family) were there, and Michael (my family) was there. So we had a grand old time drinking Spanish wine and eating for hours. People rarely seem to really relax and enjoy their food the way we did those evenings. Most people tend to eat and run. Whenever Michael and I visit Inés and George, eating becomes more or less a ceremony. Part of it is because Inés is a good cook. Also the wine is always very nice. They are good company, and finally, they're just not up-tight people. Meals should be a time to relax and so that's exactly what they do.

Because we also made a very exotic dessert called Vacherin (which must have something to do with a cow in French) everyone was really full and there was a lot of Tortilla de Papas left over. But that was no problem because everyone just packed it cold in their lunches the next day. You'll be pleased at how good Tortilla de Papas tastes—hot or cold.

Suggested Ingredients

1/2 medium onion
5 eggs
5 small potatoes, washed and peeled or unpeeled
parsley, salt, pepper, nutmeg
1/2 c. oil, to start

Utensils

A frying pan, bowl for mixing, a draining spoon (spoon with holes in it—optional), a flat board or a large plate

Fry the onion in the oil at a medium to medium-high heat. While you are doing this, scramble the eggs in a bowl with a fork, and add the seasonings. Slice the potatoes into thin (1/8-inch) slices. When the onions are tender, take them out of the oil with the draining spoon and put them into the eggs. Using the same oil, fry the potatoes until they are cooked through. (Poke 1 or 2 with a fork to test them.) All potatoes may not fit in the pan at once, so as some finish cooking, take them out of the pan and add them to the egg mixture. Pour most of the oil out of the pan but save enough to coat the bottom of the pan. (The frying oil can be covered in a jar and saved for another recipe.) Put the potato-egg combination in the frying pan, keeping the heat at medium to medium-high. When the mixture begins to congeal, in 2 to 4 minutes, put a flat board or large plate over the frying pan, remove the pan from the heat and turn the "pancake" onto the board. Then gently slide the "pancake" back into the frying pan with the uncooked side facing down. If this sounds too confusing, after the first side is done, cut the "pancake" in half with a spatula and flip each side over onto its uncooked side. Cook until the egg has solidified or another 2 to 3 minutes. Turn the "pancake" over onto a board or plate. Serve hot or cold.

Suggested Use of Leftovers

Serve cold or reheat on a pan or cookie sheet in the oven.

Potato Salad
(serves 4 or more)

Suggested Ingredients

5 large, washed potatoes
1 stalk of celery
1/2 onion

Other Suggestions

Add:
1/2 green pepper
2 hard-boiled eggs
radishes

Sauce

3/4 c. mayonnaise
3/4 c. sour cream
1/2 tsp. dried mustard or
1 tsp. regular mustard
salt, pepper, paprika, parsley
1/4 to 1/2 clove (section) garlic

Substitute Ingredients for Sauce

3/4 c. firm yogurt for 3/4 c. sour cream

or

use 1-1/2 c. mayonnaise and the juice of 1 lemon
instead of 3/4 c. mayonnaise and 3/4 c. sour cream

Utensils

A pot for cooking potatoes, a small bowl for mixing sauce, a large bowl for mixing potato salad

Put whole, washed potatoes in a pot large enough to cover potatoes with water. Boil until tender but not falling apart. Remove potatoes from the pot and cool in cold water. Peel potatoes and slice them into a bowl in the desired size chunks. Add onion, celery and other vegetable condiments. Add eggs if you like. In a separate bowl make the sauce by combining all sauce ingredients. Gently fold the sauce into the potato mixture making sure that all potatoes are moistened. Add more mayonnaise or sour cream, if necessary, to make the mixture moist. The salad will be moister than you might expect but as it "sets," some moistness will be lost. Garnish with paprika or parsley and put it in the refrigerator to cool and set.

Leftovers You Can Use
　　Leftover boiled potatoes.

Suggested Use of Leftovers
　　Potato salad will last for quite a few days when well covered and refrigerated. If it becomes dry, add a little mayonnaise.

RICE

The three types of rice most commonly seen in the supermarket have three undeniably different tastes.

　　Instant rice takes a few minutes to cook and in my opinion is hardly worth the bother because it doesn't taste like anything except possibly kindergarten paste. Noninstant white rice when mixed with other things or, at least with lots of margarine and salt, fills you up with a little bit of flavor. But brown rice is really worth incorporating into your diet. It has a good taste and a pleasant consistency. Brown rice and white rice are the same grain except that brown rice is unpolished. The nutrients contained in the husk of the rice have been left in the brown rice. Unfortunately, most Americans haven't caught on to this great flavor so it may be hard to find brown rice at a reasonable price at your supermarket. You can probably get it very reasonably if you can acquire it somewhere in bulk. All recipes which call for rice will go well with either white or brown rice. Instant rice will probably botch up a great many dishes. Store brand rice is usually quite acceptable and can be purchased in larger quantities which means you pay less per pound.

　　Depending upon the type or brand, rice expands between two and one half and four times its original volume during the cooking process. In other words, for every one cup of dry rice you combine with a specified amount of water, you'll come up with two and one-half, three, or four cups of rice after it's cooked. Unless package directions, specify otherwise, to make rice, bring water and a little salt to a boil, stir rice into the boiling water with a fork, turn the heat down, cover the pot, and simmer until done. Done is usually accomplished in twenty to twenty-five minutes for white rice—unless otherwise specified—and forty-five minutes to an hour for brown rice.

　　Brown rice sometimes takes some minor extra preparation. It

may come to you with bits of dirt in it and it might have to be washed. To do this, either rinse it in a strainer (not colander) or pour water over it and quickly strain it with your fingers cupped over it. To cut down on the cooking time (to forty-five minutes or so) soak it in the water you will cook it in, for a few hours. Brown rice sometimes needs a little more water than the recipe calls for. Add it during the cooking process if the water has been absorbed but the rice is not done. Brown rice when done will be tender on the inside but a little chewy around the outer husk.

Many casseroles call for rice as do many vegetable, meat, and fish dishes. Leftover cooked rice can be thrown in soup, fried, or reheated with a little oil. Hot or cold rice is good with milk and a sweetener. Rice can be cooked in the pot with bouillon cubes, herbs, mushrooms, and vegetables. Rice can also be added directly to steaming meats and vegetables which you are preparing in a frying pan, providing that you have twice or three times the amount of liquid as rice. Be careful of how much rice you add to something. Remember, it expands an average of three times.

Recipes which call for rice are in other sections of this chapter as well as in this section. Some recipes in the Casserole section call for rice, or often rice is suggested to be served plain as a side dish. Most of the following rice recipes are also side dishes as the major ingredient is rice and you will want to add additional dishes to your meal.

Quick Side Dish

Fried Rice

Suggested Ingredients

precooked cold rice
1 egg per 1, 2 or 3 cups of cooked rice
soy sauce
oil

Utensil
    A frying pan

Coat the bottom of a frying pan with oil. Add the cooked rice and then enough soy sauce to taste, or until the rice turns golden. Mix in the egg. Fry at a medium-high heat turning the rice often with a spatula or spoon and scraping the bottom of the pan which will turn crusty. Continue to cook until the egg is done and the mixture is hot. Cooking takes a few minutes.

Leftovers You Can Use
    Leftover rice is great for frying. I never cook rice especially to fry. I always wait until I have some leftover.

Suggested Use of Leftovers
    Refry in oil or add to soups or casseroles.

Fancier Rice

Cook rice as usual, only add a bouillon cube to the rice water, or add onions, peppers, celery, or mushrooms. If you want to add a lot of ingredients, slightly increase the amount of water used in cooking the rice. Herbs such as basil, oregano, or dill are also good to add. Vegetables and herbs such as chives, scallions, or leek tops are a good combination.

Suggested Use of Leftovers
    Refry in oil or add to soups or casseroles.

Quick Breakfast

Cold Rice and Milk

Suggested Ingredients
> **cold, cooked, brown or white rice**
> **honey or sugar**
> **milk**

Put rice in a bowl. Add sweetener and milk to taste.

Leftovers You Can Use
    Rice.

SALADS, RAW VEGETABLES AND SALAD DRESSINGS

Tuna, egg, and potato salads are given in other sections of this chapter.

Raw vegetables and fresh salads are not things which should be reserved for diets and summer. You should take advantage of the vitamins offered by uncooked vegetables and fruits all year round.

Fruit salads may be served as desserts or with the main part of your meal. Vegetable salads are good with lunch or dinner or as a snack. They're a good type of snack to have before going to bed because they are light, thus, you don't go to bed on a full stomach and wake up the next morning with a stomachache.

All salads can be prepared quickly and easily.

Green Salad

Suggested Ingredients

leaf lettuce
chicory
romaine
escarole (endive)
spinach
carrots
onions
celery
green peppers
radishes
tomatoes

Utensil

A bowl

Use a few or all of the above ingredients. Wash all vegetables in cold water and shake off excess water or pat dry with a towel. Tear lettuce into large bite-size pieces into a bowl. Cut up other vegetables and add them to the lettuce. Mix in lemon, Italian, yogurt, cheese, or other salad dressing, or leave dressing for people to put on the salad themselves. Hint: People use less salad dressing when it is mixed into the salad for them.

Suggested Use of Leftovers
    If the salad becomes too limp to use as a salad, put it in soup, or fry the vegetables in oil.

Tomato Salad

Suggested Ingredients

fresh, ripe tomatoes
several cloves (sections) of garlic, cut in halves, thirds or quarters
oil
salt
oregano

Utensil
    A bowl

Cut tomatoes into bite-size pieces into a bowl. Add cut garlic and season the salad with salt and oregano. Pour on enough oil to slightly coat the tomatoes. Mix the oil in and refrigerate the salad for a while so that the ingredients will soak into one another. The garlic should not be eaten unless you are trying to keep vampires or the landlord away. Warn people that they are in the salad. The garlic does a good job of flavoring the salad.

Suggested Use of Leftovers
    This salad will stay fairly fresh for two days.

THE EMPEROR'S NARCISSUS

I was riding the number five train from Grand Central to 180th Street in the Bronx one afternoon in October. A stereotyped drunk with three or four days growth of beard entered the car a few stops past Grand Central. Everyone in the car, pretended not to notice the man.
    "Shut up!" he screeched in a horrible high pitched voice which reminded me of a mynah bird. People quickly lowered their eyelids as he weaved his way down the aisle. He sat next to me. I sat back and began to play the cool New York subway rider. The object of the game is to act so casual that you look as if you live on the subway. My inebriated seatmate sat there—smelling like a brewery—and began to chant:

"The emperor's narcissus. The emperor's narcissus," he recited over and over again with careful intonation in his mynah bird voice. People in the car began to stiffen in attempts to suppress laughter. I couldn't resist sneaking a look at him. As I did, he looked at me in a threatening way and raised the *Daily News* he was holding over my head and laughed maniacally. I thought I was going to be sick. My cool subway rider game ended.

"You stay away from me," I stammered stupidly.

In a very prissy way, as if offended, he got up and headed for the next car. Before opening the door, he turned around and screeched: "Shut up!" while looking straight at me. The car dissolved into those giggles which had been suppressed for minutes.

If you're looking for the moral of this story or the symbolism behind it, shut up.

Quick Meal

After the Subway in Summer Spinach Salad

After dragging my body off of the subway where it's ninety degrees outside (and 110 degrees on the train) there's no way that I'm going to be able to cook or eat a hot meal. The following recipe is suggested to cool and calm you down. It's almost as good as owning an electric fan.

Suggested Ingredients

fresh spinach with stalks
radishes
green peppers
olives
cheese
celery
cold meat (ham, turkey, chicken, etc.)
carrots
pickles
escarole
chicory
tomatoes

Utensil
    A bowl

Use some (or all) of the above ingredients and add anything else you like. Wash all vegetables carefully and shake off excess water. Put ingredients in a bowl and mix in Yogurt Salad Dressing, French Dressing, or Italian Dressing. (See recipes for all three salad dressings.) This salad, depending upon what and how much you add, can make a very substantial lunch by itself, or a light dinner.

Suggested Use of Leftovers
    If the salad is too limp to use again as a salad, throw it in a soup or fry it in oil.

Apple and Carrot Salad

Suggested Ingredients
apples—cored but not peeled
carrots
nuts or sunflower seeds
mayonnaise
lemon

Utensil
    A bowl

Cut washed and cored apples and the carrots into a bowl. Sprinkle in a few nuts or seeds. Add mayonnaise—enough to thinly coat all ingredients—and lemon to taste. Serve with the meal or alone.

Suggested Use of Leftovers
    This salad will stay fresh and edible for several days.

Fruit Salad

Use Any of the Following Ingredients
grapefruits
oranges
bananas
melons
pears
apples
peaches

>   any other fruit
>   Dressing (optional):
>   lemon juice
>   cinnamon
>   nutmeg
>   honey or sugar

Utensil
> A bowl

Wash all fruits with edible skins. Squeeze some of the grapefruit and orange juice into your bowl. Throw in the pulp and the sections which have not been squeezed. Cut up other fruits and put them in the bowl. Squeeze in lemon juice and cinnamon, nutmeg, and honey or sugar according to taste. Do not put in a lot of sweetener as the fruits will become sweeter as they sit with one another. Refrigerate and allow fruits to soak into each other. If you must serve the salad immediately, it will still taste good.

Suggested Use of Leftovers
> The salad should taste good for several days.

Raw Vegetables

Suggested Ingredients
>   raw cauliflower
>   raw cabbage
>   radishes
>   celery

Utensils
> None

Serve washed and sliced raw vegetables just as they are or with thick salad dressing to dunk them in.

Green Bean Salad

Suggested Ingredients
>   green beans (fresh or frozen)
>   1 or 2 hard-boiled eggs
>   a little oil
>   a little lemon
>   salt

Utensils
> A pot for the eggs, a pot for the beans, a bowl

Hard boil the eggs. Cook the beans, drain them, and refrigerate the beans and eggs until they are cold. Then cut up the eggs and combine them with the beans. Add just enough oil to coat the beans and enough to nicely flavor them. Add lemon and salt to taste.

Suggested Use of Leftovers
> This salad will stay fresh for several days.

DRESSINGS

Italian Salad Dressing

Suggested Ingredients

> **oil**
> **vinegar**
> **salt**
> **seasonings such as oregano, basil, dill, parsley**

Use about 2 tablespoons of oil for every teaspoon of vinegar or according to taste. Mix your ingredients right into the salad. Do not overdrench the salad. Lightly coat it. If preferred, mix dressing in a bowl or jar.

Suggested Use of Leftovers
> Store any unused dressing in the refrigerator.

Cheese Salad Dressing

Follow directions for Italian Dressing. Sprinkle grated cheese into the salad and/or dressing. Toss the salad.

Suggested Use of Leftovers
> Same as for Italian Dressing.

French Salad Dressing

Suggested Ingredients

> **2 tbsp. mayonnaise**
> **2 tbsp. catsup**
> **1 tsp. vinegar or lemon**
> **sprinkles of black pepper, basil, and paprika**

Utensil
>A small bowl

Mix all ingredients together and pour over salad. Or leave in a small bowl so the dressing can be put on each individual serving of salad.

Suggested Use of Leftovers
>If you do not pour the dressing over the salad, refrigerate the dressing in a bowl, but put a cover over it so that the top does not become hard.

Yogurt Salad Dressing
(2 to 3 servings)

Suggested Ingredients
>**2 tbsp. plain yogurt (or commercial sour cream)**
>**2 tbsp. mayonnaise**
>**1 very small section** *finely* **chopped garlic (optional)**
>**1 tsp. parmesan cheese**
>**salt, pepper, and parsley**

Mix all ingredients together and pour over salad, or leave the dressing in a small dish for people to put over their own salad. The mixture may also be used as a dip for vegetables such as raw carrots, cauliflower, cabbage, radishes, and celery if your yogurt is not too thin.

Suggested Use of Leftovers
>Cover and store in the refrigerator.

SANDWICHES

It's always convenient when your leftovers will provide you with lunch for the following day. Chances are, that if you eat away from home, sandwiches are the most practical thing to carry along.

Sandwiches can be made from leftover cold fried liver, eggplant, fried fish, meat loaf, or sliced turkey or chicken. Salads for sandwiches can be made from the night before's turkey, chicken, fish, or vegetables.

Of course, there's not always something left over and even if there is, it might be difficult to make a soup sandwich. In that case you can make something like tuna or egg salad, sardine salad, or cheese, lettuce and tomato. You can also turn omelettes or scrambled eggs into a sandwich. The old standbys are peanut butter or cream cheese and jelly or jam. They still taste good, even when you're not a kid—and peanut butter and cream cheese are good for you. (Marshmallow Fluff, if you're still hung up on that, is not very good for you but would probably not do much harm if eaten occasionally.) Luncheon meats such as bologna, salami, chicken loaf, liverwurst, and others, are all overpriced and contain many fillers and preservatives. I don't recommend them. The following are some sandwich recipes, but you should be able to think of many more.

Egg Salad
(3 or more sandwiches)

Suggested Ingredients

4 hard-boiled eggs
mayonnaise
a stalk of celery
squeeze of lemon (optional)
salt, pepper, and other seasonings
such as oregano, basil, dill,
parsley, paprika

Peel and chop egg. Cut up celery, mix all ingredients together. Add enough mayonnaise to make the eggs moist but not runny. If you are low on eggs, add more celery.

Tuna and other Salads
(makes 3 or more sandwiches)

Suggested Ingredients

1 6-1/2- or 7-oz. can of tuna
a little onion (optional)
mayonnaise
1 stalk of celery
a squeeze of lemon (optional)
1 tsp. of relish (optional)
seasonings such as
pepper, paprika, dill,
parsley, oregano

Drain oil or water from tuna. Loosen tuna with a fork. Cut up celery and onion and add enough mayonnaise so that tuna is moist but not runny. Add seasonings as desired. To increase the volume of the tuna, add more celery. You can make fish salad the same way, using last night's leftover fish if you like. Or, try a can of drained, cut up sardines, leftover chicken or turkey.

Vegetable Salad

Use leftover cooked broccoli, carrots, beans, or other vegetables combined with the same ingredients as other sandwich salads. Or, just add a few pieces of vegetables to tuna, chicken, sardine, or other salads, if you want to increase their volume. Vegetable sandwiches may be a little runny, but who cares? It's good food.

Roasted Pepper Sandwiches

Suggested Ingredients

Bell or Italian peppers
salt
margarine or vegetable oil

Optional

sliced potatoes
sausage
scrambled eggs

Lightly coat the bottom of a frying pan with oil. Add sliced, raw peppers. Cover the pan and steam until peppers are tender. Add salt. Serve on a sandwich, hot or cold. For a pepper and potato sandwich, fry the potatoes first, and add the peppers when they're 3/4 done, cover and cook until tender. For a sausage, pepper and potato sandwich, cook the sausage with the potatoes, then add the peppers and cook as above. Or, add eggs to the tender peppers and scramble them up for a scrambled eggs and pepper sandwich.

Fried Egg Sandwiches

Suggested Ingredients

egg
desired seasonings
margarine

Melt enough margarine in a frying pan at medium heat to coat the bottom of the pan. Add an egg and break the yolk when done on one side, flip it to the other side and cook until not loose or runny. Season. Serve as a hot or cold sandwich. Add catsup, if desired and no gourmet cooks are looking. (You can also make sandwiches out of omelettes or scrambled eggs—see the Eggs section).

Melted Cheese Sandwiches

"Grilled" cheese sandwiches may be cooked in a variety of ways. They can be broiled, put on a grill, or fried.

Suggested Ingredients
> **slices of any type of cheese**
> **bread**
> **margarine or oil**

Utensils
> A grill or frying pan and a frying pan cover or a broiler and a pan under it

For grilled or fried cheese sandwiches, spread the "wrong" sides (the outside) of the sandwich with margarine, or oil the grill or frying pan. Set the pan at a medium high to high heat and lower it when necessary to prevent burning. Put cheese in between the bread and then fry the sandwich on one side until brown. Flip the sandwich over and cover it with the frying pan top. When the second side is done, and the cheese is melted, your sandwich is done.

For broiled cheese sandwiches, toast 2 pieces of bread on one side under the broiler. When they are brown, put the cheese on them and top with an untoasted piece of bread. Let the untoasted side face the broiler and broil until the cheese is melted. You can make open-face melted cheese sandwiches by skipping the top piece of bread and melting the cheese until it's golden brown.

Suggested Use of Leftovers
> Reheat by oiling a frying pan and steaming the sandwich with a cover at a medium heat or put the sandwich in an oven and heat until warm.

SAUCES AND GRAVIES

Through the section on Cream Sauce which follows, you should be able to get some ideas about sauces in general. Basically, they should enhance whatever you've cooked. Their purposes are to make something moister, interesting, or more interesting. Once you know how to make a few basic sauces, you can develop many more using the original recipes as guides.

CREAM SAUCE

A few recipes in this book call for cream sauce or a cream sauce base. Because cream sauce is such a helpful concoction for combining and covering something that is otherwise lacking much personality, I think it merits discussion.

Cream sauce can be created in proportions of approximately one tablespoon of flour, to one cup of liquid, to one tablespoon of margarine. These are your basic ingredients. They are combined by slowly adding the flour to the melted margarine in a pot and gradually adding the liquid and then stirring constantly on not too hot a burner. If you discover that the sauce is not as thick as you want it to be, do not just sprinkle in more flour because you will create instant lumps. Instead, mix more flour with some liquid in a separate bowl, making it a pourable consistency. Pour it into the cream sauce and continue cooking until the desired consistency is reached.

Cream sauces may be used on vegetables like spinach, asparagus, and broccoli, as a base for vegetable soup, as a thickener in stews, casseroles, and pot pies, as a base for creamed chicken, and as a topping for broiled chicken.

Some cream sauces are made with milk, while others are made with bouillon and water or soup stock (though they may not be technically considered to be cream sauce since they lack milk). Varied ingredients may be added like herbs, cheeses, eggs, and mushrooms. When making cream sauce with milk, I quite often use a store brand powdered milk mixed first with water. With the increasing price of milk (along with everything else), I do not like to "waste" whole milk. A powdered milk cream sauce tastes quite good.

Suggested Use of Leftovers

Reheat any of the following cream sauces by slowly adding more milk while stirring. Or add to soups or casseroles.

Cheese Sauce

Suggested Ingredients

a cream sauce recipe
grated or chunk cheese
paprika, salt, pepper, and other seasonings

Utensil

A saucepan

Simply add cheese, to taste, to a basic cream sauce. Heat the sauce gently so that the cheese will melt. Add seasonings. Serve over fish, vegetables, eggs, or use in casseroles.

Herb, Wine and Mushroom Cream Sauces

Suggested Ingredients

cream sauce
a little salt
herbs such as basil, oregano,
dill, thyme, or sage
or, wine
or, mushrooms

Utensil

A saucepan

For herb cream sauce, add herbs to taste to a cream sauce. Allow them to soak into the sauce before serving, so that their flavors will permeate the combination. Serve over fish, fowl, or vegetables, or use in casseroles.

For a wine-flavored cream sauce, add about a tablespoon of dry wine or any other kind of wine (including rotgut) per cup of cream sauce along with a little bit of herbs if you like. Again, allow it to soak into the sauce as it gently simmers.

For mushroom cream sauce, you need to gently fry a few mushrooms in margarine. Then add them to the cream sauce, with a little wine and seasonings if you like.

Bottom of the Pan Gravy

Juice which drips off of meat and into your baking pan can be used as a very tasty gravy. Even the stuff which crusts and dries onto the pan is excellent.

Suggested Ingredients

meat drippings
a little boiling water (to loosen drippings)
more hot water
1 tbsp. flour per cup of water
bouillon cube or soy sauce
seasonings, if needed

Utensils

The pan or a saucepan

Loosen the gravy with a *little* boiling water poured into the pan. If your pan can be used directly on the burner, cook the gravy in the pan. Otherwise, transfer the water and drippings to a saucepan. Gradually stir the flour into the drippings, and then slowly add your other water. If the combination is not thick enough, take out a little water, add more flour to it, and pour it into the gravy. Add part or all of a crushed bouillon cube or some soy sauce if the gravy needs more flavor. Season with herbs.

Giblet Gravy

Giblets are the neck, gizzard, liver, and heart of a chicken, turkey or other fowl. These pieces, when cooked, chopped up, and combined with Bottom of the Pan Gravy, make an excellent gravy.

Suggested Ingredients

giblets
a little celery, with leaves, if desired
a little onion
Bottom of the Pan Gravy recipe using your water stock
from the giblets instead of usual water
water
salt

Utensils

The baking pan and a saucepan

Put the giblets in a pot with the celery, onion, and salt and a few cups of water.

Allow the combination to come to a boil and then let it simmer for an hour or until the meat can be easily picked off the neck. Take the giblets out of the water and then save the water (which is now stock) for making the gravy.

On a cutting board cut up the heart, gizzard, and liver into small pieces. Remove and discard the gristle which you'll find on the gizzard. (No one wants a gristly gizzard—it's too much of a mouthful in more ways than one.) The meat from the neck should be stripped off as best you can, but don't expect to get all the meat off.

Make your gravy following the recipe for Bottom of the Pan Gravy, using the giblet stock instead of water. Do not oversalt the gravy, as you've already put salt in the giblet water. Add the giblets to the gravy either before or after you thicken the gravy.

Suggested Use of Leftovers

Reheat in a saucepan on the stove. Add more water to thin, if necessary.

Margarine Herb Sauce

Suggested Ingredients

margarine
herbs such as basil, parsley, oregano
a little salt and pepper, as needed

Utensil

A saucepan

Slowly melt margarine in a saucepan. Add herbs and allow the mixture to gently simmer as the flavor of the herbs soak in. Serve over vegetables—especially potatoes. Two potatoes require about 2 tablespoons of margarine sauce.

Suggested Use of Leftovers

Reheat in a pan on the stove.

Marinade or Barbecue Sauce

This conglomeration has many varieties and many different uses. Pork chops, lamb shank, chicken, and probably many other things can be doused with or soaked in this sauce.

There are choices of many ingredients to use and you will probably think of others. Some of these ingredients are:

1 part honey, molasses, brown sugar, or white sugar
1 part catsup or chili sauce
1 part soy sauce or Worcestershire sauce
drops of lemon, vinegar, or wine
pepper and other seasonings

Utensil
    A bowl for mixing

If you don't have many of these ingredients, don't worry. A sauce can be made with say, honey and soy sauce, excluding catsup or chili sauce. In fact, in some recipes, you may not want catsup, even though in my opinion it hasn't spoiled any sauce I've made. Honey or molasses would probably be the most desirable sweeteners in the sauce, though sugar, dissolved in a little hot water will pass.

    The last sauce I made was for pork chops. It was made from:

1 tbsp. honey
1 tbsp. catsup
a dash of thyme
a dash of pepper
1 tbsp. soy sauce
a squeeze of lemon

This is to say that you should only use this recipe as a guide. Put in molasses, take out the honey, add Worcestershire sauce, do whatever tastes good to you, or whatever you can do with the ingredients you've got.

    This book is a little bit about the freedom to create. So invent your own sauce.

    For use of this sauce, soak or brush any meat in the sauce—soak for 30 minutes to many hours or just brush it on and bake. Bake the meat in a baking dish or pan at 350° F. to 400° F. until the meat is done when sliced with a knife.

Suggested Use of Leftovers
    Reuse as a marinade or barbecue sauce in the same way, adding more liquid if necessary.

SOUP

Soup can play an important part in your diet. It's economical and can be served often because it is a variety of things. It can be made in many different ways, so you are not likely to tire of it.

Soup is one of those dishes that takes "hours to cook" but does not take hours of preparation. When cooking soup, you do just a little more than sit on your rear end and wait for the stove to do its thing. Your only real task when preparing soup is throwing in the ingredients, tasting the mixture several times, adding what is missing, removing meat from the bone, and skimming off the fat.

Some people think that homemade soup is a really glamorous item. I make it because it's fantastically cheap. Some weeks are so bad financially that if it wasn't for homemade soup, we would be eating nothing but potatoes and coming down with a vitamin-deficiency disease like scurvy.

There are a variety of ways of rationalizing your way out of making soup. You could say that you do not have much spare time to spend in your apartment watching some stupid pot bubble and that you are dubious about leaving an unattended stove burner on while you are out. The fact is that you can cook the soup all day long all at once, or you can cook it for a few hours at a time, or, finally, you can put the soup on the stove sporadically as you are coming and going from your apartment over a period of, say, two days. Let the soup cook while you are trimming your whiskers, or plucking your eyebrows, or whatever your thing is. Even if the soup is on the stove for only half an hour, it's cooking; all those great natural flavors of the bones, herbs, and vegetables are synthesizing and becoming one great tasting, nutritional, economical meal.

Meat ingredients for soup are usually available at the supermarket. Such items include beef and pork neckbones with enough meat on them, and, if you're lucky, you might find a ham bone with enough meat on it to make a soup. You might want to try grubbing soup bones directly from a butcher or meat market. Who knows? You might get a good deal. Chicken and turkey soup may be made from necks, gizzards, hearts, backs, and the general carcass. I usually freeze those parts each time I buy a bird until I have enough collected to make a big soup.

Aside from being cheap, soup is fun to make. It gives you a chance to utilize your creative abilities—and your leftovers. You will eventually find that no two soups you make will be alike. You will want to use the things which you have in your refrigerator at the time—unless you don't have *anything*—rather than making a special, expensive trip to the supermarket for some ingredient.

Soups may be served with biscuits, dumplings, omelettes, salads, or anything else you like. The soup recipes in this book are intended to create a generous soup which should satisfy a supper-type hunger.

Beef Neckbone Soup

This recipe may be used as a guide for making practically any meat soup. You can use a large variety of ingredients. The "suggested ingredients" are meant as a guide.

Suggested Ingredients

    3 or more neckbones with some meat on them
    1 onion
    2 or more bay leaves
    1 tsp. or more parsley
    1 tsp. or more basil
    4 carrots
    2 stalks celery
    salt as needed
    2 potatoes or raw or cooked noodles or 1 c. cooked rice
    beef bouillon cube(s) (optional)

Other Options
Practically any vegetables like escarole, spinach, beans, turnip, peas; more seasonings such as oregano, paprika, black pepper

Utensils
    A 5 qt. or larger pot with a cover

Brown neckbones in the pot using a little oil or margarine if desired. Add a little water plus onion, seasonings, and celery. Cover and let the ingredients soak into each other for 15 minutes or so. Then fill the pot a few inches from the top with water. Add your other vegetables such as carrots, and potatoes in the last hour or so. Cooked rice or raw or cooked noodles may be added toward the end. Cover and bring the mixture to a slow boil and allow the soup to cook at a low heat. If after a few hours, the soup tastes like nothing, add bouillon and more seasonings. Don't be discouraged though, because the flavor is a long time coming.

After a few hours, or the next day, if you like, take the bones out of the pot with a draining spoon and tear the meat off the bones. Throw away the obvious gristle and fat, and return the meat and large bones to the pot. The bones will continue to add flavor to the soup. Or, just leave everything on the bones and serve the soup with bones and let each person tear the meat off.

The soup may be cooked from about 4 hours to a day. When you are ready, serve immediately or remove the pot from the heat and put it in the refrigerator overnight. Wait for the fat to cake on the top of the soup and then remove the fat. The fat may or may not appear depending upon how fatty the bones were. The older the soup is (within reason), and the more times it is reheated, the better it tastes.

Serve with biscuits, salad, dumplings, omelettes, or anything you want.

Leftovers You Can Use
    Any or all ingredients used may be leftovers.

Suggested Use of Leftovers
    Reheat, adding extra water if necessary.

Pork Neckbone Soup

Suggested Ingredients
    3 or more pork neckbones with some meat on them
    other ingredients are the same as beef neckbone soup, including beef or chicken bouillon, if desired

Other Options
    dillweed
    1/2 to 3/4 c. dried barley (presoaked)
    1/2 to 3/4 c. dried beans of any variety (presoaked)

Utensils
    5 qt. or larger pot with cover, a pot and cover for cooking beans or barley.

Follow the directions for beef neckbone soup, adding more bay leaves, if needed, and adding some dillweed for a different flavor. While the soup is cooking, soak the beans or barley in 3 times as much water as beans or barley for a few hours (if you are using both beans and barley, you can soak them together). Be sure that there is enough water to cover them at all times. Cook the beans and barley in a separate pot with the soaking water, until fairly tender. Add the beans and/or barley to the soup pot along with the water they cooked in, a few hours before serving the soup. Add other ingredients as in Beef Neckbone Soup.

Leftovers You Can Use
   Vegetables and bones.

Suggested Use of Leftovers
   Reheat adding more liquid, if necessary.

Chicken or Turkey Soup

Suggested Ingredients
**chicken or turkey bones, any or all parts including the carcass, backs, and necks; these bones can be raw or cooked
gizzards, hearts, and livers (optional)
other desired ingredients as suggested in Beef Neckbone Soup**

Utensils
   A 5 qt. pot or larger with cover

Put bones in the pot and cover them with water and allow the water to come to a boil if they are raw bones. As soon as it boils, drain out the water, remove the bones from the pot, wash the pot, and then put the bones back into the pot. This seemingly ridiculous process will make sense to you as you do it. You will notice that a lot of dirt and scum will float to the top and sides of your pot. This boiling will help make a cleaner soup. If your bones are cooked, ignore this process.
   Pour water over the bones and fill the pot a few inches from the top. Then follow directions as in Beef Neckbone Soup. Add gizzards, hearts, and livers along with the vegetables.

Leftovers You Can Use
   Bones and vegetables.

Suggested Use of Leftovers
   Reheat adding more liquid, if necessary.

SOUP STOCK

Advance preparation of soup stock makes soup creation an extremely simple process. If you have some reserve stock, you can make a soup within 20 minutes. If you cook a chicken, turkey, steak, or anything with bones, save all the bones. Grab them off of people's plates. (Once the bones boil, even if people have been chewing on them, you won't be contaminated.) Raw bones can also be used for soup stock. If you are boning a chuck steak while preparing a steak as suggested in the meat section of this chapter, do not throw these precious bones away. Use them in soup stock or soup. Wash the raw bones before using them to remove bone splinters. Throw all bones into a large pot containing water, salt, bay leaf, and other seasonings, cover and cook for a few hours. You can also save various bones for up to five to seven days in the refrigerator, and then cook all your accumulated bones together as stock. Also, bones can be frozen for weeks in the freezer compartment of your refrigerator. You can mix chicken bones with beef bones—or use any combination of bones. Drain the bones from the pot and store the stock well covered in the freezer or refrigerator. Use it in various recipes as suggested in other sections of this chapter, or make it into soup. To make soup from stock, follow the next recipe.

Stock can be prepared while you are occupying yourself around the apartment. Covered, a good stock will cook in four hours. The four hours the stock takes to cook does not have to be all at once. Do it at intervals when you are in your apartment, and refrigerate the unfinished stock in the pot while you're out.

If you make your soup stock in advance, you will be able to prepare a soup meal in no time at all, as shown in the following recipe.

Quick Preparation

Soup Stock Soup

Suggested Ingredients

soup stock
onions, potatoes, carrots, rutabagas, cabbage, or any other vegetable, cut into small pieces
salt and desired herbs
a little tomato paste or other canned tomato product (optional)

Utensils
   A saucepan with cover for vegetables, a larger pot with cover

Cook all vegetables in a little water in a saucepan. Begin to heat up your soup stock and herbs in the larger pot. When the vegetables are tender, add them to the pot of stock along with the water the vegetables cooked in. Add more water to the soup to increase its volume, if desired. Also add a little tomato paste to the soup to add an extra flavor. When the soup is hot, serve it.

Leftovers You Can Use
   Vegetables.

Suggested Use of Leftovers
   Reheat adding more liquid if necessary.

Stone Soup

As a child I remember being fascinated by a fairy tale about a traveler who came hungry to the cottage of a stingy old lady who said she was out of food. He claimed that he could make a soup out of three small stones and a pot of water. Intrigued by the idea, she got some stones and he preceded to make the soup. Every so often he'd say something like: "Ah, if we only had some carrots, the flavor of these stones would be greatly improved." "Well, maybe I have a few carrots," the woman said and got them. He added the carrots to the soup and stirred for awhile and said, "Oh, for one small potato in this soup, but poor woman, I understand, you have nothing in your cupboard." "Now, I do recall that I have one precious potato left," she said, and she rounded it up. And so it went until there was actually meat in the soup and the two of them sat down to this fabulous soup which, miraculous as it may seem, was made with only three small stones.

Suggested Ingredients
3 small stones
leftover salads, vegetables, meats, bones, biscuits, pot pie, gravy seasonings, soy sauce, bouillon

Utensils
   A pot with cover

To a pot of water, add whatever happens to be in your refrigerator. Season to taste and cook for several hours until it tastes good. This is a good recipe for using up many of your leftovers.

Leftovers You Can Use
   Any ingredients.

Suggested Use of Leftovers
   Reheat in a pot adding more liquid if necessary.

Earth Soup

Beets taste very "earthy" for the obvious reason that they are grown underground. Add 2 or 3 beets to Stone Soup, Beef Neckbone Soup, or any other soup, and you will feel a communion with nature. Also, beets have a distinctive but subtle flavor which may eliminate the need for a bouillon cube.

Leftovers You Can Use
   Any ingredients—however beets used for the first time will taste more "earthy."

Suggested Use of Leftovers
   Reheat in a pot adding more liquid if necessary.

Three-Day Soup

Soup can be expanded in various ways. For example, cook any soup the first day and serve it. On the second day, add more water and some beets (earth soup). On the third day, add more water, seasonings, and tomatoes, or some other vegetable, or leftover green salad. You might even be able to stretch it to Four-, Five-, or Six-Day Soup. This is another soup in which you may use up some of your leftovers.

Leftovers You Can Use
   Any ingredients.

Suggested Use of Leftovers
   Reheat in a pot adding more liquid if necessary.

Fish Chowder

Suggested Ingredients
   1/2 lb. any type fresh or frozen boned fish
   3-1/2 c. milk (powdered or whole)
   2 bay leaves
   chives, scallions, or a small onion

salt, pepper, paprika, nutmeg, thyme,
parsley, soy sauce to taste
2 tbsp. margarine
flour
celery with or without leaves

Utensils
Medium-sized saucepan with cover

Chop celery and onion in a saucepan which is set at a medium heat. Fry them with the margarine. Add bay leaves to this mixture. Put milk in the saucepan, cut up the fish (no need to thaw it), remove skin if desired and add the fish to the milk. Turn the heat to medium-low and add all other ingredients except flour. Add seasonings in moderation, at first. Later, taste the soup and add extra seasonings if needed. Do not allow the soup to boil, since this will cause the milk to curdle. If the soup does curdle, it will still taste good. Once the soup is steaming, if a slight thickness is desired, remove 1/4 cup or so of soup, add a few tablespoons of flour to the 1/4 cup of soup, stir, and pour the mixture back into the soup and stir for a few minutes. Cover the soup, keeping it at a very low heat and cook for 20 to 30 minutes.

This entire process takes less than an hour.

Leftovers You Can Use
Fish.

Suggested Use of Leftovers
Reheat slowly.

Borscht

More than once, I've worked as a janitor to support myself. It's good work because no one bugs you and you're usually allowed to work at your own pace. When I was a student, I had a job cleaning office buildings from 6:00 to 10:00 at night. I would arrive there at 6:00, finish my work around 8:00, and then "sneak" into the bathroom to study until 10:00. My boss knew about it—in fact he might have given me the idea. My last cleaning job was a temporary one in a Clark, New Jersey, factory with a man originally from the Ukraine, named Walter (or "Valter," as he said). Walter was of an indistinguishable age. He wore a grey uniform, and I never could tell if he was fat, thin, tall, or short. I would pass Walter about thirty times a day, and each time he would smile and say, "Don't vork too hard," or "Why don't you take a leetle break?" Walter had had his job for about 10 years, and he did not look tense or overworked.

While I cleaned cigarette butts and coffee stains (and often cigarette butts ground into wet coffee) from cafeteria tables and floors, some of the workers would talk to me about their fellow workers who had made the repulsive messes and expected Walter and myself to clean them up. Walter walked in on such a conversation once. The mess never seemed to bother him—he had stoically accepted it long before. The worker, Willy, was ranting and raving about "all the slobs" and Walter calmly said to Willy:

"I seen you squash a cigarette butt under your foot dee udder day." He gave me an evil grin and winked.

"You *never* seen me do such a thing!" screamed Willy. Walter smiled.

"Doesn't it bother you?" asked Willy. Instead of answering, Walter told a story.

"I vas cleanin' da men's room one day, I had just finished vashin' da floors. A man stands by da door and says, 'Please, please, I haf to go.' O.K., says I, come on. Da man comes in like dis," says Walter. Walter at this point tucks his arms behind his back and like a little sprite-like creature, delicately tiptoes to the imaginary urinal.

"Da man does his business," continues Walter, who sways back and forth in front of the imaginary urinal, "Valks back like dis," carefully tiptoes Walter, who is now holding an imaginary cigarette, "and does like dis." Walter throws down the imaginary cigarette on the imaginary wet floor and violently squashes it with his foot. Walter's face remains calm and serene as he does this, and continues to tiptoe out of the make-believe bathroom.

" 'Oh, I'm sorry' says da man," continues Walter in reference to the squashed cigarette. " 'I forgot.' "

Walter lived in a small city, but having been accustomed to the Ukrainian countryside, he adapted some country ways to his small house lot. He had a garden there. One of his very favorite vegetables was beets. "Vee Ukrainians really like beets," he would say. As he harvested the beets, he would dig a hole and bury them, creating a mini-root cellar. For Easter, he would unearth them and his wife would make Borscht.

Suggested Ingredients

        5 beets, peeled and sliced or grated
        juice of 1 lemon
        1 onion
        2 bay leaves
        1 clove (section) garlic cut into very small pieces
        6 c. water
        spare ribs or bones with some meat on them or 3 to 4 strips of bacon (or substitute 1 to 2 c. water with soup stock)
        1/4 head of cabbage

Utensils

    3 qt. pot with cover

If you are using bacon, cut it in 1 to 2 inch pieces and fry it in the soup pot. When fairly crisp, drain out most of the fat but leave some. For other meat, fry it in the pot for a few minutes until its surface is browned. Add all other ingredients in any order except cabbage. Keep the heat at medium or medium-high. Cover the pot and wait for the soup to come to a boil. Every so often, with a metal spoon, remove the foam which forms on top of the soup. When it starts to boil, lower the heat and let it simmer for 20 to 30 minutes. During the last 15 minutes, add shredded cabbage. Taste the soup during the last few minutes. If it needs more flavor, add a bouillon cube. If it is too sour, add 1 teaspoon of sugar.

    Walter's wife also puts the Borscht in sweet cream. This, however, is not necessary. The soup does not lack anything without it. She puts 1 to 2 tablespoons of cream in everyone's bowl. She allows the soup to cool a little and then pours it over the cream. If this process is done in reverse, the cream will curdle.

    Borscht tastes very good with Eggs and Broccoli in Cream Sauce.

Leftovers You Can Use

    Meat or bones.

Suggested Use of Leftovers

    Reheat.

Vegetable Soup

    Here's a no soupbone, no fish, no stock soup invented by my sister, Cathy. You can add chopped meat to it if you want, but all it really requires is a lot of vegetables. If you have a pressure cooker, the soup can be cooked in 20 minutes. Otherwise, it takes a little longer.

Suggested Ingredients

**All quantities of the ingredients are approximate—add everything according to preference.
2 or 3 carrots
1/3 medium-size red cabbage
2 or 3 stalks of celery with leaves
2 medium-size onions
1 large (28-oz.) can whole tomatoes with juice,
or a 4-oz. can of tomato paste
2 bouillon cubes (any type, if desired)
parsley, pepper, salt, garlic, oregano, to taste
water: if using canned tomatoes, the total liquid in the pot should be 2 qt. including the juice from the tomatoes.
If using tomato paste, *add* 2 qt. water.**

Utensils

Pressure cooker or 5 qt. saucepan

Wash and slice, pare or chop all vegetables. Throw everything in the pot. Cook at a medium-high heat until the vegetables are tender. Or, cook in a pressure cooker at 15 pounds for 20 minutes.

For variety, brown about 3/4 pound of chopped meat. Drain off the excess fat and put the meat in the cooked soup. Let the mixture simmer for several minutes.

Leftovers You Can Use

Chopped meat and vegetables.

Suggested Use of Leftovers

Reheat adding more liquid, if necessary.

Bean or Pea Soup

The following recipe can be used with limas, pinto beans, lentils, split peas, and probably a few other beans. Use the recipe freely and vary it according to taste.

Suggested Ingredients

**1-1/2 c. beans or peas
1 tsp. celery seed
6 to 8 peppercorns (or pepper)**

3 bay leaves
5 cups boiling water
1 tsp. sugar
2 medium-size onions
1 ham bone with leftover meat on it, or
3 strips of bacon or pork bones
4 cloves
1/2 c. milk (or more)
sherry (very optional)

Utensils
   A 5 qt. pot with cover

In 3 times the amount of water as beans, clean and soak your beans for several hours—or follow the bean package directions. Leaving the beans in the water, add them to the bone, seasonings, and boiling water in a covered pot, and cook the combination until the beans are tender and the soup has flavor. If you use peas, you may want to press them through a sieve or strainer to mush them. Cut any remaining meat off the bone and add it to the soup. Add milk to the soup if it is too thick. Add sugar, sherry, salt, and pepper to taste. Serve with toast, crackers, or grilled cheese sandwiches.

Leftovers You Can Use
   Bone and some vegetables.

Suggested Use of Leftovers
   When reheating, you may have to thin this soup more than you do others. Thin with water or milk.

STEW

Any vegetable and/or meat combination which sits in a pot for awhile mixing its juices together could probably be classified as stew. If people cook something and they don't know what to call it, they usually end up calling it stew.

Typical stew meat can be purchased precut. You can also cut your own from inexpensive steaks which are thick enough and have enough fat so that they won't shrink up into a piece of tough shoe leather when they are stewed. This is not to say you should have a lot of fat on your stew meat. Every piece could have a little hunk of fat. Chuck steaks trimmed of some excess fat and cut into chunks, make excellent stew. They usually cost less per pound than conventional precut stew meat. If you suspect that your meat is tough, soak it in vinegar and soy sauce for at least an hour to tenderize it.

Stew meat should be thawed or partially thawed for convenient preparation.

Beef, Pork or Veal Stew
(serves 2)

Suggested Ingredients

approximately 1 c. raw meat
2 tbsp. margarine
1 bay leaf
approximately 1/2 tsp. salt
1/2 tsp. basil or oregano
1/2 tsp. dill (for veal or pork stew)
1/2 tsp. parsley
dash of wine vinegar or wine (optional)
2-1/2 to 3 c. water
1/2 onion
1 stalk of celery (with leaves if desired)
1 large or 2 small carrots
1 large or 2 small potatoes,
or a handful of noodles
1 or more bouillon cubes
flour

Utensils

A sturdy, medium-sized pot or a large frying pan, with cover

Brown meat in the margarine in the pot or pan. Add most of the water, the seasonings, onion, potatoes (but not noodles) and other vegetables. Add a bouillon cube. Later on add another if needed. Let the mixture cook covered for 20 minutes or more. Some of the water will have soaked into the ingredients or evaporated by this time so you can add more if needed. Taste the concoction and add more seasonings if desired. If you are using noodles, add them at this point and expect them to soak up much of the liquid. If you use noodles, you may not want to thicken your gravy.

Add wine vinegar or wine if desired.

A few minutes before serving, thicken the stew gravy by taking a tablespoon or so of flour and putting it in a cup. Ladle some stew liquid into the flour making a soupy mixture. Pour this back into the stew pot and bring the mixture to a gentle boil while stirring the stew. If the stew doesn't thicken as much as you would like, use more flour and stew liquid in the same way as before. Do not add flour directly to stew as it will lump.

A quick stew can be made in well under an hour but the longer you cook stew, the more flavor you get.

Leftovers You Can Use
Vegetables.

Suggested Use of Leftovers
Add a little water to cold stew and reheat in a pot.

Helen's Pepper Steaks
(serves 2 or more)

Pepper steak as cooked according to this recipe really is a variety of stew.

Suggested Ingredients
2 c. chuck steak, trimmed of most fat and cut into chunks
1 15-oz.-can tomato sauce
1 clove (section) garlic
salt, pepper, oregano
1/2 to 1 green pepper
a little oil

Utensils
A sauce pan with cover

In a medium-sized saucepan at a medium heat, brown the meat in a little oil. Add all other ingredients except green pepper. Cover and allow it to come to a gentle boil. Reduce heat and cook at a low heat at least 30 minutes—45 minutes to an hour is even better. Add sliced pepper and cook for an additional 10 to 15 minutes. Serve with noodles or macaroni, rice or potatoes and a vegetable or salad.

Suggested Use of Leftovers
Reheat in a pot and serve as before, or put stew in a roll and eat it like a sub sandwich.

Lamb Curry
(serves 4)

Suggested Ingredients

enough cooked rice for 4 people
2 tbsp. margarine
1 c. sliced onions
1 tsp. curry powder
salt
2 c. beef bouillon (this means 2 bouillon cubes and 2 c. water)
1 c. sliced celery
1 finely chopped clove of garlic
1-1/2 c. diced pieces of lamb (left over from shank or other part)
1/2 c. raisins
fresh parsley (optional)
1/2 c. salted peanuts
1 tsp. cornstarch diluted in a little cold water (optional)

Utensils

A frying pan with cover, a pot for cooking rice

Begin to cook the rice. Set it aside and keep it hot while other ingredients cook. In the frying pan, sauté onions, celery, and garlic until lightly browned. Add lamb, curry powder, and salt to taste. (Be careful of the salt because of salted peanuts.) Add the raisins and bouillon. Simmer covered for 30 minutes. If desired, thicken with cornstarch.

Serve on top of rice with sprinklings of peanuts and fresh parsley.

Leftovers You Can Use

Lamb—other meats such as beef, pork and chicken can also be used in this recipe.

Suggested Use of Leftovers

Reheat in a pot or frying pan, adding a little water if necessary. Or reheat in a greased dish in the oven, adding additional liquid if needed.

STUFFING

Bread Stuffing
(stuffs a small bird)

Suggested Ingredients
>1-1/2 c. stale bread pieces (packed down tightly into the cup while measuring)
>3 tbsp. margarine
>1/3 c. or more boiling water
>1 stalk of celery
>1/2 onion
>**seasonings such as salt, oregano, bay leaf and basil**

Utensils
> Saucepan, mixing bowl, something to boil water in

Melt margarine slowly in the saucepan. Add to it the bay leaf and chopped up celery and onion. Add the other seasonings. Let the onion and celery fry for a few minutes. Then remove the mixture from the heat. Put the bread pieces in a bowl. Add boiling water and the margarine mixture. Mix all ingredients. If bread is not moist all the way through, add more boiling water. Do not drench the mixture. It should be moist, but not runny. The stuffing is now ready for the bird. Or, bake it in a greased baking dish at around 350° F., until hot and crusted on top.

Leftovers You Can Use
> Stale bread.

Suggested Use of Leftovers
> Eat cold or fry in a little margarine, or reheat in a greased baking dish.

Saltine Stuffing
(stuffs a small bird)

Suggested Ingredients
>1-1/2 c. broken saltines
>3 tbsp. margarine
>1/3 c. or more, boiling water
>1 stalk celery
>1/2 onion
>**seasonings such as oregano, bay leaf, and basil**

Utensils
>Saucepan, mixing bowl, something to boil water in

Follow directions for Bread Stuffing.

Suggested Use of Leftovers
>Same as Bread Stuffing.

Vegetable Stuffing

This stuffing can be of different consistencies depending upon your preference. If you do not want to use any bread or saltines at all, the stuffing will not hold together like your stereotyped stuffing, but an all-vegetable stuffing will taste good. So, use any proportions you like. Use enough margarine so that when frying the vegetables, nothing will stick to the pan. Vegetables will shrink, so it will take more all-vegetable stuffing to fill a bird than it takes with a bread or saltine stuffing.

Suggested Ingredients
>**vegetables such as green peppers, celery, onion, spinach, olives, and enough stale bread or saltines to make a nonrunny mixture which holds together somewhat when combined with vegetables (optional)**
>**1 egg (optional)**
>**margarine**
>**1/3 c. or less water (no water if using all vegetables)**
>**seasonings**

Utensils
>Frying pan, mixing bowl (optional—may use frying pan to mix ingredients)

Fry vegetables and seasonings in margarine. It is not necessary to fry spinach and olives. When vegetables are crunchy, but a little cooked, add them to bread or saltines and water, plus your olives and spinach. Stuff the mixture into the bird as in the Bread Stuffing recipe, or bake as in the Bread Stuffing recipe.

Suggested Use of Leftovers
>Same as Bread Stuffing.

VEGETABLES

Gustatorially, in my opinion, meat is not an essential part of a meal. Nutritionists will debate the matter. Some will claim that you're doing near-fatal damage to your body if you don't eat enough meat, and others feel that meat is not essential to health. I find that financially, it's easiest for me to play it safe and compromise. Sometimes meat is a bargain over an all-vegetable meal, especially when eaten in small quantities and combined with vegetables. And sometimes, no matter how you look at it, you just can't buy meat without spending a fortune. I usually have between two and four meatless days a week, and I don't feel as if I'm missing anything.

Most people have a misconception about vegetarian meals. They don't think there will be anything wholesome or substantial tasting in the meal. One friend of mine has had quite a few of my vegetarian meals and upon eating them, he always says in surprise: "Hey. This is good! If all vegetarian meals were like this, I wouldn't mind becoming a vegetarian." The same fellow, in another breath, will claim that he could never become a vegetarian because a meal doesn't feel like a meal unless there's meat in it.

The fact is that most people have misconceptions about vegetarian meals. They must think that vegetarians sit around like rabbits munching on lettuce, carrots, cabbage, and celery. Well, I'd be hungry in an hour too, if that's all I ate for supper, and I'd also get very tired of crunching all those vegetables. Fortunately vegetables come in such different consistencies and can be prepared in so many different ways, that with a little careful preparation you won't have to crunch, crunch, crunch your way through a meatless meal.

Brainstorm for just half a minute and think of a few vegetables: cabbage, celery, onions, spinach, turnips, corn, tomatoes, green beans, lima beans, lettuce, carrots, broccoli, and cauliflower are a few of them. Which ones can be gassy? Cabbage, onions, broccoli, cauliflower. Which are meaty or filling? Corn, lima beans, turnips and carrots. Which vegetables are most fibrous? Celery, green beans, maybe broccoli. Knowing these few things about vegetables, which you at least subconsciously know already, can help you to create a meal to your liking. Because cabbage, onions, broccoli, and cauliflower can be gassy, chances are you don't want to heap them all together in one meal. They could give you a very uncomfortable feeling. Also, because cabbage, broccoli, and cauliflower are all members of the same family and have many similar flavor characteristics, you wouldn't get much of a flavor variety if you served them together. Your filling vegetables, if eaten all together, might give you a feeling of having a lump in your stomach without actually being filled. If you serve the semi-fibrous beans, celery and broccoli together, you may tire of their similar consistencies.

Vegetables can be very individual and special, so it would be a shame for you to not think about what you're doing with them and turn your meal into a mundane affair. If you learn to combine vegetables of different characteristics together and with sauces, batters, and imaginative seasonings, you too will wonder why people are always screaming for meat. Eggs, cheese, protein extract, mushrooms, wheat germ, whole grains, seeds, and nuts mix beautifully with vegetables. Vegetables can be boring when they are forever boiled, buttered, and served. Frying or baking a vegetable will bring out rich flavors which you perhaps never noticed before. Also, using vegetables in ways you previously only used meat, will make you begin to realize that maybe meat isn't the thing which people enjoy so much—rather it could be that nothing interesting was offered in its place.

The recipes in this section should be abundant enough for you to begin making vegetables more interesting. They include vegetable meals and side dishes which may be served with meat or other foods. Most vegetable dishes may be made in a short time for a quick meal.

If you still think you hate all vegetables, it could be that you have not been seeing their best sides. Vegetables which are frozen or canned go through quite a few changes in flavor and consistency. We all know that flavor is important. But consistency—or how something feels in your mouth, against your teeth, and going down your throat—is really an essential factor, too. You may discover that some of your vegetable hang-ups have to do with these sensory factors.

Though some techniques in vegetable cooking are mentioned in Chapter 19, it might be best to repeat some of those methods here and go into others. Most vegetables should be washed as you prepare them to remove dirt, chemical sprays, and regular old germs. Even if you peel a vegetable, dirt from the skin can get into your hands and rub onto the vegetable. If you wash the skin and your hands, this can still happen. So you might have to wash the peel and then wash the peeled vegetable. Of course, if you do not peel a vegetable, an even more thorough job of washing it will be required. Wash the vegetable in cool or cold water so it won't wilt.

You may be confused as to what you're supposed to do with some vegetables—what parts you should remove and what parts should remain. The following list should help you decide.

Gritty, poorly washed vegetables are a chore to eat. So, when following these directions, make sure you don't do a haphazard job of it.

Asparagus—Rinse asparagus well in cool water. Remove any tough white parts of the stalk and peel off any tough skin which has tender vegetable underneath. Rinse again.

Beans—(dried) Rinse beans well and throw out any rotting or otherwise funny looking beans. Soak them in clean water for a few hours, or according to package instructions.

Beans—(wax, pole, string, snap, Italian, French, etc.) Rinse beans thoroughly. You can put them in a basin of cool water to wash and sort. Remove the stems and any bottoms which look tough. Also remove and discard any section of the bean which is dried out or does not snap.

Beets—Wash thoroughly with a vegetable brush or a clean plastic dish scrubber in cool water. If all dirt is removed from the skin, little will get on the unpeeled beet. If possible, you want to avoid washing a peeled beet and losing some of the juices. Peel the beet and remove the bottom and stem. If dirt gets on the peeled beet, wash it quickly.

Broccoli—Put broccoli into a basin of cool water and wash. Cut off tough stems and peel off tough skin which is usually just near the bottom of the stem. Remove excess, long, wilting leaves. Small tender ones are edible.

Cabbage—Remove wilted or dirty outer leaf. It's hard to wash that leaf. Separate other leaves and rinse them in cool water. Cut out any dark spots in leaves. If a partially used cabbage turns dark in your refrigerator, cut the dark area off; there should be good vegetable underneath this surface spoilage.

Carrots—Carrots do not have to be peeled. Scrub them with a vegetable brush or a clean plastic dish scrubber in a basin of cool water. Notice the dirt wedged in the lines which run around the carrots, and remove it. Or, scrape or peel the skin from the carrots.

Cauliflower—Separate into sections and put them in a basin of cool water. Wash the vegetable and remove any badly darkened spots and any unusually tough looking stems. Do not cook the leaves on the base of the plant—remove that section.

Celery—Separate the vegetable into stalks. Put them in a basin of cool water and hand wash them making sure that the dirt stuck in the inner grooves is removed. Cut out any discolored spots. You can also eat the leaves.

Corn—Husk the corn and remove the silk. Wash only to remove dirt which clings to the corn.

Cucumber—Rinse skin thoroughly in cool water. Or rinse off obvious dirt and peel the skin. Do not wash the peeled vegetable unless it is visibly dirty. In that case, rinse it quickly.

Eggplant—Rinse the vegetable in cool water, or rinse off obvious dirt and peel the skin. Peeling the skin is optional. Do not wash the peeled vegetable unless it is visibly dirty. The eggplant will darken after you peel it, but that is not dirt. Remove stem and base scab.

Leafy Vegetables or Greens, Lettuce, Spinach, Collards and Others—Remove each leaf from the base of the vegetable. Discard any unusually tough appearing or discolored sections. Put the vegetable in a basin of cool water and hand wash. Shake off excess water. Leafy vegetables are real sand catchers, so two or three washings may not be out of the question.

Onion—Peel the onion removing the flaky skin and the first white layer if desired. Washing is not necessary unless some obvious dirt gets on the peeled vegetable. If peeling or cutting onions makes you cry, put onions in a wide bowl or basin of cool water, and do your peeling or slicing there.

Parsley, and Other Herbs—Put herbs in a basin of cool water. Wash thoroughly and shake off excess water.

Parsnip—Rinse off excess dirt. Peel the vegetable and remove top and bottom. Rinse after peeling if necessary.

Peas—Shell. Wash peas in a colander—just in case some insecticide penetrated the shell.

Pepper—Rinse in cool water. Slice the pepper in half, cut out the seed section. Cup your hand over the half and hit the pepper against your hand to remove seeds left in the pepper. Rinse the inside of the pepper.

Potatoes—For further information, see Potato section of this chapter. Scrub the skin thoroughly with a vegetable brush or a clean plastic dish scrubber. If you peel potatoes, rinse them thoroughly again, and put them in a basin of cool water so they do not darken.

Radishes—Put radishes in a basin of cool water. Scrub them, removing all dirt. Remove top leaves and bottom root.

Rutabagas—If waxed, peel off skin and wax. Otherwise, simply peel off the skin. Wash the peeled vegetable only if it is visibly dirty. The peeled vegetable may discolor slightly, but this is not dirt.

Squash (Summer and Zucchini)—Peel only where the skin is discolored. Wash thoroughly under cool water. Remove stem and base scab.

Squash (Winter, Acorn, Butternut)—Rinse skin quickly. Bake with the skin on, but do not eat the skin. Or, peel the skin and cook.

Tomatoes—Wash thoroughly, but lightly, under cool water. Remove stem and base scab.

Turnips—Peel the vegetable only if desired. Remove the bottom root and the top. Save young top greens and tender stems and follow leafy vegetable directions for preparation. Wash the peeled turnip only to remove obvious dirt.

COOKING TIME

Because vegetables are of many different consistencies, they require different amounts of time for cooking. The size of the pieces will also determine the time it will take your vegetables to cook. Most vegetables should be cooked until they are tender but still together, and if tasted, are the slightest bit crunchy. Do not cook them so long that they become mush. Of course you may prefer vegetables with more or less crunch. Just remember that vegetables will continue to cook very slightly between the time you taste them, drain them, and eat them because of the heat which surrounds and penetrates them.

Follow the above general cooking rule in most cases, but not for potatoes and turnips which you intend to mash. Cook these vegetables a little bit longer. It's also hard to follow the rule for many greens, as they cook so rapidly. Just cook most of them a few minutes. If they steam when you take the lid off the pot, then they are most likely done. Collards must be cooked longer than most greens or any other vegetable. See page 233 for details on cooking them.

As you know, not all vegetables must be cooked, and a few you would probably never want to cook. Cucumbers and iceberg lettuce, as far as I know, would be best left uncooked. I've cooked radishes, but that seemed to zap all the flavor out of them. Asparagus, beans, beets, broccoli, corn, eggplant, parsnips, peas, potatoes, rutabaga, squash, and turnips are vegetables that we would think of as those which we cook. However, tender asparagus, beans, corn, peas, and summer and zucchini squash are good raw when nibbled in small quantities. If any of these vegetables are exceedingly sweet and tender, put them in salads. Cabbage, carrots, cauliflower, celery, many leafy vegetables, onions, parsley and other herbs, peppers, and tomatoes, are excellent raw or cooked.

There are several methods of safeguarding your vegetables against cooking them into a state which is beyond recognition. Remember, one reason you may feel you do not like vegetables is because they were cooked improperly. Most greens or leafy vegetables should be sprinkled with water, put in a saucepan and steamed for a few minutes. Escarole, kale, and mustard greens will take longer to cook than dandelion, spinach, young turnips and beet greens. Collards do not cook like greens at all. (Again, see page 233.) The thicker a green is in leaf and stalk, the longer it will take to cook. Most greens should be cooked between one and seven minutes after they become hot. Greens can also be fried in a lightly oiled frying pan for a few minutes, or cooked in a casserole.

Broccoli, cabbage, cauliflower, celery, onions, and summer and zucchini squashes require a relatively small amount of water to cook. Add from one-fourth to half an inch of water to a pot if you are cooking an average amount (two to four servings) of vegetables. Of course, if you use a lot of vegetables, you'll need more water. Bring the water to a boil and then add your vegetables. Reduce the heat and allow the vegetables to gently steam. If the water evaporates, add more and keep your heat lower next time. Cook the vegetables until tender, usually no more than fifteen minutes. The abovementioned vegetables can be fried in oil also. You might want to parsteam or parboil broccoli, cauliflower, and celery for two to three minutes before frying.[1]

Green and yellow beans, as well as beets, carrots, parsnips, peas, potatoes, rutabagas, winter squash and turnips, require a bit more water. Put enough water in the pot when cooking these vegetables so

---

[1] To parsteam or parboil something, simply partially steam or boil it. Steam or boil vegetables for two to three minutes.

that they will float. You can crowd the vegetables together—but they should float. These vegetables usually require a bit more cooking time than other vegetables.

I've never steamed or boiled eggplant. I've always fried it according to the recipe in this section. Tomatoes and peppers can be steamed in a saucepan or frying pan, carefully, with no water.

If you can rig up a good method, put your colander or strainer in a saucepan, fill your pan one-quarter to one-third full with water, allow the water to boil, and then put any type of vegetables in the colander section. Cover the pot and steam the vegetable without it ever directly touching the water. Carrots, potatoes, rutabagas, and turnips will take longer than other vegetables through this method, unless cut into very small pieces, so it may not be worth it to you to steam these vegetables. This method is almost foolproof for keeping as many vitamins in your vegetables as possible and preventing the vegetables from burning. Vegetable steamers can be purchased in some stores. This will eliminate the colander or strainer. If your colander or strainer simply does not fit easily into your pot, you might want to consider buying a steamer or asking for one for your birthday. Last time I checked, they sold for under three dollars.

Try anything you want with vegetables. Just remember that overcooking them and oversaturating them with water will most likely destroy their vitamin content and their flavor.

Asparagus Pancake
(serves 4 or more)

Suggested Ingredients

1 dozen or so fresh asparagus
1 beaten egg
any type of cheese—shredded or grated—to taste
(start with 1 tbsp.)
1 c. white or whole wheat flour
1/2 tsp. baking powder
salt, pepper, nutmeg, basil
enough milk to make a thick but spoonable batter
(start with 1/4 c.)
oil

Utensils
A bowl for mixing, a frying pan or griddle, a small saucepan with cover

Wash asparagus and cut them into 1/2- to 3/4-inch pieces. Throw away any *tough* white sections of the stalks. If the skin is the only tough section, peel it off and use the understalk. Put the asparagus into a small saucepan with a little salt and water and let them cook until barely tender.

Meanwhile, combine all other ingredients except oil. Drain off any of the excess water from the asparagus and add them to the batter. Heat your frying pan from a medium-high to a low-high heat. When a drop of water thrown on the pan spits and bounces off, coat the pan with oil. Spoon out little, two-inch diameter pancakes. Let them cook on one side and then check each pancake to see if it is brown on that side. If so, flip it over and cook until the other side is brown. Keep them warm in a low oven, or serve them at room temperature. These pancakes may be served instead of potatoes, rice, or noodles.

Leftovers You can Use
Asparagus.

Suggested Use of Leftovers
Reheat in a baking dish in the oven, or eat them cold.

Other Vegetable Pancakes

Other vegetables may also be used to make these pancakes. Try using celery, cauliflower, broccoli, and spinach or other greens. Most greens do not have to be parboiled. They can be put directly into the batter. Celery, cauliflower, broccoli, and a lot of other nonleafy vegetables should be parboiled before adding them to the batter.

Possible Leftovers Used in This Recipe
Vegetables.

Suggested Use of Leftovers
Reheat or eat them cold.

Baked Lima Beans
(serves 2)

This is not a time-consuming recipe to prepare. Beans can be thrown in a bowl and soaked overnight or while you are out (5 to 7 hours) with no work on your part. However, if you feel you do not have time to soak them and boil them, use a can of lima beans, preferably the white ones, although the canned beans will probably cost you more money. Canned beans do not have to be boiled and baking time may be slightly reduced. Beans are nice because they are a good meat substitute. They provide essential protein and cost less than meat.

Suggested Ingredients

1/2 lb. dried baby lima beans
1 to 1-1/2 tsp. sugar or molasses
1 tbsp. soy sauce
a little thyme or another interesting herb
salt to taste

Utensils

Saucepan for boiling beans, baking dish for baking beans

Follow directions on lima bean package for general preparation of beans, or rinse and sort beans, picking out the bad ones. Soak limas overnight in 3 times as much water as beans, boil until tender, and then drain some liquid leaving 1/2 cup to 1 cup. Add all other ingredients and bake at 350° F. in a greased, covered casserole until the liquid soaks into the beans and the mixture is hot—about 30 to 45 minutes. Uncover during the last 15 minutes or so if the liquid has not been absorbed by the beans.

Suggested Use of Leftovers

Reheat limas with a little extra water in the same baking dish. Also add other ingredients such as celery and onion for variety.

Quick Side Dish

Boiled Beets

Suggested Ingredients

peeled, sliced beets
salt
a dash of vinegar (optional)
margarine

Utensils

Saucepan with cover

Put beets in boiling salted water which will barely cover the beets. Cook until tender. Add a dash of vinegar if desired. When the beets are done, add some margarine.

Suggested Use of Leftovers

Reheat in a pan on the stove in the same liquid, or use beets in soup.

Quick Side Dish

Beet Greens

Suggested Ingredients

**washed beet tops and stems
a dash of vinegar (optional)
margarine**

Utensils

A saucepan with cover

Steam greens in a little water until tender, a few minutes should do it. Add vinegar and margarine.

Suggested Use of Leftovers
Use in soup.

Eggs and Broccoli in Cream Sauce (serves 2 to 3 as a side dish)

Suggested Ingredients

**4 hard-boiled eggs
2 washed, large stalks of broccoli
1 c. cream sauce (see page 199.)
oil
2 tsp. soy sauce
seasonings such as sweet basil, paprika, nutmeg**

Utensils

Frying pan, saucepan

Hard boil your eggs. Coat a small or other frying pan with a little oil. Slice small pieces of broccoli into the pan, season with soy sauce, cover and let steam at a medium-high heat. Make sure the broccoli doesn't burn. Make your cream sauce and season it with desired herbs. When the broccoli is tender, turn the heat down to medium-low. Slice your hard-boiled eggs into the frying pan on top of the broccoli. Cover the eggs with cream sauce. Put the lid on the pan and leave the pan on the heat until the ingredients bubble slightly. Serve as a side dish to soups, meat, fish or anything else, or, increase proportions and serve as the main part of the meal with a salad.

Advance Preparation
Prepare hard-boiled eggs in advance to create a quick meal.

Leftovers You can Use
Broccoli.

Suggested Use of Leftovers
Reheat in a pan on the stove, or in a dish in the oven.

Eggs and Vegetables in Cream Sauce

Peas, spinach, cauliflower, celery, and many other vegetables can be creamed with eggs by following the Eggs and Broccoli in Cream Sauce recipe. Fresh or frozen peas should be parboiled for a few minutes and spinach needs only a few minutes of frying. Add enough vegetables so that the cream sauce is not the major ingredient.

Advance Preparation
Prepare hard-boiled eggs in advance to create a quick meal.

Leftovers You can Use
Any leftover vegetables may be used.

Suggested Use of Leftovers
Reheat in a pan on the stove or in a dish in the oven, or add it to a casserole.

Stuffed Cabbage
(serves 2 to 3)

This recipe substitutes wheat germ, cheese, and egg for the traditional meat and rice which usually makes up the main body of stuffed cabbage. These substitutes not only provide the necessary protein, vitamins, and nutrients, but they also provide for a filling and tasteful meal.

Suggested Ingredients
>6 thin 2" × 4" pieces of outer leaves of cabbage
>2/3 c. wheat germ
>2 tbsp. cheese, grated or chopped
>1 egg
>seasonings such as salt, pepper, basil, nutmeg
>tomato sauce made with 1 28-oz. can whole tomatoes or tomato sauce, 1 bay leaf, seasonings, such as: oregano, basil, nutmeg, salt, pepper

Utensils
>A large frying pan or medium-sized saucepan, a bowl for mixing, wooden toothpicks

The cabbage leaf measurement is only a guide. Do not bother to measure it. Wash and dry cabbage pieces. Combine in a bowl the wheat germ, cheese, seasonings, and egg. Add enough water to make a spreadable paste. Combine tomato sauce ingredients in the frying or saucepan and allow them to come to a gentle boil. Lay the cabbage pieces flat and spread some of the wheat germ mixture on each piece. Do not spread it to the edges of the cabbage. Roll up the cabbage like a blanket roll, and put a wooden toothpick through each one. Place them with a spoon into the tomato sauce. Make sure the sauce continues to gently bubble. Cover and cook for 20 minutes or until the cabbage is done. Serve with noodles or rice and another vegetable.

Suggested Use of Leftovers
>Reheat in a frying or saucepan.

Quick Side Dish

Orange Glazed Carrots
(serves 2 to 3 generously)

Suggested Ingredients
>6 medium or 8 small carrots
>2 oranges
>1 to 1-1/2 tsp. cornstarch

Utensils
>2 saucepans

Wash the carrots. Slice them and put them in boiling water to cook until tender. Meanwhile, squeeze the juice of the oranges into the other saucepan. If you like, also put the pulp in with the juice. Stir in your cornstarch. Put the mixture on a medium heat and stir until thickened. Drain the carrots and pour the orange mixture over the carrots. Serve as you would any other side dish vegetable.

Quick Side Dish

Fried Cauliflower

Suggested Ingredients
>fresh cauliflower washed and cut up
>margarine
>a little crushed garlic
>a few bread crumbs
>salt, pepper, paprika, parsley

Utensil
>Frying pan

Prepare cauliflower. Heat frying pan to a medium heat. Add enough margarine to generously coat the bottom of the pan. Lower the heat if the margarine is in danger of burning. Add garlic, the cauliflower, and seasonings. Fry until cauliflower is tender but still a little crunchy. Add bread crumbs during the last few minutes. The smaller the cauliflower pieces, the shorter the cooking time.

Suggested Use of Leftovers
>Reheat in a pan on the stove or in a dish in the oven, with a little water if needed, or add to a casserole or soup.

Fried Broccoli

Follow directions for Fried Cauliflower using broccoli.

Suggested Use of Leftovers
>Same as for Fried Cauliflower.

Collards

Collard greens are a very popular dish in the southern part of this country. If you don't know how to cook them, they can be pretty disappointing. While a VISTA (Volunteer in Service to America) in the rural area outside of Rochester, New York, I worked with people who had formerly been seasonal farm laborers and had traveled from the South to the North with the crops each year. I stayed with a woman named Jessie Mae Butler who had come from the South a few years before to live permanently in New York state. Jessie has a way about her which is beautiful. She would invite anyone into her home, no matter who the person was. Jessie has a wonderfully inviting smile. She lets you know you are welcome. She is also just about the most spontaneous cook I've ever met. Piles of people—including hungry VISTAs—would wander into her home on a Sunday afternoon. Jessie would come up with a fantastic meal which was abundant enough to feed her guests. Among the things she cooked were Southern Fried Chicken (page 160) and collards.

Suggested Ingredients
>**a bunch of collards—make sure they are fresh and green, neither yellow nor limp**
>**a few strips of bacon**
>**or some salt pork**
>**or any fatty hunk of meat**
>**a little salt**
>**a little sugar**

Utensil
>A large pot

Separate collard leaves and wash them individually. Stack 8 to 10 on top of one another, roll them together lengthwise and slice them into thin strips. Stack another bunch of leaves and follow the same procedure until you've sliced all the leaves. Fry the meat in the pot. If you are using bacon, cut it into 1- or 2-inch pieces. When the meat starts giving off a lot of fat, add the collards, a little salt and 1 teaspoon of sugar. The water which remains on the leaves after washing may be sufficient for steaming the collards. Cover the pot and allow collards to steam at a medium heat for a while. If they begin to stick to the bottom of the pan, add a little water. Continue steaming for at least half an hour, checking periodically to see if more water is needed. Collards taste best when they've been cooked over an hour. If they are not cooked long enough, they may be tough. Taste the collards. If they are tender, they are done. Add more sugar if they seem unpleasantly bitter. If you got a bum batch of collards and after a few spoonfuls of sugar, they are still too bitter, add a dash of vinegar. If your collards look fresh and green, not yellow, they will most likely taste good.

Suggested Use of Leftovers
>Just keep reheating them. They're better every time.

Fried Eggplant
(serves 2 or 3 as a side dish)

Suggested Ingredients

8 1/4-inch-slices of eggplant, with or without peel
1 egg, beaten
2-1/2 tbsp. flour } or 4 tbsp. of either one
1-1/2 tbsp. bread crumbs
1 tbsp. Parmesan or other dry grated cheese
seasonings such as salt, pepper, oregano, basil and parsley
oil

Utensils

Frying pan, a bowl for egg and a bowl for flour mixture

Wash the skin of the eggplant if you intend to keep it on. Slice the eggplant. Beat the egg in a small dish. Combine flour, bread crumbs, cheese, and seasonings in another dish. Heat the frying pan coated with oil to medium high. Lower the heat if the oil begins to burn. Add more oil as needed. Dip each piece of eggplant into egg and then into the flour mixture. Fry them until brown on both sides. Place the fried pieces on a paper bag to absorb excess oil. Then place them on a dish in a warm oven, or serve at room temperature. Serve cold in sandwiches, if desired.

Suggested Use of Leftovers

Reheat in a baking dish in the oven, or use on sandwiches.

Eggplant Sort of Parmesan
(serves 2 or more as the main part of the meal instead of the meat portion)

Suggested Ingredients

3/4 to 1 28-oz. can whole tomato
or tomato sauce, seasoned with salt,
pepper, oregano, slices of mozzarella or any other cheese,
parmesan or any other grated cheese, or a combination of both
8 1/4-inch slices eggplant, with or without peel

Utensils
    Frying pan and baking dish, and bowls for mixing ingredients

Fry eggplant as in the Fried Eggplant recipe. Put a layer of eggplant into the baking dish, spread a layer of sauce over the eggplant, ending with the cheese layer. Continue until you use up all of the eggplant. Bake in a 350° F. oven until the cheese melts and everything bubbles.

Suggested Use of Leftovers
    Reheat in the same baking dish in the oven or put the eggplant on sandwiches.

Quick Side Dish

Boiled Onions

    This recipe may sound really dull, but it isn't. Discovering the onion as a very edible vegetable by itself is a pleasant experience.

Suggested Ingredients
onions
margarine
any seasonings desired, such as salt, pepper, paprika, parsley

Utensils
    Saucepan with cover

Peel onions and cut them in halves or quarters. Add them to a small amount of boiling water. The onions do not have to be covered with water. Cook them covered until tender—15 to 20 minutes might be a fair estimate. Drain the onions and season them as desired. Top with margarine. For onions in cream sauce, make the cream sauce (page 199) and add your desired seasonings to it. Then, drain the onions and mix the cream sauce into them.

Suggested Use of Leftovers
    Reheat in a pan with a little water if needed, or add to soups or casseroles.

Quick Preparation

Julia Mae's Southern Fried Green Tomatoes

    While working with VISTA in New York state, my husband, Michael, and I managed to eke out a small garden in a suburban development. As we were digging up the last piece of sod, the friendly neighbor stopped by to tell us that when the developer had purchased all the land in the area, which had previously been farm land, he had scraped off all the top soil and had sold it. This, of course, meant that most of the good nutrients which are essential for a successful garden, did not exist where we planned on planting. Later, as we raked over the soil, we discovered a generous layer of clay, which added to the doubtful success of our garden. We decided to plant anyway. Aside from the parsley, which was drowned during the rains which swept through the area and badly flooded the state to the south of us, everything came up—in miniature. We found we could boast about our vegetables: "Yep, we have string beans which grow to be half an inch long," we would say. Or, about our watermelons, why seeing was believing. They made a softball look big. Everything tasted just fine. Our tomatoes were fairly successful. They were anywhere from the size of peewee marbles you collect as a kid, to about the size of a hardball. We did manage to do some tomato canning that year. It was very simple. The business we did through our job entailed going to people's homes. We visited about five families one afternoon and all of them begged us to take some of their ripe, luscious, tremendous tomatoes before they went bad. That night, we canned twenty-four quarts of tomatoes. Maybe, five tomatoes were from our garden. Meanwhile, the frost was not far off, and little hard, green tomatoes hung from our vines. We mentioned our dilemma to a friend of ours, Julia Mae King. "Bring 'em over to me," she said. "My family loves green tomatoes fried in corn meal." That sounded terrible to me. We brought over pounds of green tomatoes to Julia Mae. She was very happy. I never fried green tomatoes until the following year when we again had a garden—this time a two hour drive from our apartment in the Bronx. Those last few dozen tomatoes never ripened, so I finally decided to fry up some. They were fantastically delicious—not at all bitter, as I had expected. In fact, they were mildly and pleasantly sweet. You may, at some time, have access to green tomatoes. Many people in cities even rent a little land for gardens. But you don't need a garden to get green tomatoes because some people will often give them away.

Suggested Ingredients

green tomatoes
cornmeal
oil

Utensil
    Frying pan

Slice, washed green tomatoes. Pat them on both sides with cornmeal. Heat an oil coated frying pan to a medium heat. Lower the heat if the oil begins to burn. Add tomatoes and fry them until the cornmeal is light brown. Drain off the excess oil by putting the fried tomatoes on a paper bag.
    Serve the tomatoes as a side dish—as you would any other vegetable.

Suggested Use of Leftovers
    Reheat fried tomatoes or put them in a casserole.

Quick Preparation

Vegetable Hash
(serves 4)

Suggested Ingredients

oil
3 to 4 carrots
4 to 6 eggs, beaten
seasonings
2 tbsp. nonfat dry milk
spinach or escarole
2 stalks celery
1 onion
1/2 large can whole tomatoes (or 14 oz.)
brown, white, or fried rice, or
noodles or potatoes
cheese

Utensils
    Large frying pan or saucepan, small bowl for mixing eggs

Coat the bottom of the pan with oil. Set the burner at a medium heat. Slice carrots, onions, and celery into the pan. Slice carrots very thin. Cover the pan and let the vegetables steam until the carrots are still crunchy but not raw. Mix the eggs with the powdered milk and desired seasonings. Put them into the pan and stir them into the vegetables. They should begin to scramble. Add the tomato and spinach or escarole. Stir the combination to get the eggs to scramble. Add other seasonings to taste. Top the whole thing with cheese. When the cheese melts, serve the hash with one of the above listed starches.

Leftovers You Can Use
    Vegetables.

Suggested Use of Leftovers
    Reheat in a pot on the stove or in a dish in the oven, or add it to a casserole or soup.

Quick Preparation

Scrambled Vegetables
(serves 4)

Suggested Ingredients
    2 to 2-1/2 c. vegetables such as carrots, onions, celery, broccoli, cauliflower, and greens, cut up into very small pieces
    1 tbsp. milk
    6 to 8 tbsp. white or whole wheat flour
    3 eggs
    salt and any other desired seasonings
    oil

Utensils
    Large frying pan, bowl for mixing

Wash and cut up all vegetables. Mix them with other ingredients. Add more milk if the mixture does not stir easily. Heat your pan to a medium heat. Coat the bottom with oil. Pour the mixture into the pan and scramble it around. Stir often until all parts are done. Serve with a side dish such as a salad or simple soup.

Leftovers You Can Use
    Any vegetables.

Suggested Use of Leftovers
    Reheat in a pan on the stove or in a dish in the oven, or add it to a casserole or soup.

Vegetable Loaf
(serves 2 to 3)

Suggested Ingredients
>1 c. very finely cut, or ground carrots
>1 large chopped onion
>1 stalk of celery, chopped fine
>1/2 c. nuts, sunflower seeds, or 1 tbsp. crunchy peanut butter
>2 beaten eggs
>1/4 c. water or soup stock
>1 c. whole wheat bread crumbs or wheat germ
>2 tsp. melted margarine or oil

Utensils
>Baking dish, mixing bowl, and a small dish for beating eggs

Preheat oven to 350° to 375° F. Combine all ingredients. Put them in a greased baking dish and pack it down well. Bake for 30 minutes or until the combination is solidified. Serve as a substitute for the meat portion of your meal.

Suggested Use of Leftovers
>Fry slices in oil until brown.

Quick Preparation

Zucchini Parmesan

Suggested Ingredients
>fresh zucchini squash
>margarine
>a little parmesan or other dry, grated cheese
>salt, pepper, basil, and other seasonings

Utensil
>Saucepan

Cut up zucchini. Do not peel. Cook it in a little water until tender. Drain off excess water. Add margarine, cheese, and seasonings.

Suggested Use of Leftovers
>Add to a casserole or soup.

Baked Acorn Squash
(serves 2 as a side dish)

Suggested Ingredients
>1 small acorn squash
>2 tsp. honey or brown sugar
>sprinkles of nutmeg and/or cinnamon

Utensil
>Baking dish

Preheat oven to 375° to 400° F. Slice squash into halves or quarters. Remove seeds. With the skin down, place the pieces in a greased baking dish with a little water in the dish. Season each piece with honey and nutmeg and/or cinnamon. Cook until squash is tender. If you bake the squash in a covered dish, it will take about 50 minutes. In an uncovered dish the baking time is an hour or so.

Suggested Use of Leftovers
>Peel, slice, and fry in margarine.

CHINESE-STYLE VEGETABLES

The use of soy sauce and a few other condiments in vegetables, which are cooked so slightly that they still maintain their "crunch," can create a dish with a characteristically Chinese flavor.

You can cook many different vegetables Chinese style. You can cook them separately, together, or with mushrooms, bits of fish, or meat. Vegetables and their condiments, which are fried in oil at a fairly high heat in a frying pan, get the characteristic consistency which is of the Chinese style. Some vegetables will cook faster and more effectively if they are parboiled before they are fried. Asparagus, broccoli, cauliflower, carrots, and string or wax beans should be washed, trimmed of any tough stalks or sections, and then steamed or boiled in water for about two to three minutes. After they are parboiled, they should be immediately drained and then rinsed in cold water to inhibit any further cooking. In-between vegetables, such as cabbage and celery, can be rinsed in steaming hot water before frying, or, stick them in a pot of vegetables which is parboiling during the last thirty seconds and then drain them and rinse them in cold water with the rest. Leafy vegetables and other fast-cooking vegetables can be put directly in the frying pan after they are washed.

Cornstarch is used instead of flour as a thickener for the Chinese-style vegetable sauce. It makes a clearer, lighter sauce which blends in well with all of the other ingredients.

One thing which makes Chinese-style cooking so attractive to the eye is the way in which the vegetables are cut up. They are often sliced at angles or in the case of cauliflower and broccoli, the flowerets are carefully kept intact. Cabbage is not hacked or chopped—it is left in bite-size, leaf layers. Bits of meat are cut in square chunks and mushrooms are sliced lengthwise—stem and button together.

Quick Preparation

Broccoli and Spinach— Chinese Style (serves 4)

This recipe can be adapted to fit many different vegetable combinations. The soup stock listed as an ingredient can be a stock which you made by following the directions in the soup section of this chapter. Or you can use a bouillon cube for every cup of water, or you can use a half cup of stock or bouillon mixed with a half cup of wine or sherry. The proportions in this recipe are meant simply as a guide. You may discover, for instance, that the cup plus of liquid creates more sauce than you would like to have for your vegetables. You may want to use three-fourths of a cup of stock and cut your other ingredients down proportionately. Or, you may find that you'll want to use more or less soy sauce or cornstarch. If your sauce is too thin after you've used your cornstarch and you want to thicken it more, add a little cornstarch to cold water and then pour it in with the rest of the sauce.

Suggested Ingredients

3 c. broccoli
2 c. spinach with stems
4 to 6 tbsp. oil
1 c. soup stock (or bouillon and water)
1 to 2 tsp. sugar (optional)
4 tbsp. soy sauce (3 tbsp. with stronger soy sauces)
2 tsp. cornstarch

Utensils

A saucepan with cover, medium to large frying pan with cover, 1 or 2 little dishes or cups for mixing condiments

Clean and prepare vegetables. Parboil the broccoli for 2 to 3 minutes. Mix stock, sugar and soy sauce together. Mix cornstarch with a little cold water and add it to the stock.

Put your frying pan on the burner and set it for a medium-high heat. When you feel that the pan is hot, add your oil. If your oil spits a bit, add your broccoli. Cover the pan for about 2 to 3 minutes, then lift off the lid and poke a broccoli with a fork. After you've gotten used to this recipe, you'll know when it's done. The broccoli should be in your opinion about half as done as you would normally eat your vegetables. Add your sauce and stir it until it thickens. If it does not thicken enough, add more cornstarch to some cold water and then to the sauce. Lay your leaves of spinach on top of the broccoli and cover the pan for 30 seconds. If the pan is getting too hot at any point, lower the heat. Remove the cover after steaming the spinach. Put a little of the sauce from the sides or bottom of the pan on top of the spinach. Serve with fried or regular rice.

Suggested Use of Leftovers

Reheat in a pan on the stove or in a dish in the oven or add it to soup. Of course you'll lose the "crunch."

Quick Preparation

Cabbage and Onions— Chinese Style

Suggested Ingredients

4 to 5 c. cabbage and onions
4 to 6 tbsp. oil
1 c. soup stock (or bouillon)
1 to 2 tsp. sugar (optional)
4 tbsp. soy sauce (3 tbsp. with stronger soy sauces)
2 tsp. cornstarch

Utensils

Medium to large frying pan with a cover, 1 or 2 little dishes for mixing condiments

Clean cabbage and peel onions. Rinse them in hot or boiling water. Follow directions as in Broccoli and Spinach recipe.

Suggested Use of Leftovers
    Same as for Broccoli and Spinach recipe.

Create other Chinese-style vegetable recipes adding precooked meat chunks and any vegetables. Add a *pinch* of ginger for an added flavor.

BREADS, BISCUITS, PANCAKES, PIZZA, AND OTHERS

Home baked bread is always a pleasure. We no longer buy commercially baked breads. Warm, steaming bread is a temptation we can rarely resist, especially if the bread comes out of the oven in time for an evening snack. When we first baked homemade bread, we used to devour over half a loaf when it came out of the oven. Making bread is really a fun thing to do especially with a friend or even a group of friends. Working together with people to make bread has the mysterious effect of cementing relationships. The two most beneficial results of baking bread with someone you love is the exploration of something new and fun, and the bread itself.

    Most yeast breads have similar ingredients. Flour is the main bulk of the bread. Yeast, either cake or dry, will make the dough rise. It is also that mysterious rising action of the yeast that makes your bread light, instead of dense and hard. Sweeteners such as honey, white sugar, brown sugar and molasses help yeast to continue working. Sweeteners also give breads a pleasant taste. Salt controls the action of the yeast and sugar. (I have found that some breads which have not risen properly do not necessarily need more yeast. The addition of more sweetener and/or the absence of some salt would have given the dough the proper chemical balance so that it would have risen.) Water or milk moisten the dry ingredients to make the dough. The right amount of milk or water will give the bread a smooth texture. Oil or margarine (or butter if you have the money) will contribute to the bread's consistency and good flavor. Herbs, spices, fruits, and nuts add exotic tastes to the bread. Fruits and nuts also give you surprises to look forward to in the bread.

    In most bread recipes, you will find that the wet ingredients will be mixed together and then the dry ingredients will be gradually added, sometimes all together, and at other times, at intervals. The reverse procedure of adding the liquid to the dry ingredients is called for only occasionally.

After you have set out the bowls you'll need for making bread, the yeast should be prepared. For one bread recipe, place about one-quarter cup hot tap water in a cup. Then stir in the amount of sweetener the recipe calls for. The addition of the sweetener will cool down the water. When the liquid is lukewarm, add the required amount of yeast and stir. Yeast cannot react with water unless the water is at least 85° F., but temperatures above 105° F. will kill the yeast. Allow this combination to react—eventually it will foam and the foam and liquid will be of equal volume. If, after 10 to 15 minutes the foam is not at least half of the liquid's volume, then something has gone wrong, but don't panic. First, feel the cup. If it is not warm, chances are, the water, sweetener, and yeast weren't given a chance to react—maybe the liquid was too cool when the yeast was added. Put the cup in a warm place, such as on top of a warm stove or radiator, and allow the combination to become warm but not hot. Then wait for the yeast to react. If the cup was warm when you felt it, then give the ingredients within a vigorous stirring. However, if enough foam does not form after either of these two attempts, chances are that you killed the yeast with water which was too hot, or your yeast was too old or just not good. To add a nonacting yeast to your bread will only result in disappointment (like a brick instead of a bread). So make a new batch of yeast rising it according to the directions in this paragraph.

All of the dry ingredients used—flour, cornmeal, salt, sugar, herbs, nuts, and fruits should be at room temperature when used. To make your bread higher and lighter, warm up the flour in the oven on a cookie sheet and warm up the bowl that you will mix your ingredients in. Be sure that both the flour and the bowl are warm—not hot—because too high a temperature will kill the yeast. A warm bowl and warm flour is supposed to get the yeast to react quickly and most reliably. However, this warming-up process is not necessary.

Generally you will add the flour to all of the combined wet ingredients gradually—not all at once. As you mix in each portion of flour, be sure to get it wet. A large spoon made of wood, metal, or plastic, is good for mixing in the flour. Before you add any more flour, be sure that you don't see any patches of dry flour in the dough. Also, do not chop up the dough because this could destroy the texture of the bread and hinder the rising action of the yeast. Gently scoop dry flour toward the center of the bowl and then push a wet part of the dough into the dry flour without causing a separation in the dough. Continue this process until no more flour is dry. After a while you will put some flour into the bowl that you won't be able to get to mix with the dough. At this point you should stop using the spoon and use your hands. Place the dough on a lightly floured, smooth, clean surface, such as a bread board, counter, or stove top. Knead the dough by placing your right hand under the right quarter of the bread. Lift this section of the dough and then push it into the center of the dough. Then, placing your left hand under the left quarter of the dough, lift this section and push it into the center. Do the same with the top and bottom quarters, and then start again with the right quarter. Add flour when there is very little dry flour in the dough. Also, put flour on your hands and the kneading surface if the dough sticks on either of them. As a rule of thumb, the dough will be of the proper consistency when it no longer sticks to your hands or in the case of fine flour, when it is smooth and silky.

After the bread has been kneaded, then the dough must go through two rising periods. During these rising periods the yeast, which has been mixed throughout the dough, rises and causes the entire bread dough to enlarge, making the bread light. You will want the bread to double its volume during rising. Place the dough in a lightly oiled bowl which is at least twice as large as the dough. Cover the bowl with a dish towel. Place the dough in a warm (but not hot) place, and wait for the yeast to do its thing.

When the dough has doubled in size (about an hour), punch it down and knead it for a few minutes on a smooth surface. Then place the dough in a greased bread pan. With your hands, push the dough down until it evenly covers the bottom of the bread pan. If you are making a two-loaf mixture, cut the dough in half and place each half in greased bread pans.

The dough will go through its second rising in the bread pans. Put the pans in a warm place and cover with a dish towel. In less than an hour, the dough should once again double in size. At this point, the dough is ready to be baked. Place each bread pan in an unheated oven, and set the temperature as indicated in each recipe. The breads are finished when a broomstraw or long pronged fork is stuck into the bread and comes out without any dough on it. When finished, remove the breads from the pans and allow them to cool. If you do not take the breads from the pans right away, then the steam in the bread will condense on the insides of the pans, leaving you with soggy bread. (You can dry out soggy bread by placing it in an oven set at a low heat.) The loaves can cool down on their sides or tops, or better still, they can be placed on cool stove burners or on a cooling rack. In this way air can circulate around the bread allowing it to cool evenly.

Whole Wheat Bread
(makes 2 loaves)

Whole wheat bread is our sandwich staple. The texture makes eating a totally aware process. If you become addicted to whole wheat bread, you'll never again be able to go back to Wonder Bread. This bread is also good toasted or when slightly cooled after just coming out of the oven.

Suggested Ingredients

1/2 c. hot water
2 pkg. dry yeast (or 2 tbsp.)
1/2 c. honey or brown sugar
2 c. lukewarm water
1/4 c. oil
6-1/2 c. (or more) whole wheat flour
1 tbsp. salt
a little oil
vegetable shortening

Utensils

Measuring cup, regular cup, large mixing bowl or large pot, 2 bread pans

Mix the honey or brown sugar with the 1/2 cup hot water in a cup. When the mixture is lukewarm, add the yeast. While the yeast is foaming, put the 2 cups of lukewarm water and the oil in the mixing bowl. When the foam above the yeast is at least half the volume of the liquid, stir it into the water and oil. Whole wheat does not have to be sifted. Add 2 cups flour to the liquid and mix well with a large spoon. When no flour is dry, measure 2 more cups of flour, but before adding it to the dough, add the salt to the flour (be sure to mix the salt throughout the flour). Now add this flour-salt combination to the liquid. Mix with a spoon until all the flour is wet. Add 1 more cup of flour and mix as before, but this will take a little longer time. On a clean, smooth surface, place the dough. Spread some flour on this surface and coat your hands with flour. Add another cup of flour and knead the flour into the dough. If needed, add another 1/2 cup of flour. No more flour is needed when the dough will not stick to your unfloured hands. Add more flour, 1/4 cup at a time, if the dough is still sticking to your hands.

Knead the dough for about 5 minutes after you stop adding flour. Lightly oil the mixing bowl and let the dough rise in the mixing bowl. When it is twice its original size, punch the dough down, knead it for a few minutes, cut the dough in half, and place each piece in a bread pan which has been greased with vegetable shortening. Cover the pans with a dishcloth and put them in a warm place. When the dough reaches the top of the pans, place them in the oven, set the heat at 375° F. and bake for 45 to 50 minutes, or until a broomstraw or long pronged fork, when inserted into the bread, comes out without any dough on it. Remove breads from the pans and allow them to cool thoroughly before wrapping.

Whole Wheat and White Flour Bread

If you prefer a whole wheat bread which is lighter in color and is less grainy than the above recipe, then substitute a few cups of white flour for the whole wheat flour. Follow the directions for Whole Wheat Bread, except use 2 cups of sifted white flour the second time the recipe calls for 2 cups of flour. If you want an even lighter bread, substitute even more sifted white for whole wheat.

Italian Bread
(makes 2 loaves)

This bread was adapted from a family recipe from the Italian side of my in-laws. To appreciate the Old World touches of the original, I've included it also. This bread is light and rich tasting. It makes a good sandwich bread, but it is also excellent toasted. This bread does not taste like the typical white flour bread.

Suggested Ingredients

1/4 c. hot water
2 pkg. dry yeast (or 2 tbsp.)
2 tbsp. sugar or honey
1/4 c. milk
1 tbsp. oil
1 egg
2 c. lukewarm water
1 tsp. salt
7-1/2 c. or more white flour (sifted)

**sesame seeds (optional)
a little oil
vegetable shortening**

Utensils

Large mixing bowl or pot, measuring cup, regular cup, 2 bread pans

Put the 1/4 cup of hot water in a cup with the sugar or honey. When the liquid is lukewarm, add the yeast. While the yeast mixture foams, combine in the mixing bowl the milk, 1 tablespoon oil, egg, 2 cups water, and salt. Beat all of these together with a fork. When there is at least 1/2 as much foam as liquid on the yeast mixture, add it to the liquid in the mixing bowl. Sift the white flour and then measure it. Add 2 cups at a time until 6 cups are used. Each time 2 cups are added, mix the flour with a large wooden, metal, or plastic spoon into the dough. More flour should be added only when there is no more dry flour in the dough. When 6 cups have been mixed into the dough, put the dough on a lightly floured clean, smooth surface, such as a bread board, counter, or stove top. Add more flour, 1/2 cup at a time, and mix it in with your hands until the dough is smooth and no longer sticks to your hands. Lightly oil the sides of the mixing bowl and place the dough in there to rise, and put the bowl in a warm area. In about 45 minutes to an hour the dough should have doubled in size. Punch the dough down and knead it for a few minutes. Cut the dough in half and place each half in a bread pan that has been greased with vegetable shortening. Press each half into the pan until it evenly covers the bottom of the pan. If you wish, sprinkle the tops of the breads with sesame seeds. Cover with a dish cloth and let rise in a warm place. When the dough has doubled in size, put the pans in the oven, set the oven for 350° F. and bake for 35 to 40 minutes. The loaves are done when either a broomstraw or long pronged fork comes out clean after being inserted into the bread. Take the loaves from the pans as soon as they are removed from the oven so that they will not get soggy.

Italian Bread— Old World Recipe (makes 10 loaves)

This recipe is great to make with a few friends on some cold, winter weekend. It might take all the people there to decide what the recipe is saying—but don't worry—it's hard to botch this recipe as long as you add enough yeast. You'll need a very large pot to mix the ingredients in. You can probably borrow one from a neighbor or friend. Besides putting some dough in pans, make some round loaves and braid others and bake them on cookie sheets. Do whatever your imagination tells you to and remember, the object of my including this recipe is so that you can have fun making it.

Suggested Ingredients

10 lb. white flour
6 to 8 eggs
1 c. warm water
1/2 handful salt
oil, 4 times around the pot
1-1/8 c. milk
1/4 lb. yeast
1 c. sugar

Utensils

Very large pot such as a canner, a bowl for the yeast, bread pans, and cookie sheet

As opposed to most recipes, this one requires that you add liquid to the flour and no spoon is used for mixing—just use your hands. Put all of the flour into the pot. Add the salt and sugar and mix together. Dissolve the yeast in the water. Combine the milk, eggs, and oil and add them to the flour. When adding these ingredients, do not simply dump them in one area of the dough. Pour them all around the dough so that each section will have all of these ingredients. When the yeast dissolves (it won't foam much), mix it into the flour. Then add water slowly until the dough is smooth. Knead the dough in the pot for 30 to 50 minutes (everyone should take a turn at kneading—now you know why this is a good recipe for doing with others). Let the bread rise (covered) in a warm area until double in size. Separate the dough and put it into 2 pots if necessary. After it has risen, punch it down and place all or part of the dough on a floured bread board or other smooth surface and knead for 10 minutes. Divide the dough as best you can into 10 pieces of equal size. (Loaves of different sizes will have different cooking times. If you want to make loaves of different sizes, just be aware of this.) Form dough into loaves of whatever shape you desire and when the dough has doubled in size, bake the bread for 35 to 40 minutes at 350° F. You probably will not be able to put all 10 loaves in the oven at the same time, so put as many in as you can without the pans being crowded. Bread which does not go into the oven with the first batch, may begin to rise over the tops of pans. Push the bread down and allow it to rise again if this happens. After each loaf comes out of the oven, take it out of its pan or off its cookie sheet and allow it to cool in a manner in which air will circulate freely around the bread. These loaves can be frozen for a few weeks before they lose their flavor.

Herb Bread
(makes 2 loaves)

The addition of herbs to Italian Bread makes a great treat. Follow the directions for Italian Bread. Just before adding the flour to the liquid, stir in about 3 tablespoons of any herbs you like—oregano, basil, thyme, dill, etc. Oregano in this bread will give your apartment the pleasant smell of a pizzeria. You can combine different herbs such as 1-1/2 tablespoons of oregano and 1-1/2 tablespoons of basil. I like about 3 tablespoons of herbs in this 2-loaf recipe, but you should use more or less according to your own tastes. This bread is excellent toasted or for sandwiches.

Raisin Bread
(makes 2 loaves)

The Italian Bread recipe is a very versatile recipe. You can have a raisin bread by simply adding 1-1/2 tablespoons cinnamon and 1/4- to 1/2-cup of raisins to the Italian Bread. (Omit the sesame seeds on top though.) To separate raisins, rinse them in a strainer in warm water and them mix them with the milk, oil, egg, and water. The cinnamon should be stirred into the first 2 cups of flour. Then follow the directions as given for Italian Bread.

Corn Bread
(a baking powder bread)

This is really the best corn bread recipe I've ever tasted. It is a quick bread because you use baking powder instead of yeast. No time is needed to allow the bread to rise. It's quite sweet so it makes a great dessert when topped with fruit. It also can be eaten hot or cold with margarine, or just plain. This recipe was given to me by my friend Joanne who got it from a friend of hers.

Suggested Ingredients

>3/4 c. sugar or less,
>according to taste
>1/4 c. margarine
>2 eggs
>2/3 c. cornmeal
>2 tsp. baking powder
>1-2/3 c. flour (sifted, if white)
>1/4 tsp. salt
>1 c. milk

Utensils
    2 bowls for mixing ingredients, a 9 x 11 (or so) cake pan

Preheat the oven to 350° F. Cream together with a fork, the sugar and margarine. Then add the eggs. Sift dry ingredients into the other bowl. Add them alternately with the milk, to the sugar, egg, and margarine mixture. When blended well, pour the mixture into a greased pan and bake for 25 minutes or until done.

Suggested Use of Leftovers
    Top with fruit, Creamed Chicken, or other vegetable and meat dishes.

Baking Powder Biscuits

Suggested Ingredients
>**2 c. sifted white flour**
>**3 tsp. baking powder**
>**1/4 c. sugar**
>**1/3 c. shortening**
>**1 egg, beaten**
>**1/2 tsp. salt**
>**1/4 c. milk or enough to make a dough**

Utensils
    Mixing bowl, rolling pin, greased and floured baking sheet

Preheat the oven to 425° F. to 450° F. Mix together dry ingredients. Add shortening and stir it in with a fork. Your mixture will not be smooth. Add egg and milk and stir until as smooth as possible. The mixture will be thick and you may want to mix it with your hands. Put a little flour on your clean counter or board, place the dough on it, and roll it out 1/3 to 1/2 inch thick. If you cannot get all of it to roll out evenly, reroll, after you've cut some biscuits. Cut the biscuits out with a cookie cutter or with the rim of a drinking glass pressed down against the dough. Make as many biscuits as you can, rerolling the dough as needed. Bake until golden brown or 9 to 10 minutes. Serve with margarine, jam, or honey, if desired.

Suggested Use of Leftovers
    Eat cold or reheat by putting a few tablespoons of water in a paper bag and then shaking it out. Then put the biscuits in the bag and heat in a 400° F. oven for a few minutes.

Baking Powder Biscuits, Variations

Follow the recipe above, using 1/2 whole wheat or graham flour instead of all white flour, if desired. You can also omit the sugar and add herbs such as parsley, oregano or chives. Or, omitting the sugar, add 1/4 cup of cheese.

Quick Preparation

Whole Wheat Pancakes
(8 medium pancakes)

Suggested Ingredients

3/4 c. whole wheat flour
1/2 c. white sifted flour
3 tsp. baking powder
1 tbsp. honey or sugar
1/2 tsp. salt
1 beaten egg
1 c. milk
2 tbsp. oil, melted shortening, or margarine

Utensils

2 bowls for mixing, a griddle or frying pan, a spatula

Grease your pan a little and heat it to a high heat, lowering the heat when necessary to prevent burning. Combine all dry ingredients, and combine all wet ingredients. Mix wet ingredients with dry ingredients. The mixture might be a little lumpy. Don't worry. When the pan is hot, spoon batter onto the griddle. Flip the pancakes when bubbles, that form on them, break and hollow out. Flip the second side when it is brown. Serve with margarine, and honey, jam, syrup or cinnamon and sugar.

If preferred, use all white flour.

Leftovers You Can Use
Milk which has gone sour.

Suggested Use of Leftovers
Reheat in the oven.

Quick Preparation

Yogurt Pancakes

Follow the previous recipe using 1/2 to 3/4 cup yogurt and 1/2 to 1/4 cup milk instead of the 1 cup milk called for in Whole Wheat Pancakes.

Quick Preparation

Apple Pancakes

Follow the recipe for Whole Wheat Pancakes or Yogurt Pancakes. Add thinly sliced apples to the batter. Peaches, berries, bananas, and other fruits may also be used.

Mush
(serves at least 4 as a side dish)

Cornmeal mush made in the following way may be served as a substitute for rice, potatoes, or noodles. It tastes good when served with baked lima beans and practically anything else.

Suggested Ingredients

1 c. cornmeal
1 c. cold water
1 tsp. salt
2-1/2 c. boiling water
1 tbsp. soy sauce
paprika to taste
4 tbsp. grated cheese
or 2 slices American cheese or other cheese

Utensils

Double boiler (If you do not have a double boiler use 2 saucepans. Put one inside of the other and fill the outer pot about 1/4 of the way with water.), an oven dish, something to boil the water in

Mix the cornmeal, cold water, and salt in the pot. When the mixture is smooth, add the boiling water. Simmer for 30 to 45 minutes or until the consistency is like that of a thick, hot cereal. Add 1/2 cup additional water if the mixture seems too thick. Season with soy sauce, paprika, and cheese. Put mush in a greased oven dish or pie plate. Allow it to cool and solidify at room temperature. Heat in a 350° F. oven until hot.

Suggested Use of Leftovers

Reheat in the oven. Top with margarine or cheese if desired.

Quick Preparation

French Toast
(makes about 6 pieces of toast)

Suggested Ingredients

1 c. milk
1 egg
a little salt
a little sugar or honey (optional)
a little cinnamon (optional)
margarine or oil for the pan
bread

Utensils

A frying pan or griddle

Mix all ingredients except bread. Heat your pan to medium high or high and lower it when necessary. Oil your pan. Dunk the bread in the batter. Remove it and put it on the pan. When brown, flip the bread over to the other side. For your second batch of toast, oil the pan only if necessary. Serve with margarine and jam, honey, syrup, or cinnamon and sugar.

Pizza
(makes 1 large pizza)

This recipe was invented by my friend Inés. It is easier and works better than any other pizza recipe I've tried.

Suggested Ingredients

Dough

1 c. lukewarm water
1 package dry yeast
1 tsp. sugar
2 tbsp. vegetable oil
approximately 3 c. flour

Sauce

1 small can or 1/2 large can of whole tomatoes
or a can of tomato sauce
1/2 to 1 garlic section finely chopped
a little salt, pepper, oregano

Possible condiments for the top

mozzarella cheese (or any other cheese)
grated, cut or sliced
sliced onion
green pepper
olives
sliced fresh tomatoes
thinly sliced celery
pimento
thinly sliced ham
capers
anchovies

Utensils

A cookie sheet with sides, or a large round platter, bowl for mixing dough

Dissolve the yeast and sugar in the lukewarm water. When it just begins to foam or is at least fully dissolved, add it to the flour and salt and mix and knead with your hands until you have a smooth, not sticky, silky dough. Add more flour if necessary. Put the oil in a bowl and place the dough on top of it. Cover the bowl with a dish towel, and put it in a warm place to rise for about 30 minutes.

If you have a blender, throw all sauce ingredients into the blender. The tomato and garlic will be chopped up in a few seconds. Otherwise, use a can of tomato sauce or hand chop whole tomatoes fine, chop garlic and add other ingredients. No cooking of the sauce is necessary. Set sauce aside.

Preheat the oven to 400° F. After the dough has risen, roll it out on a board or spread it out with your fingers to the approximate shape of the pan. Place it on a well-oiled cookie sheet or platter and with your fingers, shape it to the pan, stretching it and evening it where necessary. Push some dough toward the sides of the pan to create the crust. Ladle half of the tomato sauce onto the pizza, and place it in the oven and bake for about 30 minutes or until the crust is slightly golden. Remove the pizza from the oven (do not turn off the oven) and add the remaining sauce, condiments, and cheese. Return the pizza to the oven and bake it until the cheese melts and the condiments are hot.

Advance Preparation
    To make a pizza in advance, freeze it and then reheat it.

Leftovers You Can Use
    Use leftover cooked tomato sauce. Add water to make it thin.

Suggested Use of Leftovers
    Freeze pizza uncooked, partially cooked, or fully cooked to be used at a future date. Reheat in a 400° F. oven. Or reheat leftover pizza which has been refrigerated.

Sample menus for two weeks
(with luncheon suggestions for each week)

DINNER SUGGESTIONS:

DAY 1: Lamb Shank Marinade
Orange Glazed Carrots
Rice
Salad

DAY 2: Stuffed Peppers
Stove Top Macaroni and Cheese
Fruit Salad

DAY 3: Meat Loaf, using leftover raw chopped meat from Stuffed Peppers
Boiled Potatoes
Fried Cauliflower
Salad

DAY 4: Lamb Pot Pie, using leftover lamb from Day 1 (save the lamb bone and put it in the refrigerator or freezer for a future soup) and leftover boiled potatoes from Day 3
Apple Sauce

DAY 5: Quick preparation:
Poached Fish
Reheated Glazed Carrots from Day 1
Fried Rice, made from leftover rice from Day 1
Salad

DAY 6: Pizza, using leftover raw pepper from Day 2
Salad

DAY 7: Quick preparation:
Scrambled Vegetables, using leftover cauliflower from Day 3 and leftover onion, greens, and celery from a salad
Radishes and carrots with Yogurt Salad Dressing

DAY 8: Broiled Chicken
Zucchini Parmesan
Asparagus Pancakes
Tomato Salad

DAY 9: Quick preparation:
Omelette
Leftover Asparagus Pancake from Day 8
Salad

DAY 10: Creamed Chicken, made from leftover chicken from Day 8
Save the chicken bones and make a soup stock along with the lamb bones.
Rice
Salad

DAY 11: Eggplant, Sort of Parmesan
Beet Greens
Mashed Potatoes
Salad

DAY 12: Soup with leftover and fresh vegetables and leftover lamb and chicken bones
Corn Bread
Apple and Carrot Salad

DAY 13: Stuffed Cabbage
Southern Fried Green Tomatoes
Fried Rice, made from leftover rice from Day 10
Salad

DAY 14: Quick preparation:
Reheated Soup

Reheated Green Tomatoes from Day 13
Cheese
Sunflower Seeds
Celery
Carrots

LUNCH SUGGESTIONS:

Make sandwiches from leftover chicken, eggplant, and omelette. Take cold asparagus pancakes in a lunch.

Make sandwiches from leftover stuffed peppers, meatloaf, and fish (make it into a fish salad).

Eat cold or reheated pizza instead of a sandwich.

part 4
COUNTRY LIVING IN THE CITY

Some are by nature urban folks who enjoy a city's offering of constant activity and entertainment, while others prefer the quiet serenity of the country. My grandmother, for instance, when she visits the country, is kept awake late at night by crickets and awakened early by the chirping of birds. However, she sleeps right through the noise of the garbage trucks outside her city apartment at dawn. Just the same, most of us would ideally want a little bit of city in our rural environments and a country flair mingling with the city.

When people think of canning fruits and vegetables, making jams and ice cream and growing herbs, they tend to associate these things with the country. The truth is that these things can be done in the city. In fact, your access to good fresh fruits and vegetables may be better than that of your cousin in the country who doesn't have a garden, a berry patch, or fruit trees. Quite often the produce sold in the country supermarkets is far inferior to that which may be bought in the city. When I was a kid living in a rural town in Connecticut, my city aunt and uncle used to bring fresh fruit to us when they came to visit. We used to flip out over the cherries, plums, and grapes, the likes of which we had never seen in the country. The reason for this irony is that fruit and vegetable-producers would probably prefer to do most of their business in the city and within their own areas. This leaves northern rural areas without good produce in the winter and nonagricultural rural areas in pretty poor shape all year round. Large farm markets which offer a varied selection of fruits and vegetables which are grown throughout the country (and the world) are most often centered near cities because that's where the business is. You can pick up bushels or pounds of good produce for canning and jamming at these markets, especially during the summer and early fall. So as far as variety goes, you definitely have an advantage over the country folks.

Some of these things will save you money. Others will give you pleasure in the preparation and results. The chapters that follow will take you back to things which are reminiscent of our prairie or hill origins. I can almost smell the fresh air and the cow manure.

22
INTRODUCTION TO CANNING AND PICKLING

Canning certain fruits and vegetables—when they are available to you at a low price and in bulk—might save you money. It is also very convenient to have a good supply of ready-to-use foods at your finger tips. The following sections will give you some basic information about canning, but you'll probably want to get additional information through pamphlets or books. A few canning bulletins that are available to you, are listed at the end of this chapter.

EQUIPMENT

Canning does not have to be a mundane, long, and difficult task —providing that you are selective in those things which you can. The equipment you need for the type of canning I do is actually quite limited. You'll need one or two large (eight-quart or more) pots with covers, canning jars with rims and lids, kitchen tongs (those used for turning chicken and steaks), towels, a ladle, a saucepan and, if you want, a jar funnel (jar funnels fit into the rims of jars and facilitate the pouring of food into the jars).

WHAT TO CAN

I usually can such things as pickles, tomatoes, and fruits because they are easy to prepare and they taste good after they are canned. I do not can green or other vegetables because they require special equipment such as a pressure canner. With most vegetables the cooking temperature must be extremely high to prevent botulism—a disease which can be contracted due to improper canning of vegetables—especially beans. I also don't can vegetables because they just don't taste that great after they've been boiled and processed to death. The information given below is for foods such as pickles, tomatoes, and fruits. If you are interested in doing other vegetables, definitely read other sources before going ahead with the canning.

STERILIZATION

When canning anything, precautions must be taken to prevent and detect spoilage of foods. Because microscopic organisms can get into food and jars, it is essential that everything be sterilized through a high heating process. Also you must make sure that all lids seal properly. If they do not, you should reseal them.

Jars can be sterilized in two ways. Wash them in detergent and water and rinse them in clear water. Then, for a few minutes place them in a pot of boiling water or put them in your oven at a low temperature. I find that by using the oven, I need fewer pots and I don't crowd the stove burners. Do not remove jars from their hot environment until you are ready to put the food in them. Lids and rims can be sterilized in the boiling water in a saucepan and removed when needed. Jars, lids, and rims should be removed with tongs.

SELECTION
OF FRUITS AND VEGETABLES

Firm but ripe fruits and vegetables should be used in canning. Tomatoes that are bruised or wormy can be used providing that all bad sections are cut out. But a cucumber which is slightly soft, will make a very unsuccessful pickle. All solid foods should be packed fairly tightly into the jars and, if required, well covered with liquid. Foods should be packed to a level that is half an inch from the top of the jar.

SEALING
AND PROCESSING

Edges and rims of the jars should be wiped with a damp cloth before they are sealed if even the slightest amount of food spills on them. Food that clings to these areas could prevent a proper seal from being made.

Processing of foods, once in the jar, is necessary in some cases. Put jars in a large pot with a lid and make sure that water covers the tops of the jars. Most eight-quart pots are not deep enough to do this with quart jars but are fine when using pint jars. Boil the water with the jars for the required amount of time. This processing will help to make a proper seal and will kill bacteria.

The day after you can, test the lids to see if proper seals were made. Unscrew the rim and slowly turn the jar over. If there is any leakage, throw out the lid, sterilize a new lid in boiling water, put it on the jar and then process the jar. Also test for improper seals by checking the lid—if the center of the lid bulges out, push it down. If it does not stay down, remove the lid and put on a new lid following the above instructions.

SPOILAGE

Spoilage of canned foods is indicated through bulging lids, leakage, liquid that spurts when the jar is opened, mold, or an unpleasant smell. Botulism, which does not occur in pickles, tomatoes, or fruits, is colorless, odorless, and tasteless. It should be noted that botulism bacteria cannot exist in fruits or acidic solutions. Tomatoes are naturally acidic and the vinegar added to pickles is acidic.

The following recipes are pretty standard ones. You'll be able to find similar ones in most canning books.

Pickles

Suggested Ingredients

> 5 lb. very hard, small cucumbers
> 3/8 c. salt
> about 3/8 c. pickling spice or your own seasonings,
> or a large sprig of dill plant with seeds
> 2-1/2 qt. water
> 5/8 c. vinegar
> a clove of garlic for each jar

(For larger batches just multiply all measurements by the number of times larger you want to make your batch.)

Utensils

See section on Utensils in this chapter

Wash and scrub all cucumbers. Sterilize jars according to one of the methods in the Sterilization section in this chapter. Boil lids and rims. Heat liquid ingredients to the point of boiling. Put dry ingredients in each jar and then pour in your liquid to within half an inch of the top of the jar. Wipe off rim of the jar and then put your hot lid and rim evenly and firmly on the jar. Put all jars in a pot of water which covers the top of the jars. Cover the pot, bring the water to a boil, and process from one to ten minutes.

Remove all jars from the pot and allow them to cool for about twelve hours. If you can, put the jars on cool oven burners or on racks, so air will circulate freely around them. But do not put the jars in a draft.

In twelve hours, or the next day, test the seals as in the section under Sealing and Processing. If seals are not proper, reseal and then reprocess the improperly sealed jars. Reprocess only one minute after the water reaches the point of boiling. These pickles are ready to eat a few weeks after canning and will last indefinitely.

Fruits

Suggested Ingredients

**firm fruit
sugar or honey and water or fruit juice,
(about 4 c. water or juice to 3 c. sugar
or 1-1/2 to 2 c. honey)**

Utensils

See Utensil section in this chapter

Peaches and pears should be peeled. Most other fruits do not have to be peeled. To easily remove peach peels, follow peeling directions as with Tomato recipe. All fruits should be washed and then sliced and pitted, if desired. The sugar and water can be either cooked with the fruit in a large covered pot, or it can be heated until boiling and poured over raw fruit.

For Cooked Fruit: Fruit, when cooked quickly, becomes juicy, so little sugar and water will be needed. Cook fruit with sugar and water (in desired proportions) until the mixture gently boils. Sterilize jars, pour fruit into jars, seal, and process for 10 minutes.

For Cold Packed Fruit: Heat a sugar and water syrup to boiling. Sterilize jars, pack cold fruit into jars, pour boiling syrup over fruit. Seal and then process for about 25 minutes. Canned fruits will last indefinitely.

Tomatoes
(cold packed)

Suggested Ingredients

**tomatoes
1 tsp. salt for every qt. jar**

Utensils

See Equipment section in this chapter

Pour boiling water over a dish of whole, unpeeled, uncored tomatoes. Let them stand in the water for 30 to 45 seconds. Submerge tomatoes into cold water. The skins can be peeled off easily. Core tomatoes. Add salt and then raw tomatoes to jars. Then follow directions as in the Pickle Recipe to seal and process. Canned tomatoes will last indefinitely.

Stewed Tomatoes

Suggested Ingredients

tomatoes
green peppers
salt
other desired seasonings
basil
onions
a little sugar

Utensils
See Utensil section in this chapter

Peel and core tomatoes as in the previous recipe. Put ingredients in any proportions into your large pot. Use lots of tomatoes because they boil down to nothing. Cook tomatoes until a lot of foam forms on top. Pour the sauce into sterilized jars (see Sterilization section of this chapter) and put on your lids and rims. No processing is necessary. If desired, process 1 minute after water comes to a boil.

Use these tomatoes as you would tomatoes in casseroles, fish, and sauce. These stewed tomatoes will be of a very thin consistency. Tomato paste will thicken the tomatoes when added to a recipe. These tomatoes will last indefinitely.

MAIL ORDER CANNING INFORMATION

Ball Corporation
Muncie, Indiana 47302
Ask for the *Ball Blue Book on Canning*. It was fifty cents last time I checked.

Office of Information
U.S. Department of Agriculture
Washington, D.C. 20250
Ask for *Home and Garden Bulletin #8* to get information on fruits and vegetables.
Ask for *Home and Garden Bulletin G92* for pickles and relishes.

23
HOMESTEADING FOODS

Homemade bread, jam and cakes and other foods that remind you of a country grandmother are fun to make. Food gifts are also cheap presents for the holidays. When simply, but attractively wrapped, food gifts should look very enticing.

When I'm wrapping a jam as a gift, I simply cover the top of the jar with a neatly cut piece of aluminum foil and then attach a bow to the top of the foil with a doubled-over piece of tape stuck to the back of the bow. A bow can be made by folding thin ribbon in layers and tying it together with a small piece of ribbon.

Breads can be neatly wrapped in aluminum foil or plastic wrap. Ribbon can be put around the bread in the same way you would for any other package you would wrap.

Granola and Earth Snacks also make great gifts. The comments you get from people are terrific: "My. That certainly was an interesting gift you gave me. It tasted great. No, it really did." Why people think grains, nuts, seeds, and dried fruits are not supposed to taste good, and are strange, I'll never know. Even when some people discover that they like them, they still feel weird about eating these things. (I, for one, feel weird about eating a Hostess Twinkie.) These types of natural snacks can be plastic bagged, and ribboned. I also usually include a piece of paper inside the bag to inform the person of the ingredients in the gift.

Recipes for these things, and more, follow.

JAMS, JELLIES, PRESERVES, AND MARMALADES

Jams, jellies, preserves, and marmalades can be made successfully with almost any fruit, sugar, and a store-bought pectin that jells the juice of the fruit.

Pectin is a natural gelatin that is present in some fruits such as apples, cranberries, currants, gooseberries, guavas, quinces, and the inner peels of oranges, lemons, and grapefruits. Pectin is absent from strawberries and raspberries. One can make pectin extract with hard, ripe apples, skins, or cores, or the white inner peel of citrus fruits, but at the time of this writing, I've never tried this and have always relied upon commercial pectin.

The most foolproof recipes I've used are included with boxes of Sure-Jell and bottles of Certo. Both are commercial pectins. Sure-Jell is preservative free, but Certo is not—so I no longer use Certo. Some home-invented recipes I've tried do not jell at all for me, so unless you've got some other good recipes, you're bound to do well by closely following the recipes offered by makers of Sure-Jell and Certo.

Homemade jam, jellies, preserves, and marmalades can be poured into canning jars and sealed as described in Chapter 22. Or more simply, you can use any glasses or jars available to you. They do not need covers. They can be sealed with paraffin which is available at many supermarkets. Place broken pieces of paraffin in a clean, empty tomato sauce or other can. Place this can in a small pot one-quarter filled with water. If the can floats, remove some of the water. Heat the paraffin slowly, and make sure that the water does not evaporate. But if it does, add more water. Beware of high heats, as paraffin is very flammable. Never put a can of paraffin directly onto a stove burner—it could burst into flames. To facilitate pouring the paraffin, press the top of the can with two fingers to form a spout. Do this while the can is still cool.

After the jam, jelly, preserve, or marmalade has been poured into each jar, clean any drippings or splashes from the inside of the jar. Then pour about one-eighth to one-quarter of an inch of paraffin over each jam, jelly, preserve, or marmalade. This will seal them from any bacteria or dust. Store the jams, jellies, preserves, or marmalades in a place that is not too warm. Jams, jellies, preserves, and marmalades that have been properly sealed will last indefinitely.

Banana Bread
(makes 2 loaves)

Nel (maker of granola) devised this recipe. It is delicious—especially when it is not overcooked. Nel recommends that you cook it for one hour and 10 minutes. I found an hour to be enough. It really depends upon your oven. Don't worry about the crack which may form down the center of the bread. That's supposed to mean you have a good bread. To test the bread to see if it's done, poke a broomstraw through the center. If it comes out gooey, it's not done. If it comes out fairly clean, but a little moist, then the bread is done. Flip it out onto a cake rack, a cool burner, or on one of its narrow sides onto the stove or counter, and allow it to cool before wrapping. Banana breads can be refrigerated or frozen—they will last for weeks in a good freezer and for two weeks in the refrigerator.

Suggested Ingredients

>4 c. whole wheat or white flour (sifted, if white)
>4 tsp. baking powder
>1/2 tsp. baking soda
>1 tsp. salt
>a pinch of cinnamon
>2/3 c. shortening
>1-1/3 c. honey or sugar
>4 beaten eggs
>1/3 c. wheat germ
>1-1/2 c. very ripe bananas
>1-1/2 c. apple sauce

Utensils

>2 mixing bowls, 2 bread pans, a cup to mash bananas

Preheat oven to 350° F. Sift or stir together dry ingredients, except wheat germ. In a larger bowl, mix shortening and honey. Add beaten eggs and wheat germ. Mix well.

Mash bananas. Alternate, combining the mashed bananas and dry ingredients with the wet mixture. Stir well. Pour the mixture into well-greased bread pans. Sprinkle the tops with cinnamon. Bake at 350° F. for an hour to an hour and 10 minutes or until done.

YOGURT

Some people think yogurt is a dieter's food. Others think of yogurt as a fruit pudding or dessert. Yogurt can be these things, but it's a lot more. It can be a breakfast with granola and/or fruit; it is a major ingredient in some salad dressings or pancake mixes; and it can be used instead of sour cream or milk. (See Salad Dressing, Pancakes, and Nel's Granola recipes for yogurt uses.)

Homemade yogurt usually has a somewhat different texture. It is a little thinner than the commercial varieties. This makes homemade yogurt more appealing to some people—and less appealing to others.

In order to make your own yogurt, you must start with a small amount of existing yogurt. Yogurt contains something called yogurt culture. When a small amount of this culture is placed in milk, the culture multiplies so that after five to eight hours you have yogurt instead of milk. The only readily available source of yogurt culture is existing plain yogurt. The first time you make yogurt, you will have to buy a plain commercial yogurt (or borrow some from a friend). After you have made your own yogurt, always leave at least three tablespoons of yogurt in the refrigerator for your next batch and be sure that it is still fresh. If, after a few batches, your yogurt becomes too thin or old, start again with commercial yogurt. Try the previously mentioned salad, pancake and granola with yogurt, or serve it with vanilla and honey or brown sugar or jam. Or, freeze it with fruit in cups with sticks or spoons in them to make yogurt pops.

Yogurt
(makes 1 quart)

Ingredients

1 qt. powdered, whole, 2% or 1% milk
3 heaping tbsp. of fresh, plain yogurt
at room temperature

Utensils

Saucepan, earthenware with lid

If you are using powdered milk, mix it according to directions on the package. Heat the milk to *near* boiling. Pour it into an earthenware bowl and cool to lukewarm. Stir in the room temperature yogurt, cover the bowl and place it on a warm blanket, or cover it with a terry cloth towel, or put it in a large pot that has warm water in it. Yogurt that is setting must be kept warm—ideally around 100° to 120° F. The pilot light on a gas stove does a good job in keeping setting yogurt at that temperature. If the earthenware bowl is warm to your touch, you can assume that it is at the proper temperature. Homemade yogurt forms a thin layer of liquid (whey) on top. Don't worry about it. When the yogurt reaches a consistency of heavy cream (or thicker), put it in jars and refrigerate.

YOGURT CHEESE

I first discovered yogurt cheese when, having prepared yogurt the night before, I checked out the results and to my distress there was a lot of whey floating on top and runny small curds sitting down below. This flop can occur for many reasons including: The yogurt culture was killed due to overheating; the yogurt was not warm enough while setting; or the yogurt used as starter was of inferior quality. Deciding that the reason for my failure was the fact that the apartment had gotten cool during the night, I put the disaster in a pot and attempted to reheat it. You can't do that to yogurt and expect it to continue to be yogurt. Within seconds, all liquid surfaced and the curds solidified to the consistency of ricotta or pot cheese. I strained the combination through an old (but clean) pair of nylon underwear (any fine material will do) and ended up with a lot of whey and about a cup of cheese. I used the whey instead of milk in cooking. The cheese can be used like cottage cheese seasoned with salt, pepper, and herbs or in lasagna or other cooked dishes.

I vaguely remember some story from when I was a kid with a title similar to *How Cheese Was Discovered*. The claim through this saga was that an Eastern European peasant put his daily supply of milk in a bag made of cow's stomach and went out to tend his flock. Because the day was warm and the bag moved back and forth as he walked, as the sun warmed the milk it turned into cheese. Cow's stomachs have something called rennet in them that contributed to this cheese process. Anyway, this story about a humble peasant discovering cheese while in his pastures is somehow more appealing than mine of discovering it on a gas burner in the Bronx. Besides, yogurt cheese had been discovered previously, I later found out. Anyway, yogurt cheese tastes good and you might as well do something with your botched yogurt.

Orange (Bronx Cheer) Cake with Raspberries

My husband invented this cake one year for my birthday. You can use any fruit as topping, although if you don't use raspberries it will spoil the name of the cake. Make this cake on a special occasion because it's expensive in comparison to most recipes in this book.

Suggested Ingredients
1-1/2 c. white or whole wheat flour (sifted, if white)
1/2 tsp. salt
1-3/4 tsp. baking powder
3/4 c. sugar
6 tbsp. melted margarine
1/4 c. orange juice
1/4 c. water
1 tbsp. lemon juice
2 beaten eggs

Topping

1/4 pt. medium or heavy cream,
with 1 tsp. sugar and 1/2 cap vanilla
(sugar and vanilla are optional)
1/2 to 3/4 c. fresh raspberries
or drained frozen raspberries

Utensils

2 bowls for mixing, a small saucepan for melting margarine, 1 8- or 9-inch round or square cake pan, an egg beater

Preheat the oven to 375° F. Combine flour, salt, and baking powder in a bowl. In another bowl, mix sugar, melted margarine and then the remaining batter ingredients. Combine the 2 bowls of ingredients. Put the mixture in a greased cake pan and bake at 375° F. for 30 minutes or until a straw stuck through the center of the cake comes out almost dry.

Remove the cake from the oven and flip it out onto a rack or plate. When the cake is cool, top it with whipped cream and raspberries. To make the whipped cream, beat heavy or medium cream until it peaks. Add sugar and vanilla to the cream as you beat it, before it thickens.

If you decide to bake the cake with whole wheat flour, you will get a cake with an extremely nice consistency. However, the orange flavor is a lot stronger when you use white flour. Try the cake both ways—you'll find that it tastes like two different cakes.

Suggested Use of Leftovers

Leftovers from this recipe are obvious—but when you do have leftovers there are a few things you'll want to know. This cake should be refrigerated. You'll also probably want to cover the top so that the cream won't take on the flavors of everything else in your refrigerator.

Pumpkin Pie
(makes 2 pies)

This recipe was given to me by my mother-in-law. I usually make two pies at once because they don't last long—even with only two of us eating the pies. Pumpkin pies, if kept for more than a day, should be refrigerated. I once had one that had been left out to turn moldy on me—that was when I cooked four pies at once.

Suggested Ingredients

Pie Crust
(for 2 pies)

approximately:
3-1/2 c. sifted flour
1 tsp. salt
1 c. shortening
2/3 c. cold water

Filling
(for 2 pies)

4 beaten eggs
1 c. brown sugar
1 tsp. salt
1/2 tsp. cinnamon
1/2 tsp. nutmeg
1/2 tsp. ginger
1/4 tsp. ground or grated cloves
1 13-oz. can evaporated milk
1 29-oz. can (1 lb. 13 oz.) unseasoned pumpkin

Utensils

Mixing bowls, something to sift the flour, a rolling pin, 2 8-inch pie plates

Combine the dry pastry ingredients. Add the shortening and with a fork blend the shortening into the flour. Gradually add enough water to make a pliable—but not soggy—dough. Flour a clean counter surface or a board. Divide the dough in half. Put some flour on your rolling pin. Put one portion of dough on the floured surface and roll out the dough as evenly as you can to about 1/8-inch thick. Carefully pick up the rolled out dough and place it in the pie plate. Trim or fold under the edges. Press the trimmed edges down to the plate with the prongs of a fork. Roll out the second portion of dough and follow directions as with the first portion. Do not be surprised if there is a little leftover dough.

Preheat your oven to 450° F.

Combine in a mixing bowl, beaten eggs, sugar, salt, and spices. Mix well and then add the pumpkin and milk. When the mixture is smooth, pour half into one pie shell and half into the other.

Put the pies in the oven and bake at 450° F. for 10 minutes. Reduce the heat to 375° F. for 40 minutes or until the filling begins to brown and crack.

Suggested Use of Leftovers

Leftover dough can be rolled out and molded into shells or turnovers. Fill dough with jams, apple sauce seasoned with cinnamon, sugar, and nutmeg, or other fruits and spices. Bake in a 375° F. oven until the crust is brown and the fruit bubbles.

MABEL IN CEREALLAND

There was once a housewife whose name was Mabel Fitch. Mabel went to the supermarket one day in her section of the Bronx to buy some meat, eggs, cereal, and "terlit" paper (as she would say).

As Mabel was pushing and scraping her three and one-half wheeled grocery cart (the only one left in the store) and fantasizing about winning "Let's Make a Deal" and kissing Monty Hall, she realized that she had come to the cereal aisle and would be forced to make the big decision of the day. Her son Harold had mentioned that he wanted the cereal with the man with the funny hat on the package. Jessica, her daughter, wanted Cocoa Krispies but Alfred, her husband, hated them, and the ants seemed to like Cocoa Krispies the best. Mabel's head began to whirl inside her curlers, and she stared at the cereals and wiped her brow with her hand. Cornflakes, Wheaties, Rice Krispies, Quisp (charged with B vitamins and iron), Puffed Rice, Pebbles, Super Orange Crisp, Pink Panther Flakes, Red Berry, Booberry, Frankenberry, King Vitamin, Count Chocula, Sir Grapefellow, Cap'n Crunch, Crunchberries, Lucky

Charms, Trix.... Mabel leaned her plump little body helplessly against her grocery cart and futilely attempted to get down to the business of making a decision. Gradually, the cereal aisle closed in on Mabel as marshmallows, Booberries, raisins and Cocoa Hoots floated through the air....

Sir Grapefellow appeared in a purple satin tuxedo with sequins on it. He looked like Liberace except that his face, teeth, and eyes were all purple. He carried a staff with a grape the size of a grapefruit on top, and with an evil grin and squinty eyes he sauntered up to Mabel, the fair lass, and within a second had unpinned her golden hair which billowed to the floor.

"Help," she whimpered in a barely audible voice. Her abundant and tempting youthful breasts heaved in terror. Sir Grapefellow stared at them, licentiously grinned, and bit Mabel on her delicate white neck.

"Oh," squeaked Mabel. As Sir Grapefellow squinted his horribly lustful eyes at Mabel's eighteen-inch waist, thunder rumbled in the background. Suddenly a heroic knight appeared through a spark of lightning. "I have come to save you from this gloop!" he said triumphantly. Mabel, though breathless and distraught, managed to surmise—from the sword glittering with B_1's, B_6's, A's, C's and E's, phosphorous and iron—that this glorious savior was indeed King Vitamin. Sir Grapefellow raised his grape-laden staff—but it was too late. As King Vitamin gouged his sword through the villain, purple milk spurted from Grapefellow's body and trickled onto Mabel's sneakers....

Mabel blinked several times, sadly felt her thirty-two-inch waist with her hands, and sighed:

"Damn you, King Goody Two Shoes, you spoiled my fun." Sadly she stared at the fading image of Sir Grapefellow on the supermarket floor.

Mabel picked up a box of corn flakes and wheeled her cart into the long check-out line.

Nel's Granola

Granola is a multi-grain and seed cereal which can be eaten with milk, yogurt, or yogurt and fruit. It can also be eaten as a snack just as it is. A variety of foods, such as ice cream, pudding, and fruit salad, are highlighted when granola is sprinkled on them. If you are making a crumb cake, use the granola for the crumb part. Besides being so deliciously versatile, it's also very nutritious. Since granola is quite filling, you only need to use about half as much as you would use of another cereal such as corn flakes.

The recipe below makes a large batch. You may want to reduce the proportions by one-half or more. The granola which is available in the supermarkets usually does not contain most of the ingredients in this recipe. Many of the ingredients in this recipe can be eliminated if you do not have them. Oats, honey, and oil are the only essential ingredients. Granola is best stored in a jar with a lid, or in a plastic bag.

Suggested Ingredients

1/2 to 3/4 c. vegetable oil
1/2 c. honey
1 tbsp. vanilla
3/4 to 1 c. sesame seeds
5-1/2 tbsp. instant milk
1 c. coconut shreds
1 c. sunflower seeds
1 c. chopped walnuts, slivered almonds,
or raw or roasted peanuts
8 cups rolled oats
2 tbsp. brewer's yeast (optional)—
for vitamin supplement

Utensils

A large mixing bowl, a small saucepan, cookie sheets

Mix together in a large mixing bowl all the dry ingredients and nuts. In a small saucepan, heat together the oil, honey, and vanilla until thin. Gradually add this to the dry ingredients.

Spread thin layers of the cereal on one or more baking sheets and toast them in a 225° F. to 250° F. oven, turning the granola over often with a spatula. All of the granola will not fit on one baking sheet, so you will have to repeat the process until all of the granola has been toasted. If you have more than one baking sheet, you may put two of them in the oven at the same time. The granola is done when it becomes a golden brown color. Be sure not to burn it.

Granola #2

Follow directions as in Nel's Granola eliminating such things as coconut, sunflower seeds, or other ingredients which might be costly and add 1/2 cup raisins. Also, melt 2 heaping tablespoons of peanut butter along with the oil, honey, and vanilla.

Earth Snacks

There used to be a natural food store in New Milford, Connecticut, called Frog Meadows Earth Snacks. They also sold each ingredient separately so you could make your own snacks. Not all natural food stores sell these exact ingredients, but you should use your imagination and vary the contents of Earth Snacks. Also, to save a little money, look for some ingredients (such as wheat germ and raisins) in a supermarket. Earth Snacks taste great—you can eat them like popcorn or candy, but you won't get as fat and your teeth won't fall out as fast. In fact, they are great for you.

Suggested Ingredients in Any Proportion
sunflower seeds
pumpkin seeds
wheat germ
unroasted peanuts
toasted soy beans
light or dark raisins
dried figs
dried pineapple
raw cashews
sea salt, kosher salt, or regular salt

Pour some wheat germ in a bowl, cut up the pineapple, figs, or other fruit and coat them with the wheat germ to prevent the fruit from sticking together. Leave all these ingredients in the bowl. Add the raisins, also coating them with the wheat germ. Add all other ingredients and salt the mixture according to taste. Store in jars, or plastic bags.

GROWING BEAN SPROUTS

Sprouts are great vegetables because you can have them fresh all year round. You can easily grow them in your dark city apartment. Sprouts can be steamed or sautéed (gently fried) and are good in combination with meats, fish, and other vegetables, or by themselves.

Types of Beans to Use: Mung, soy, kidney, lentil, or any other dried bean. Beans are obtained in packages and can be purchased wholesale through a co-op or at some large farm markets, in bulk.

Utensils

A bowl, a screen, colander, or a cloth which can be made taut, a catch basin (bowl)

Directions

1. Soak beans overnight or all day in three times as much water as beans. The water should be warm.
2. Pour the water off after soaking. Rinse the beans carefully.
3. Spread the beans on a screen, colander, or on a taut absorbent cloth with a catch basin below.
4. Rinse the beans approximately every 4 to 6 hours (don't get up in the middle of the night to do it—they are not like a baby whose diaper has to be changed). Make sure when you rinse the beans that as much water as possible is drained off. The catch basin should take care of the excess water.

Keep the beans in a warm dark place such as a dark, stuffy closet, or put them in a corner near a pipe or heat duct with a box over them.

Beans usually take 60 to 80 hours to sprout. Mung sprouts will be 3 to 4 inches long, soys 2 to 3 inches, and lentils about an inch.

If you wish, expose the sprouts to indirect sunlight for a few hours to form chlorophyll. Too much sunlight will toughen the sprouts.

Grow as many sprouts as you want at a time, though half a pound should be a sufficient supply. Store sprouts in the refrigerator in a bag.

The bean does not have to be removed from the sprout when the process is completed. It too can be eaten. If you wish, detach the bean and sprout and use them separately. For instance, sprouts can be steamed with other vegetables and the beans can be cooked with meat. Often the beans, after having been exposed to a lot of water, become saturated and spoil. Limas and kidneys have a tendency to do this. Throw the beans away if they become mushy. The sprouts, however, will still be usable.

Sprouting beans sometimes smell funny. Don't let the smell bother you. Once the sprouts are rinsed, the smell should disappear.

24

A FEW COUNTRY THINGS

TERRARIUM

Imagine green ferns and moss, partridge berries, violets, shelf mushrooms and decaying wood blending into your city apartment. Even if you don't know what some of these things are, the prospects of having something very green in your apartment should make you happy.

If you've ever been out in a fertile woodland in the spring or summer, you've probably noticed an obviously serene, lush, and alive atmosphere. You can hear the birds chirping far above your head. Flowers are scattered in clusters, everything is moist or humid and very, very green. Your terrarium can be a re-creation of this atmosphere, minus the birds. Like the woodland, it will remain very green and moist. I even have an earthworm living in mine. I discovered him one day leaning against the side of the terrarium jar. He's probably keeping my terrarium soil very fertile and healthy.

Making a terrarium will require a trip to the country unless you live in a city where you can find plants and earth without digging up someone's lawn. A jaunt in the country will probably do you some good anyway. The fresh air might revive some dormant receptacle of your spirit.

The word terrarium is copied from the word aquarium. Aquariums are water tanks and terrariums are earth tanks. If you've ever taken a Latin based language in school you can probably figure out what "aqua" and "terra" mean. As for the "rium" it doesn't mean tank, but you get the idea.

More explicitly, you can make your own terrarium with an old fish tank that is covered with a piece of glass, or you can create a terrarium with a covered glass jar or bowl. Covering the glass container creates the moist atmosphere that keeps the plants constantly thriving, because they feel as if they are in their own environment. (If you think that my ascribing human characteristics to a plant is unnecessary anthropomorphism, you might have a point. But plants really do have feelings in the sense that if they're not comfortable, they'll die.)

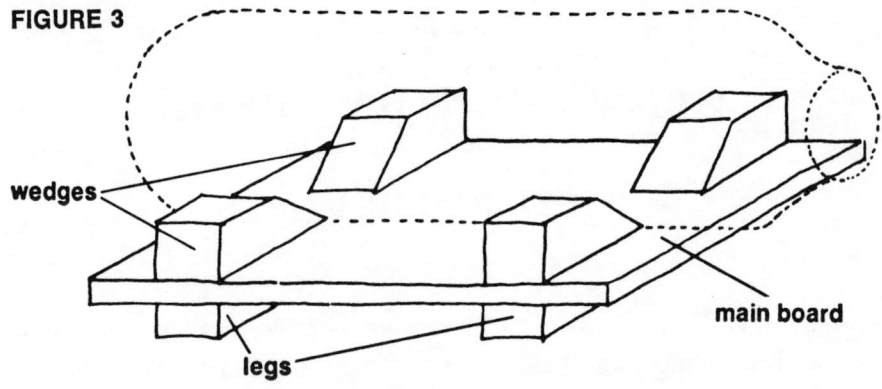

FIGURE 3

The most uncomplicated and usually the least expensive terrarium is one made out of a jar. Unless you can get an old aquarium cheap or free, you'll probably spend too much money to make your terrarium worth it. However, if you can get an aquarium, it's O.K. if it has a few leaks in the seams. Your terrarium does not have to be totally airtight. Large institutional mayonnaise or other glass gallon jars make ideal terrariums. If you choose taller plants, the jar can stand upright. If your plants are shorter, you'll want to lay the jar on its side. If the jar lies on its side, it will have to be put on some sort of stand or holder so that it does not roll off the table. My husband made a beautiful wooden stand for my terrarium out of old, weathered wood. For a diagram of the stand, see Figure 3. At any rate, choose your container. Jars that lie on their sides must have a lid or some other covering. Containers that stand upright may be covered with glass or clear plastic.

To make the terrarium stand, you'll need: four wedges (cut at right angles) to support the jar bottom; a main board which is four or five inches longer than the jar; and two small rectangular pieces for the legs. Nail the legs on their sides to the bottom of the main board at each end. Nail wedges to the top of the main board at each end. These wedges, when placed face to face, will cradle the bottom of the jar as it lies on its side.

Next, you'll want to think about what type of plants you want in your terrarium. All the plants you choose should be from similar or the same environments and you should remember that flowering plants will not always be in bloom in this atmosphere. If you do choose a flowering plant for your terrarium you should also appreciate its appearance when it is not blooming. Whatever type of plants you use, as you are digging them up, take along some of the soil from that vicinity to use in your terrarium. The plants will have a better chance of survival, since they are used to that particular composition of soil and it is probably nutritionally balanced for them. In my opinion the most beautiful as well as successful terrariums are those that are created of moss and other woodland plants. But you must decide for yourself what plants you want to look at.

When you dig up your plants, be careful to keep the roots intact and leave large clumps of soil around the plant whenever possible. After you've gathered your soil and plants, put them in a plastic bag until you can place them in the terrarium. Get them to the terrarium as soon as possible.

Place a layer of earth at least an inch high in the bottom of small terrariums and more in larger ones. Next, gently put the plants into the soil leaving the earth that has clung to the plants on them, thus adding soil to the layer in the terrarium. As you plant, arrange everything in a way which looks attractive to you. Water the plants and earth *very well* and then cover the terrarium with the lid or glass. Your garden is now completed.

Woodland terrariums can be kept in poorly lit places, though some light will be beneficial to them. Do not expose any terrarium to strong sunlight.

If water begins to condense on the glass of your terrarium, fogging it so you can't see your plants, remove the cover for a while until the glass clears. Some condensation will be beneficial—like a spring shower. You may wipe the glass with a cloth if you wish, but be careful not to harm the plants. If the cover is removed for any length of time, the plants and soil should be watered. Under average circumstances the terrarium should not require watering.

Some plants in your terrarium may die for various reasons. One reason may be that their life cycle has simply ended. Remove those plants and replace them with others.

POTTED HERBS

If you think that picking fresh herbs in the middle of winter and using them in your meals is an enjoyable prospect, then you should definitely start growing your own herbs indoors. Not only do fresh herbs taste great, they also add a subtle, pleasant aroma to your apartment. Some of them are even an aid in keeping certain bugs away. It's a neat sort of feeling to be cooking something (let's say fish) and deciding on the spur of the moment that some fresh parsley would taste great with it. All you have to do is pinch some sprigs off your plant and you have an exciting addition to your meal.

Many different herbs can be planted indoors. Your best guide for each herb is to follow the directions on the seed packets for depth of planting and any other specific directions for things such as watering, thinning, and amount of sunlight. Then follow the general rules for inside planting that are given below. Although I have only planted basil, chives, parsley, and oregano indoors, the treatment I give all four of these plants is very similar. So I assume you can adapt my experience through these plants to many other types of herbs.

Though you eventually may want a clay plant pot or a metal pot with holes punched in the bottom for your mature herbs, you can start your seeds in cardboard milk cartons which are cut down to the desired size, or in styrofoam egg cartons. When using gallon milk containers, remove the top staple so that the top is entirely open. Then cut the container from top to bottom lengthwise to get two rectangular containers. Staple the ends of each container together. One side of a half-gallon or quart container can be removed to make a good rectangular planter. Poke a few holes in the bottom of the containers to allow air to circulate throughout the cartons. Egg cartons can be used as they are—top and all. Just poke a few pin holes in the bottom of each section.

Plants require adequate drainage so you'll need pebbles, broken pieces of pottery, or a layer of kitty litter in the bottom of your plant containers. The egg carton containers, because they are so shallow, will require an extremely small amount of drainage material.

If adequate planting soil is available to you, use it. Adequate soil would be earth near or in a garden or other fairly fertile area. If you can get to a park or a back yard garden, you might be able to get fertile soil there. Look for areas that get some shade or an area where there is a layer of leaves covering the soil. If leaves fall and gather in an area, they decompose and naturally enrich the soil. In general, any soil that is dark when not wet should be good soil for growing herbs. Bring two bags with you to the park or garden. Put one bag inside the other so that if one bag breaks the other will still contain the soil. You do not need special tools to dig up the soil. Simply use old spoons.

Potting soil can be readily purchased if soil is not available to you. It usually costs a lot less when purchased in larger quantities. Buy the average, sometimes called "type 1" potting soil, since no special enrichments are needed for herbs.

When purchasing seeds, just buy seeds in packets that you'll commonly see in the supermarket during the spring and summer. Packets may sometimes be purchased at discount prices at other times of the year. Buy the smallest seed packets you can since you wouldn't need all the seeds unless you have to season the food for a family of 100. Or if you prefer, order your seeds from a seed catalog. A few companies are listed at the end of this section. You can write to them and order the specific herbs you want, or just ask for their catalog and then make a choice and order. Many seeds may be used the following year, but if your plants are successful the first year, many of your herbs will not have to be planted the second year, so chances are you'll be giving away many of your seeds as they are usually not reliable after about fifteen months.

The only other materials you need are clear plastic (bags, wraps, or meat trays) or glass—to cover your containers with while they germinate—and trays to put under your containers so they don't leak all over the place. To summarize, you need the following:

covers for the tops of containers	pebbles or kitty litter for drainage
seeds	containers for plants
soil	dishes or trays for bottoms of containers

You are now ready to grow your seeds. Prepare your containers by cutting them to size as described above and poking small holes in their bottoms. Line the bottoms with one of the suggested drainage materials. Prepare anywhere from one-half to one container for each type of herb planted. About fifty to sixty percent of all seeds planted will probably germinate. Fill your containers with soil which is free of rocks, weeds, or other things that might interfere with the growing process. The dirt can be packed within a quarter of an inch of the top of egg cartons and within three-quarters of an inch or so of the milk containers. Pack the soil fairly firmly. Next press your seeds into the soil. Seed packet instructions usually indicate that you should put the seeds about one-eighth to one-quarter of an inch into the soil. Follow those instructions. Plant about two to three seeds in each egg carton section and about one to two seeds every half inch in the milk cartons. If you have clumsy fingers, use a tweezer to poke your seeds into the soil. Spacing your seeds in the beginning will eliminate excessive thinning later. Make sure your seeds are covered with soil and then carefully water the soil well. You'll want to make sure that the seeds do not wash away. If you have a fine mist sprayer, use that. Otherwise, just be very careful. Now cover your containers with the plastic or glass. You can use the egg carton's own covers. The covers should be kept on the containers until the seeds begin to pop up. Occasionally, the covers will have to be removed for a few hours during the day if mildew appears on the soil. Once you see signs of life, the containers no longer have to be covered unless you discover that something is eating your plants. In that case cover the plants periodically by placing jars over them or loosely wrapping them with plastic.

Herbs take a long time to germinate (or spring through the soil). So don't be surprised if you wait well over two weeks and still don't see any signs of life. During this waiting period, as during the entire life of the plant, water the soil when it seems to be getting dry; but do not overwater as the seeds may drown or become mildewed.

Once they germinate, keep your plants as close to an average supply of sunlight as possible. If sun brightly or strongly pours into your window, do not subject your plants to the strongest rays.

When most of your plants first begin to germinate, you will notice that they have a particular type of leaf which does not in anyway resemble the plant in its mature stage. For instance, the first leaves of the parsley will not have the characteristic parsley leaf shape. In the case of chives though, the leaves do not undergo a dramatic change. At all phases they resemble grass. When the leaves undergo a change or the plants develop their "true leaves" (as they are called), they are ready for thinning.

As you thin plants, those close by can be weakened—this should be avoided as much as possible. In the case of an herb like chives, thin them along with other plants sown at the same time or when they first look sturdy (which is a hard thing to define). Most plants will be ready for thinning after about thirty days after you planted them. Do not be surprised if your plants take much longer before they are ready to be thinned. Thin the plants so that there is one plant in each egg carton section and about one plant every one to two square inches in the milk cartons. Carefully pull out the puniest-looking plants making sure that you do not pull up the other plants. Firm the soil around the plants which have not been thinned out. If all your plants look healthy and you hate to sacrifice any of them, you are not doing them a favor by leaving them all crowded together. If you want, transplant uprooted plants into other containers. When your plants become tall and willowy, about forty-five to sixty days after planting, prepare other containers or clay pots and put the plants in their own individual pots.

In preparation for transplanting, water your plants well so that the soil will be loose. Choose your healthiest plants for transplanting. Fill your new containers with soil and then hollow a hole in the soil. With a fork, carefully remove the plant to be transplanted. If soil stays with the root of the plant, that's O.K. If you break the root, choose another plant. Place the plant in the hollow and pack the soil around it. Water the transplanted plant and, if you like, cover it with a jar for a few days. This will protect it from the elements (such as they are in your apartment). Water your plants as needed. One or two plants of each variety should provide you with a more than adequate supply of herbs. As soon as your plants develop many leaves and they begin to look as if they're thriving (between eighty-five and 100 days), you can begin pinching off leaves and using them in your meals. In some cases, the stem that the leaves grow on should also be removed. Leaves should be used frequently, as the pinching process keeps the plants bushy and healthy. Pinching, in the case of oregano, keeps the plant in top shape. Many people claim that you *must* pinch off the leaves or flowers rather than twisting, tearing, or ripping them off. When you pinch the plant with the nails of your thumb and index finger, you seal the "wound" created and prevent the loss of fluid to the plant. Occasional spraying of the leaves of the plants with water will also help them to thrive. This is sort of like a spring shower to them.

Plants in general fall into three different categories. They are annuals, biennials, or perennials. Basil for instance is an annual, parsley is a biennial, and chives and oregano are perennials. Annuals supposedly last for a year, biennials for two years, and perennials for a longer period of time. The rule, however, does not necessarily follow when you plant indoors. Indoor annuals, for instance, have been known to last over two years—probably because they are not subjected to the extremes of season changes. Theoretically, you could have a plant which lasts for years, but in the case of many plants, after about three years they will turn woody, and you'll want to begin new plants.

If at any time your mature plants begin to look unhappy and

you've been watering them, giving them sun, and you feel that they are not due to die, there is a possibility that the nutrients in the soil have been depleted or that the pots they are in are too small for them. In this case, it's probably best that you change your soil and/or pots. Water your plants very well and carefully loosen as much soil as you can from the roots. Then put these plants in new soil in fresh, larger pots. These changes may revive your plants.

MAIL-ORDER SEED COMPANIES

W. Atlee Burpee Co., Philadelphia, Pennsylvania 19132
Gurney Seed and Nursery Co., Yankton, South Dakota 57078
Joseph Harris Co., Inc., Moreton Farm, Rochester, New York 14624
J. W. Jung Seed Co., Randolph, Wisconsin 53956
Geo. W. Park Seed Co., Inc., P.O. Box 31, Greenwood, South Carolina 29646
Vita Green Farms, P.O. Box 878, Vista, California 92083.

DRYING HERBS

If you acquire or grow a fairly large amount of herbs you might want to dry some of them as gifts or for your own purposes. Fresh parsley, basil, oregano, or practically any other herb can be dried in one of several ways. The prime time to dry most herbs is just as they begin to flower. They are at the height of flavor at this time, and because the drying process causes some flavor to be lost, you'll want to dry them at this most opportune time.[1] Of the three drying methods below, I find the first method to be most successful.

Method 1: Keep herb leaves on the stalks they grow on. Wash the "branches" in cold water and thoroughly shake off the excess water. Hang the herbs in your apartment. You can wrap a string around the top of the herbs and hang them from whatever you choose to tie the string to. After the herbs are no longer wet from their washing, to prevent them from getting dusty, you can cover them with small bags. Poke a hole in the bottom of the bag so that the stem can remain attached to the string, and draw the

---

[1] Parsley should be dried before it begins to flower because it starts to turn bitter as it begins to flower. Soon after, the parsley plant dies.

stem and string through the hole. The bag and plant will be arranged in the same way a bag hangs over dry-cleaned clothing. Allow the herbs to hang and dry out until a leaf will easily crumble. This could take two weeks or more. When the herbs are done, crumble them into jars and cover the jars.

Method 2: Rinse fresh herbs and shake off excess water. Pinch leaves or sections from the stalks. (In the case of small-leaved plants such as oregano, keep them on the stalks.) Lay the leaves or leaves and stalks on a screen and allow them to dry out—near a sun source—until a leaf will crumble. This could take two weeks or more. Crumble the leaves and store them in covered jars.

Method 3: Rinse herbs and shake off excess water. Pinch leaves or sections from the stalks or leave small-leaved herbs on their stalks. Put the herbs on a screen or flat surface and allow them to dry for a day or two. Then put the leaves or stalks and leaves in a flat pan in the oven. If you have a gas stove with a constantly lit pilot, just put the herbs in the oven without turning on the stove. If you have no pilot light or have an electric stove, set the stove at the lowest possible heat. Leave the herbs in the oven until they dry out. This will take anywhere from a number of hours to a day. They are ready for use immediately. Crumble the leaves and store herbs in jars.

DECORATIVE HOUSE PLANTS

Chances are that after you plant your herbs, you'll really start getting into the idea of having plants all around your apartment. If you go to a florist and look around at all the house plants, you'll notice that most of them are very pretty—and outrageously expensive. Do not despair. You may still be able to have house plants without spending money for anything except soil and containers (if you can't grub those two things for free). There's a very convenient little thing about most plants. If you pinch a stem which has one or more leaves on it from a parent plant, you can develop a new plant. Put such a clipping in water so it can develop its own roots. This becomes a new plant which can then be potted on its own. Chances are you have at least one relative or friend who has many house plants. Just ask this person for clippings from his or her begonias, African violets, geraniums, or any other plants. Put the clipping in water in such a way so that the stem will be submerged but the leaf or leaves will remain dry. When a few roots an inch or more long begin appearing on the stem, just pot your plant.

Seeds and pits from fruits such as oranges, lemons, grapefruits, and mangoes, can be planted and produce very nice green plants. Seeds or pits should be soaked in water for twelve hours or so before they are put in soil. Water all house plants every two or three days or when they seem to need a drink.

If your plants begin to look unhealthy, transplant them, changing the soil and putting them into larger pots if needed. Spray leaves of plants with water and expose the plants to indirect sunlight. Expect some fatality in your plants. I for one, have a brown thumb at times. But some plants, no matter how green or brown your thumb is, will kick off regardless of anything you might do in an attempt to aid in their survival.

SPICED-ORANGE AIR FRESHENER

When I was in first grade, we made air fresheners out of oranges and cloves for our parents as Christmas presents. At the time, I remember feeling ripped off by the choice of gift we were to make because the smell of cloves annoyed me. To me, they smelled like mothballs. I think an appreciation for the fragrance of cloves is most easily developed in people who are not children. Children seem to like smells like flowers or cookies baking. Teen-agers might like the smells of car fumes, gasoline, and popcorn, while other people might prefer scents of evergreen, trees, grass, hay, and cloves.

Cloves combined with oranges give off an intoxicating but subtle and pleasing aroma. If you hang the orange somewhere in your apartment, you may forget about it until it sends a gentle whiff your way.

Take an orange and a box of cloves and stick the cloves side by side into the skin of the orange until the fruit is covered with cloves. Tie a ribbon or string around the orange, or put it in a net-type bag (such as the kind oranges come in) and hang it up in a place you walk past often. Or, put it in a closet. It doesn't smell like mothballs, and will not prevent holes in your woolen clothing, but it sends off a pleasantly strong odor when confined to such a small place.

CANDLES

Homemade candles can be made easily and imaginatively if you know a few basics of candlemaking. You might really enjoy an evening of creating weird and interesting candles. Floating, multicolored, and multi-shaped candles are just a few you can create. The basics are given here and you can proceed from these few directions. After all, if I told you all the various designs for candlemaking, I'd probably stifle your creativity.

Before you proceed in making the candles, note all of the following.

Basic Equipment Needed
large chunks of paraffin (wax)—sometimes called petroleum blocks—can be purchased at many retail department stores
a large can—such as a coffee can—for melting the wax
a pot to put the coffee can in when melting the wax
Stearic acid or stearin to harden the candles (3 tbsp. for every pound of wax, or according to package directions)
wicks or string
weights to hold down wicks—or pieces of coat hangers
molds, such as milk cartons (reinforced on their corners so they won't collapse), glass jars, cans, or anything you can think of
candle release, silicon spray, or spray oil, such as Pam (depending upon your mold, this spray may be optional)
coloring (candle dye or bits of crayon)
scents (optional)

Wax Melting Procedures
The wax can be melted by first cutting it into small chunks. To do this take a screwdriver or other tool and put its end on the paraffin block. Next, hit the top of the screwdriver with a hammer until the paraffin breaks. Put the pieces into the coffee can and then put some water in a pot that you don't value too much (it might get a little waxy). Place the can with paraffin in the pot of water. If the can floats, take out some water or add more wax. Next, heat your wax until melted, but be careful of high heats, as paraffin is very flammable.

Wick Preparations
Commercial wicks are usually better than your homemade string-type wicks as they don't burn out as quickly. Follow directions on wick packages or use one of the following methods.

Method 1: Cut your wick an inch longer than the candle will be. Dip it in liquid wax and lay it on a flat surface. Allow the wax to harden. When the molded candle hardens but is still warm, insert a piece of straight wire coat hanger (or equivalent) down the center of the candle. Next, insert your hardened wick and pour on additional wax.

Method 2: Cut your wick about two to three inches longer than the candle will be. Use molds which have a small hole in the bottom. Before pouring candle, put the wick through the hole, leaving an inch or so on the bottom. Tape the hole closed. Next, pull the other end of the wick to the top of the mold. Leave one or two inches at the top and attach the top of the wick to a piece of coat hanger that will lay across the mold. (See Figure 4.) You are now ready to pour your candle.

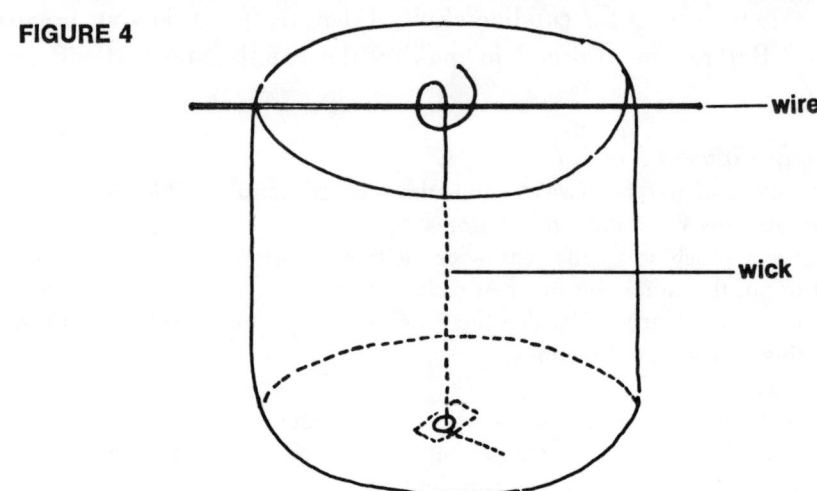

FIGURE 4

Method 3: Weight down the wick at the bottom of the mold with something you do not value that will stay in the candle. A small stone will do. Bring the wick up to the top of the mold and attach it as in Method 2.

Preparing Your Molds

Milk-carton molds do not have to be sprayed with silicon or oil. If you intend to use decorative jars or containers that the candles will stay in, then, of course, you won't have to lubricate those molds. And, if you make floating candles out of paper cupcake liners, you won't need a lubricant. Otherwise, spray the inside of your containers.

You now have everything ready to make your candles. Add color (a little at a time, until you reach your desired shade), to your melted wax. Add the stearic acid to the wax. Bend your melting wax can so it forms a spout (or pour it into a smaller can which you've bent), and pour the wax into the mold. Allow the wax to solidify and then add more wax until your candle does not hollow out on the top. Eliminating the hollow may take several additional layers of wax to accomplish. When the candle is fully hardened, remove it from the mold.

Floating Candles

Put cupcake paper liners in a muffin tin. Add your wick to the mold using the desired method. You can use Method 2 but just hold the wick while you pour the wax rather than bracing it with a piece of wire. Next, pour your wax, according to previous directions. Make the candle no more than an inch and a half high. When the wax dries, candles may be lit and can float in a bowl or basin of water.

Chunk Wax Candles
Use old chunks of colored wax to create a colorful and different textured candle. Put these chunks at the bottom of your mold. Using Method 1, 2, or 3, attach your wick. Pour undyed or a light-colored wax over the chunks and follow other candle-making directions.

Multicolored Candles
In several different cans, melt wax—each a different color. Follow your usual wick and wax directions. Add a layer of one color of wax to the mold. Allow it to solidify. If a well forms, add some more of the same color until no well or impression forms. Next, add another color layer and allow it to dry, adding more wax until no well forms. Do this until you reach the top of the mold. This process takes a long time but you can make other candles while you're waiting for this one to be completed.

CARNIVAL

Welcome to the carnival of the transportation district.

Mobs of young fashionsetters crowd off subways and merge together into a bazaar of clothing past the subdued nun who endlessly sits at the stairway with her tin cup. Boys and girls limp and clump up the stairs swaying arms in jerky ways which aid to balance their bodies. They are prisoners of the purple, green, sparkly, toeless, heelless, or middleless platform shoe.

The thin breeze of the open air is met by the dance of yellow-robed people who want to share a meal and a dance and say they don't need money—unless, of course, you have it.

"Here, sister. Next time your old man knocks you up, call this number." The bearded, smiling man slips a piece of paper into the hand of a passerby.

A few blocks over winos line the sidewalks. As dusk appears, movie-house lights flash intensely, and the mobs of people merge platformed, baggied, hip-huggered, bleached, naturaled, straight, greased, white, black, and in-between. Whistles, screams, and exhaust fumes pierce the air.

Some of the same crowd, but mostly different people—more serious and less boisterous beings—create the human obstacle course of solicitors in the bus terminal. The sellers of truth and paraphernalia line the main rooms, passageways, and stairways.

"Would you like to know the truth? . . . this book . . . only six dollars . . . yes, at first I thought it was a lot . . . my life has changed . . . I was a nonbeliever before I saw the light . . . six dollars you'll blow on a movie or a chick . . . don't throw away your life . . . the time is now. . . ."

"Register to vote. Get the commies out of city government. . . ."

"I wrote this life-giving book of poetry . . . I'm a starving artist. . . ."

"It's like this, man . . . I really didn't have it together before I heard the word of Raja Hatma Phatama. . . ."

"Pray for Nixon. Only fifty cents."

INDEX

Abbreviations, 100
Air freshener, 47–48, 288
Aluminum foil, 45
Ammonia, 43, 48
Annuals, 285
Ants, 38, 50
Apartment(s), 13–29
  cleaning, 23
  expenses, 13–14
  finding, 15–16
  fixing up, 23–29
  furnishing, 26–29
  and landlord, 16–17
  and lease, 14–15, 16
  measuring, 24
  moving into, 18
  painting, 23–24
  plastering, 24
  rent, 17
  repairs, 23, 25–26
  rights, 17
  security deposits, 13–14, 16
  utilities, 18–19
Apple(s),
  baked, 123–124
  and carrot salad, 192
  pancakes, 254
  with pork chops, 154–155
  sauce, 124–125
Appliances, used, 26
Apricots, dried, 101
Asparagus, 223, 226, 228
  Chinese style, 241
  with lemon, 86
  pancake, 227–228

Baking powder, uses, 77
  biscuits, 252–253
Baking soda, uses, 38, 41–42
Banana(s),
  Bread, 268–269
  Graham cracker ice box cake, 121–122
Banking, 31–34
Barbecue sauce, 202–203
Basil, uses, 89, 90
  hamburgers, 145
  planting, 285
  substitutions, 97
Bay leaf, 89, 90
Bean soup, 214–215
Bean sprouts, 277–278
Beans,
  dried, 223, 226
  See also individual names
  green, wax, etc., 223, 227

Beef, 139–140. *Also see* Meat
  basil burgers, 145
  bones, 140, 205–206
  cheeseburgers, 145
  chopped, 142–147
  chuck cuts, 139–140
  hamburgers, 145–146
  liver, 151–154
  meat loaf, 142–144
  roasts, 139–142
  seasonings, 90
  steaks, 139–141, 217
  stew, 216–217
  stuffed peppers, 144–145
  substitutions, 97
  and vegetable protein, 142
Beet(s), 223
  boiled, 229–230
  Borscht, 211–213
  earth soup, 210
  greens, 60, 230
Beer, substitutions for, 98
BHT, 101
Beriberi, 63, 64
Berries, substitutions, 98
Beverages, 112–115
Biscuits, 252–253
Bleach, 43
Bones,
  beef, 140, 205–207
  in chicken soup, 156
  in stock, 208
Bookcases, how to make, 28–29
Boric acid, 37–38
Borscht, 211–213
Botulism, 262, 264
Bouillon cube(s), 83, 113, 188
Bread, 244–252
  banana, 268–269
  board, 47
  corn, 251–252
  crumbs, 45
  herb, 251
  Italian, 248–250
  raisin, 251
  rising, 244, 246
  stuffing, 219–220
  testing, 46
  texture, 244
  white, 248–251
  whole wheat, 247–248
  yeast in, 245
Breakfast, 65, 115. *Also see individual names*
Broccoli.
  consistency, 221

293

Broccoli—*cont.*
 how to cook, 70, 226
 and eggs, 230–231
 fried, 233
 with lemon, 86
 and macaroni, 166–167
 omelette, 130
 how to prepare, 223
 and spinach, 242–243
 substitutions for, 97
Budget, 30–35
 and checking account, 31–34
 and credit, 35
 planning, 30–31
 sample, 32
 and savings account, 34
Burns, how to treat, 41
Butter, 98. *Also see* Margarine

Cabbage,
 consistency, 221
 how to cook, 223, 226
 and onions, 241, 243–244
 how to prepare, 223
 raw, 226
 stuffed, 231–232
Cake,
 banana Graham cracker ice box, 121–122
 orange, 271–273
 testing, 46
Calcium,
 deficiency, 63
 in diet, 65
 foods containing, 67
Candle(s), 289–291
Canisters, 42–43
Canned goods, storage, 75
Canning, 260–266
 equipment and processing, 262–264
 fruits, 263, 265
 pickles, 264–265
 spoilage, 263–264
 sterilization, 263
 tomatoes, 265–266
 vegetables, 263, 266
Caraway seed, 97
Carrots,
 and apple salad, 192
 Chinese style, 241
 consistency, 221
 how to cook, 223, 227
 orange glazed, 232
 how to prepare, 223
 raw, 226
Casseroles, 115–120. *Also see* Stews, Vegetables, Pasta, Beef, Lamb, Chicken
 broccoli macaroni, 166–167
 chicken, vegetable, and rice, 116–117
 pot pie, 119–120
 potted chicken, 161–162
 scalloped potatoes, 118–119
 tuna, 117
 vegetable, 117
Cauliflower, 223–224, 226
 Chinese style, 241, 242
 consistency, 223
 and eggs, in cream sauce, 231

fried, 233
pancakes, 228
how to prepare, 223–224
raw, 226
Celery, 224, 226
 Chinese style, 241
 consistency, 223
 and eggs, in cream sauce, 231
 pancakes, 228
 raw, 226
 substitutions, 97
Certo, 268
Checking accounts, 31–34
Cheese,
 macaroni and, 175–176
 parmesan, and eggplant, 236
 salad dressing, 194
 sandwiches, 198
 sauce, 200
 substitutions, 98
 yogurt, 270–271
Chicken,
 baked, 159–160
  with vegetables, 160
 breaded, 159
 broiled, 158–159
 how to cook, 157, 158
 creamed, 164
 how to cut, 157–158
 fried, 160–161
 giblets, 156, 201–202
 and lemon, 86
 potted, 161–162
 roasted, 163
 soup, 156, 161–162, 207
 stew, 161–162
 stuffing, 209–210
 substitutions, 97
 vegetable, and rice casserole, 116–117
Chinese-style vegetables, 241–244
Chives, 285
Chopped meat, 142
 in hamburgers, 145–146
 in meat loaf, 142, 144
 in stuffed peppers, 144–145
 substitutions, 97
 in Swedish meatballs, 146–147
 and vegetable protein, 142, 144
Chowder, fish, 210–211
Chuck beef, 139–140, 141–142, 217
 substitutions, 97
Cinnamon, 89, 90
Clam sauce and macaroni, 171–172
Cleaning,
 agents, 43–44
 apartment, 23
 crusty pots, 44
 stove, 46
Cleanser, 43
Clothes, 32, 48
Cloves, 288
Cobbler, fruit, 122–123
Cockroaches, 15, 27, 36–38, 50
Cole slaw, and lemon, 86
Collards, 224–225, 233–234
Cooking, 68–72, 91–94
 using a recipe, 109–111

Cooperatives, 51–54
Corn, 224
  consistency, 221
  raw, 226
Corn bread, 251–252
Cornmeal, 74, 77
  mush, 254
Corn oil, 81
Cornstarch, uses, 77
Cream sauces, 199–200
  cheese, 200
  herb, wine, and mushroom, 200
Credit, 35
Cucumbers, 224
Currants, substitution, 98
Curry, 89, 90
  lamb stew, 218
Cutting board, 40–41
Cyclamates, 103

Deposit,
  security, 13–14
  for telephone, 18
  for utilities, 14
Desserts, 120
  apple sauce, 124–125
  baked apples, 123–124
  banana bread, 268–269
  banana-Graham cracker ice box cake, 121–122
  earth snacks, 277
  fruit cobbler, 121–122
  fruit salad, 192–193
  granola, 275–276
  puddings, 120–121
  pumpkin pie, 273–274
  yogurt, 269–270
Diet, balanced, 63–67
Dill weed, uses, 89, 90, 97
Dinner menu, 65, 257–259
Dips, yogurt salad dressing, 195
Dressings,
  poultry, 219–220
  salad, 194–195

Egg(s), 47, 125–131
  benedict, 131
  and broccoli, 230–231
  creamed, 130
  frambled, 128
  fried, 127
  hard boiled, 126
  herbs and spices for, 90
  omelette, 129–130
  salad, 196
  sandwich, 127–128
  scrambled, 127–128, 197
  soft-boiled, 125
  and vegetables, 231, 239
Eggplant, 224, 226, 235–236
  fried, 227, 235–236
  parmesan, 236, in menu, 258
  sandwich, 234, 235
Endive. *See* Escarole
Equivalents, chart, 100
Escarole, 97, 226

Expenses. *Also see* Budget
  apartment, 13–14
  food, 58–60
  realtor fees, 16
  sharing with roommate, 17–19

Fire extinguisher, 41
Fish, 131–138
  baked, 134
  chowder, 210–211
  cuts of, 131–132
  fried, 134–135
  herbs and spices for, 90
  leftover, 105, 107
  with lemon juice, 86
  mackerel, 137–138
  poached, 132–133
  sandwiches, 135
  soufflé, 136
  stuffed, 135–136
  substitutions, 97
Fixing up apartment, 23–29
Flour, 66, 75–76
  in bread, 244–245
  Graham, 75, 76
  rye, 76
  how to store, 74
  white, 75, 76
  whole grain, 75
  whole wheat, 75
Food,
  balanced meals, 63–67
  as gifts, 267
  nutrients in, 66–67
  preservatives, 101–103
  quantity to prepare, 71
  removing from sticky pots, 44
  staples, 74–87
  storage, 74–75
  substitutions, 95–98
  taste, 70–71
Food and Drug Administration, 60, 103
Food buying club, 52. *See also* Cooperatives
Food co-op, 52–53. *Also see* Cooperatives
Fruit(s). *Also see individual names*
  canned, 263–265
  salad, 192–193
  spices, 90
  substitutions, 98
  vitamins in, 66–67
Furnishing an apartment, 26–29
Furniture, 26–29
  wax, 44

Giblets, 156, 201–202
Gifts, 267
  candles, 289–291
  orange air freshener, 288
  special food, 45
Goodwill, 28, 72
Granola, 275–277
Grapefruit, planting seeds, 288
Gravy, 200–202
  bottom-of-the-pan, 200–201
  bouillon cube, 154
  giblet, 201–202
  soy sauce, 83

Green beans, 226–227
  Chinese style, 241
  with lemon, 86
  salad, 193–194
Green peppers, *See* Peppers
Groceries, how to buy, 57–62
Ground meat, *See* Chopped meat

Ham, 147–150
  baked, 148–149
  basting, 148
  butt, shank end, and whole, 147–149
  picnic, 149–150
  roast, 147
  and trichinosis, 147
Hamburgers, 145–146
  basilburgers, 145
Herb(s), 88–90. *Also see individual names*
  amounts to use, 88
  bread, 251
  chart, 90
  how to clean, 224
  sauce, 200, 202
  and spices, 88
  how to store, 50, 285, 287
Herbs to plant, 281–287
  containers, 282
  drying, 286–287
Home fries, 178–180
  with vegetables, 180
Honey, 79
  substitutions, 98
Hospitalization, in budget, 30, 31, 32
Household hints, 40–48. *Also see* Recycling
Housing Authority, 17
Human Rights Commission, 17

Indigestion, and baking soda, 42
Insecticides, 37, 102
Insects, precautions against, 36–39, 43. *Also see* Cockroaches
Instant foods, 60–61
Insurance, in budget, 30–31, 32
Iron, foods containing, 67

Jam, Jelly, 267–268

Kale, 226
Kneading, 47, 246
Knife sharpening, 47
Kosher salt, 84

Lamb,
  curry, 218
  herbs and spices for, 90
  in sample menu, 257
  stew, 218
  substitutions, 97
Landlords, 13–14, 16–17, 25
Lasagna, 167–171
Lease, 14–16
Leaving home, 9–12
Leeks, 78
Leftovers, 104–107. *Also see* Leftovers Section at end of each recipe
  chart, 106–107

Legal Aid Services, 71
Lemon, 85–87
  lemonade, 112–113
  and liver, 153
  and mayonnaise, 86
  to remove smells, 40–41, 86
  seeds, 288
  substitutions, 97
Lentil soup, 214–215
Lettuce, 224. *Also see* Salads
  how to clean and prepare, 224
Lima beans, baked, 228–229
Linoleum, 25
Liver, 151–154
  fried, 151–154
  with lemon, 153
  with milk and egg, 152–153
  and onions, 153–154
Loans, 35
Lunch menu, 65, 259

Macaroni,
  and broccoli, 166–167
  and cheese, 175–176
  and clam sauce, 171–172
  poor man's lasagna, 170–171
  with tomato sauce, 170–171
Mackerel, 137–138
Margarine, 84
  herb sauce, 202
  substitutions, 84, 98
  uses, 84
Marinade, 202–203
  lamb shank, 150
Marmalades, 267–268
Mayonnaise, 83–84
  different from salad dressing, 83
  substitutions, 98
Meal planning,
  for unexpected company, 99–100
  menus, 257–259
  and nutrition, 63–67
  and vegetables, 221–222
Measurements (ingredients), chart, 100
Measuring, a room, 24
Meat. *Also see* Beef, Chicken, etc.
  beef, 139–147
  bones, 138, 140, 156, 205–207
  buying, 60
  chopped, 142, 145–147
  cuts, 140
  freezing, 140
  in gravy, 154
  ham, 147–150
  lamb, 150, 218
  leftover, 105–107, 154
  liver, 151–154
  meat loaf, 142–144
  nutrients, cooking to retain, 66
  pork, 154–155
  stew, 215–218
  substitutions, 97
  tenderizing, 82
  turkey, 156
  and vegetable protein, 142
Meatballs, 146–147, 174

Meat loaf, 142–143
  in sample menu, 257
  and vegetable protein, 143–144
Menus, samples, 65, 257–259
Mice, 39
Milk, 98
  dry, uses, 82
  hot, 114–115
  nutrients in, 66, 67
  in sample menu, 65
  how to sour, 82
  substitutions, 98, 105–106
Molasses, substitutions, 98
Money, *Also see* Budget, Credit, Expenses
  borrowing, 18, 35
  in checking account, 31–34
  in interest, 35
  lending to roommate, 18
  in sample budget, 32
  in savings account, 34
Moving, away from home, 9–12
  into apartment, 18
Mush, cornmeal, 254
Mushrooms, substitutions, 97
  Chinese style, 242
  cream sauce, 200
  uses, 92

Nails, 25
Newspapers, recycling, 44, 49
Niacin, in foods, 67
Noodles
  how to cook, 165–166. *Also see* Pasta
  and tuna casserole, 117
  and vegetable casserole, 118
Nutmeg, uses, 89, 90
Nutrients,
  in food, 63–67
  in soil, 286
Nutrition, 63–67
  books on, 67
Nuts, 66, 67, 98

Oat(s), 76–77
  flour, 76
  in granola, 276–277
Odors,
  in air, 47–48, 288
  decaying wood, 15
  removal of, 40–43, 86
Oil, 80–81
  polyunsaturated, 81
  preservatives in, 81
  substitutions, 98
  uses, 80–81
  varieties, 80, 81
Olives, black, substitutions, 97
Omelette(s), 129, 130
Onion(s), 46, 224, 226
  boiled, 236
  and cabbage, 243–244
  consistency, 221
  raw, 226
  how to store, 75
  uses, 77–78
  varieties, 78

Orange,
  air freshener, 288
  cake, 271–273
  glazed carrots, 232, 257
  orangeade, 113
  seeds, to plant, 288
Oregano, 89, 90, 97, 285
Oven, 46
  temperatures, 47, 69–70

Painting apartment, 23–24
Pancake(s), 253–254
  apple, 254
  asparagus, 227–228
  potato, 228
  quantity to make, 71
  vegetable, 228
  wholewheat, 253
  yogurt, 253
Paper towels, 49–50
Paprika, substitutions, 97
  uses, 89, 90
Paraffin, in candlemaking, 289
  to seal jars, 268
Parsley, how to prepare, 224
  planting, 285
  uses, 89, 90, 226
Parsnip, 224, 226–227
Pasta, 164–177. *Also see individual names*
  cooking time, 165–166
  equivalents of dry and cooked, 166
  garlic and onion, and, 175
  lasagna, 167–171
  macaroni, 166–167, 171, 175–176
  with meatballs, 174
  how to prevent sticking, 165–166
  with tomato sauce, 172–173
  y fagiole, 164–165, 176–177
Pastry. *See* pie crust
Pea(s), 224, 226, 227
  and eggs, in cream sauce, 231
  raw, 226
  soup, 214–215
Peaches, substitutions, 98
Pectin, 267–268
Peppers, green, 224, 227
  and potato, 197
  how to prepare, 224
  raw, 226
  roasted, 197, sandwich, 197
  and sausage, 197
  stuffed, 144–145
  substitutions, 97
Pepper, red, 97
Perch, substitutions, 97
Perennials, 285
Pickles, 264
Pickling, 262–264
Pie crust, 273–274
  for pot pie, 119
Pie, pumpkin, 273–274
Pimento, substitutions, 97
Pineapple, substitutions, 98
Pinto beans, soup, 214–215
Pizza, 255–257
  in sample menu, 258
  sauce, 256

297

Plants,
    bean sprouts, 277–278
    herbs, 281–287. *Also see* Herbs
    house, 287–288
    seeds, citrus fruit, 288
    Tansy, 38
    terrarium, 279–281. *Also see* Terrarium
Plastering, 23, 24
Plastic bags, 45, 61–62
Plastic wrap for meat, 60
Plumbing supplies, 27
Pollution, 61, *See also* Recycling
Polysorbate, 80, 101
Pork,
    chops, with apples, 154–155
    chops, with sauce, 203
    herbs and spices for, 90
    liver, 151–154
    neckbone soup, 206–207
    stew, 216–217
    substitutions, 97
Potato(es), 46, 177–186
    baked, 181
    boiled, 180, 181
    how to cook, 171–178, 226–227
    fried, 178–180
    home fries, 178–180
    leftovers, 107
    mashed, 182
    pancake, 182
    how to prepare, 177, 178, 224–225
    roasted, 181–182
    salad, 185–186
    with sausage, and peppers, 197
    scalloped, 118–119
    how to store, 75
    varieties, 178
Pot pie, 119–120
Pots for plants, 282
Potting soil, 282–283
Poultry, substitutions, 97. *Also see* Chicken, Turkey
Preservatives, 101–103
Preserves, 267–268
Prices, food, 57–60
    unit, 58, 59
Protein, in foods, 67
Prunes, nutrients in, 67
Pudding, 120–121

Quantity of food to prepare, 71

Radishes, 225
Raisin(s), 98
    bread, 251
Raspberries, 98
    topping for orange cake, 272
Rats, 39
Realtor, 15, 16
Recipes,
    about, 109–111
    changing, 110, 111
    how to read, 91
    substitutions of ingredients, 95–98
Recycling, 44, 45, 49–50
Refrigerators, 26

Rent. *Also see* Apartment(s), Landlords, Budget
    comparing, 16, 17
    deposit on, 13
    in exchange for chores, 17
    and Housing Authority, 16, 17
    and landlord, 13–14, 16–17
    and utilities, 14
Repair(s), 23–26, 41
Rice, 186–187
    with bouillon cube, 188
    brown, 186, 187
    with chicken and vegetables, 116–117
    cold, with milk, 188
    how to cook, 186, 187
    expansion of, 186, 187
    flour, 76
    fried, 187–188
    leftover, 107
    in sample menu, 257
    with tuna, 117
    and vegetables, 118, 188
Roommate, 17–18
Rug cleaners, 44
Rummage sales, 27
Rutabaga, 225–227

Saccharin, 103
Salad(s), 189–195
    apple and carrot, 192
    egg, 196
    eggs, with green beans, 193–194
    fruit, 192–193
    green, 189–190
    green beans, 193–194
    potato, 185–186
    spinach, 192–193
    tomato, 190
    tuna, 196–197
    vegetable, 197; raw, 193
Salad dressings,
    cheese, 194
    French, 194–195
    fruit, 192–193
    Italian, 194
    mayonnaise, 83–84
    yogurt, 195
Salt, 38, 75, 84
Salvation Army, furniture, 28
    utensils, 72
Sandwiches, 195–196
    cheese, melted, 198
    chicken, 159
    egg, 127, 128, 196, 197
    eggplant, 234, 235
    fish, 135
    jam, 149
    meat loaf, 143–144
    omelette, 129, 130
    pepper, roasted, 197
    sausage, 197
    tuna, 196–197
    vegetable salad, 197
Sauce(s), 198–203
    barbecue, 202–203
    cheese, 200
    clam, 171–172

Sauce—cont.
　cream, 199–200
　　for fish, 135
　　herb, 200, 202
　　marinade, 150, 202–203
　　mushroom, cream, 200
　　for pork chops, 203
　　pizza, 256
　　Tartar, 134–135
　　tomato, 172–173
　　wine, cream, 200
Sausage, with peppers and egg, 197
　substitutions, 97
Savings Account, 34
Scallions, uses, 78
Screwdrivers (tools), 25
Scurvy, 64
Security deposit(s), 13–14, 16
Seeds, nutrients in, 66, 67
　substitutions, 98
Seeds, planting, 283–284, 286
Shopping, 57–62
Silver spoons, flavor, 44
Simmering, 69
Smells, *See* Odors
Snacks, earth, 277
Sodium benzoate, 101
Sodium nitrate, 101
Sodium nitrite, 101
Sorbic acid, 101
Soup, 204–215
　barley, 207
　bean, 207, 214–215
　beet, 210, 211–213
　bones, 140, 156, 205–207
　chicken, 156, 161–162, 207
　chowder, 209–210
　from leftovers, 105, 210
　pea, 214–215
　stock, 208–209
　stone, 209–210
　turkey, 207
　vegetable, 213–214
Sour cream, substitutions, 83, 98
Sour milk, how to, 82
Soybeans, in pasta y fagiole, 176–177
Soy flour, 76
Soy sauce, gravy, 82–83
　substitutions, 98
Spaghetti, 164, 165. *Also see* Pasta
　leftover, 107
　and meatballs, 174
　how to prevent sticking, 165–166
　sauce, jarred, 80
　tomato sauce, 174–175
Spices, 88–90. *Also see individual names*
Spinach, 224, 226
　and broccoli, 242–243
　and eggs, in cream sauce, 231
　omelette, 129
　pancakes, 228
　quantity to cook, 71
　salad, 191
　substitutions, 97
Squash, 225–227, 240–241
　acorn, baked, 241
　summer, 225, 226

　winter, 225, 226–227
　zucchini, parmesan, 240
Stained pots, 42
Staples, food, 74–87
Steak, broiled, 141
　chuck, 139–140
　pepper, 217
　sirloin, 97
　substitutions, 97
Stew(s), 215–218
　beef, 216–217
　chicken, 161–162
　lamb, curry, 218
　meat, 215, 216
　pepper steak, 217
　pork, 216–217
　veal, 216–217
Stock, 208–209
Storage, of food, 42, 74–75
Stove, 26, 46
　temperatures, 69–70
Strawberries, 98
String beans, 241
Stuffing, 219–220
　bread, 219
　fried, 219
　leftover, 107, 219
　saltine, 219–220
　vegetable, 220
Substitutions, 95–109
　chart, 97–98
Sugar, 78–79
　brown, 98
　honey, used instead, 79
　storage, 74
　substitutions, 98
　white, 78–79
Sulfur dioxide, in dried fruit, 101
Supermarket, shopping, 57–62
Sure-Jell, 268
Swedish meatballs, 146–147
Sweeteners, 78–79, 98

Tables, making your own, 29
Tansy, 38
Tartar sauce, 134
Taste, of food, 70–71
Tea, 114
　pots, stain removal, 42
Telephone, 18–19
Temperatures, oven, 47, 69–70
　control, 66–70
Tenderizing meat, 82
Terrarium, 279–281
　equipment, 279–280
　making your own, 279–280
　plants, 280–281
　　digging up, 281
　stand, 280
　woodland, 281
Thyme, uses, 90
Time, baking, 46
　for cooking vegetables, 225–226
　saving, in cooking, 108
Tomatoes,
　canning, 262, 263, 265–266
　green, fried, 236–238

Tomatoes—*cont.*
 how to prepare, 225–227
 raw, 226
 salad, 190
 varieties, 79–80
Tomato paste, 79; puree, 79
Tomato sauce, 79–80, 172–173
 and meatballs, 174
 and pasta, 172, 173
 substitution for, 98
 varieties, 79–80
Tools, 25
Tortilla de Papas, 183–184
Transplanting plants, 284–285
Transportation, in budget, 32
Tuna, noodle casserole, 117
 rice casserole, 117
 salad, sandwich, 196–197
 store brand, 59
 substitutions, 97
Turbinado, substitutions, 98
Turkey, soup, 207
 substitutions, 97
Turnip, 92, 225, 226–227
TV dinners, 60–61

Utensils, 26, 42, 72–73
Utilities, 14, 16, 32
Utility hooks, 25–26

Veal stew, 216–217
 substitutions, 97
Vegetable(s), 221–244. *Also see individual names*
 appetite helpers, 99
 how to buy, 60
 casserole, 118
 Chinese style, 241–244
 combining, 221, 222
 consistency, 222
 how to cook, 225–227
 hash, 238
 herbs and spice, 90
 leftovers, 105, 107
 loaf, 240
 in meal planning, 221–222
 nutrients in, 66, 67
 oil, 80–81
 pancake, 228
 protein, in meat loaf, 142, 143–144

 raw, 226
 with rice, 188
 salad, 189–194
 scrambled, 239
 how to serve, 221
 soup, 213–214
 stuffing, 220
 substitutions, 97
Vinegar, 40–41, 81–82
Vitamins, 63–67
 A, foods, 66
  overdose, 64
 B_1, foods, 64, 65, 66
 B_2, foods, 65, 66
 B_6, foods, 65, 67
 B_{12}, foods, 65
  in balanced diet, 63–64, 65
 C, foods, 65, 67
  deficiency, 63, 64
 chart, 66–67
 cooking to retain, 66
 D, in milk, 65, 67
 E, foods, 67
 and minerals, books on, 67

Walls, 23–25
Wax, furniture, 44
Wax beans, 241
Wheat germ, nutrients in, 66, 67
Whole grain flours, 75–76
Wholesale buying, 52, 53
Whole wheat bread, 248
 flour, 74–75, 76
 pancakes, 253
Window shades, reviving, 41
Wine, cream sauce, 200
 substitutions, 82, 98

Yeast, 244–245
Yellow beans, how to cook, 226–227
Yogurt, 269–271
 cheese, 270–271
 culture, 270
 homemade, 270
 pancakes, 253
 salad dressing, 195
 uses, 270

Zucchini, parmesan, 240
 in sample menu, 258